THE PROMISES OF GOD

THE PROMISES OF GOD

A New Edition of the Classic Devotional
Based on the English Standard Version

CHARLES SPURGEON

Revised and Updated by
Tim Chester

 CROSSWAY®

WHEATON, ILLINOIS

The Promises of God: A New Edition of the Classic Devotional Based on the English Standard Version

Copyright © 2019 by Tim Chester

Published by Crossway
          1300 Crescent Street
          Wheaton, Illinois 60187

Cover design: Jordan Singer

First printing 2019

Printed in the United States of America

Hardcover ISBN: 978-1-4335-6324-9
ePub ISBN: 978-1-4335-6327-0
PDF ISBN: 978-1-4335-6325-6
Mobipocket ISBN: 978-1-4335-6326-3

Library of Congress Cataloging-in-Publication Data

Names: Spurgeon, C. H. (Charles Haddon), 1834–1892, author. | Chester, Tim, editor.

Title: The promises of God : a new edition of the classic devotional based on the English Standard version / Charles Spurgeon; revised and updated by Tim Chester.

Other titles: Cheque book of the bank of faith

Description: Wheaton : Crossway, 2019. | Originally published as The cheque book of the bank of faith. It has been reprinted, revised, etc. with various titles generally using "promises" in the title. | Includes index.

Identifiers: LCCN 2018037955 (print) | LCCN 2018054418 (ebook) | ISBN 9781433563256 (pdf) | ISBN 9781433563263 (mobi) | ISBN 9781433563270 (epub) | ISBN 9781433563249 (hc)

Subjects: LCSH: God (Christianity)—Promises—Meditations. | Devotional calendars—Baptists.

Classification: LCC BS680.P7 (ebook) | LCC BS680.P7 S68 2019 (print) | DDC 242/.2—dc23

LC record available at https://lccn.loc.gov/2018037955

Crossway is a publishing ministry of Good News Publishers.

LSC		29	28	27	26	25	24	23	22	21	20	19
15	14	13	12	11	10	9	8	7	6	5	4	3	2	1

EDITOR'S INTRODUCTION

For as long as I can remember, my father has had a plaster bust of Charles Haddon Spurgeon (1834–1892) in his study. Like my father and me, Spurgeon was a Reformed Baptist pastor, and Spurgeon has always been one of our heroes. When, in 2017, my father preached his last sermon, he passed the bust on to me. So, as I write these words, Spurgeon is looking down on me.

Known as "the Prince of Preachers," Spurgeon attracted large crowds, often speaking to over ten thousand people at a time before the days of amplification. His preaching was characterized by the directness of his address and the vividness of his language. In 1861, his congregation moved to the specially-built Metropolitan Tabernacle with seating for five thousand people and standing room for a further thousand. It would remain his base for the next thirty-eight years until his death in 1892.

Spurgeon founded a pastor's college to train church planters, opposed slave ownership, and opened an orphanage. He also fiercely opposed liberal theology. He paid a price for this workload and the controversies it brought, suffering for many years physically with gout and emotionally with depression. It is to these struggles that he alludes in his preface for this volume.

Spurgeon reached a still wider audience through his writings. His sermons were transcribed by stenographers as he spoke and on sale for a penny the following day. Among his many works was *The Cheque Book of the Bank of Faith*.

It was not Spurgeon's first book of daily devotional readings. In 1865, he published *Morning by Morning*, followed three years later by *Evening by Evening*. Soon they were combined into *Morning and Evening*, selling over 230,000 copies during his lifetime and many more since.

Twenty years or so later, Spurgeon wrote *The Cheque Book of the Bank of Faith* as a follow-up. And this was my father's favorite. He used to read it to our family during my childhood.

In *The Cheque Book of the Bank of Faith*, Spurgeon likens the promises of God in the Bible to checks (or "cheques" as Spurgeon himself would have spelled it). A check is a promise in written form. It promises to give the recipient the stated sum whenever they present it at a bank. The promises of God, says Spurgeon, are like checks waiting to be cashed in "the bank of faith."

In 2003, Crossway published an edition of *Morning and Evening* updated by Alistair Begg using the English Standard Version of the Bible. I have taken the liberty of doing the same with *The Cheque Book of the Bank of Faith*. I have replaced archaic words, shortened sentences, used modern word ordering, and added references to biblical allusions. I have also changed the title, partly because checks are becoming dated and partly to prevent a fight with my publishers over the spelling of "cheque" (the UK spelling) and "check" (the US spelling)! Apart from this, the content is the same. Only occasionally have I retained an archaic phrase to retain the poetic power of the original text. My aim has been to let Spurgeon speak to a new generation. Why? Not as an historical curiosity. But so the promise-making and promise-keeping God of the Bible speaks words of comfort to his people. As Spurgeon says in his preface,

> I have written out of my own heart with the view of comforting their hearts. . . . May the Holy Spirit, the Comforter, inspire the people of the Lord with fresh faith!

Many thanks to Richard Chester (my father) and Tamsin Faiers for reading my draft to ensure it sounded contemporary while retaining the "voice" of Spurgeon.

Tim Chester
2018

AUTHOR'S PREFACE

A promise from God is like a check payable to order. It is given to the believer with the view of delivering to him some good thing. We are not meant to read it at our leisure and then forget about it. No, we are to treat the promise as a reality, as someone treats a check.

We are to take the promise and endorse it with our own name by personally receiving it as true. We are to accept it by faith as our own. We seal the deal by believing that God is true and true to this particular word of promise. We go further, believing that we have the blessing by having the sure promise of it. And therefore we put our names to it to acknowledge the receipt of the blessing.

This done, we must present the promise to the Lord in faith, as someone presents a check at the counter of the bank. We must plead it by prayer, expecting to have it fulfilled. If we have come to heaven's bank at the right date, we will receive the promised amount at once. If the date should happen to be in the future, we must patiently wait until it arrives. But meanwhile we may count the promise as money, for heaven's bank is sure to pay when the due time arrives.

Some fail to place the endorsement of faith upon the check and so they get nothing. Others are slack in presenting it, and they also receive nothing. This is not the fault of the promise, but of those who do not use it in a common-sense, business-like manner.

God has given no pledge that he will not redeem and encouraged no hope that he will not fulfill. To help my brothers and sisters to believe this, I have prepared this little volume. The sight of the promises themselves is good for the eyes of faith. The more we study the words of grace, the more grace we will receive from the words. To these encouraging scriptures I have added testimonies of my own, the fruit of trial and experience. I believe all the promises of God, but many of them I have personally tried and proved. I have seen that they are true, for they have been fulfilled to me. This, I trust, may be encouraging to the young and not without comfort to those who are older. One person's experience may be a great help to another. This is why the man of God of old wrote, "I sought the LORD, and he answered me" and "This poor man cried, and the LORD heard him" (Ps. 34:4, 6).

I commenced these daily thoughts when I was wading in the surf of controversy. Since then I have been cast into waters "deep enough to swim in" (Ezek. 47:5) which, but for God's upholding hand, would have proved waters to drown in. I have endured tribulation from many sources. Sharp bodily pain succeeded mental depression, and this was accompanied both by bereavement and affliction in someone as dear to me as life itself. The waters rolled in continually, wave upon wave. I do not mention this to win your sympathy, but simply to let the reader see that I am no dry-land sailor. I have traveled many times across those stormy oceans. I know the roll of the waves and the rush of the winds. Never were the promises of Jehovah so precious to me as during this time. Some of them I never understood until now. I had not yet reached the date at which the promise matured, for I myself was not mature enough to perceive their meaning.

How much more wonderful is the Bible to me now than it was a few months ago! In obeying the Lord and bearing his reproach outside the camp (Heb. 13:13), I have not received new promises, but the result to me is much the same as if I had done so. For the old promises have opened up to me with richer stores.

Oh, that I might comfort some of my Master's servants! I have written out of my own heart with the view of comforting their hearts. I would say to them in their trials: "My brothers and sisters, God is good. He will not forsake you. He will bear you through. There is a promise prepared for your present emergencies. And if you will believe it and plead it at the mercy seat through Jesus Christ, you will see the hand of the Lord stretched out to help you. Everything else will fail, but his Word never will. He has been so faithful to me in countless instances that I must encourage you to trust him. I should be ungrateful to God and unkind to you if I did not do so."

May the Holy Spirit, the Comforter, inspire the people of the Lord with fresh faith! I know that, without his divine power, none of what I say will be of any help. But, under his life-giving influence, even the humblest testimony will fortify feeble knees and strengthen weak hands. God is glorified when his servants trust him implicitly. We cannot be too much like children before our heavenly Father. Our young ones never question our will or our power. Instead, having received a promise from their father, they rejoice in the prospect of its fulfillment, never doubting that it is as sure as the sun. May many readers, whom I may never see, discover the duty and delight of such childlike trust in God while they are reading the little bit which I have prepared for each day in the year.

May our Lord Jesus accept this, my service for his sheep and lambs, from his unworthy servant.

Charles H. Spurgeon
1888

JANUARY

JANUARY 1

I will put enmity between you and the woman,
and between your offspring and her offspring;
he shall bruise your head,
and you shall bruise his heel.

Genesis 3:15

This is the first promise to fallen humanity. It contains the whole gospel and the essence of the covenant of grace, God's eternal plan to save his people. It has been in good measure fulfilled. The seed of the woman, who is our Lord Jesus, had his hell when his heel was bruised, and a terrible bruising it was. How much more terrible will be the final bruising of the serpent's head! This was mostly done when Jesus took away sin, vanquished death, and broke the power of Satan. But it awaits a still fuller accomplishment at our Lord's second coming and in the day of judgment.

To us the promise stands as a prophecy that we will be afflicted by the powers of evil in our bodily life, and thus bruised in our heel. But we will triumph in Christ, who sets his foot on the old serpent's head. Throughout this year we may have to learn part of this promise by experience as we experience the temptations of the devil and the unkindness of the ungodly, who are the devil's offspring. They may so bruise us that we are forced to limp with our sore heels. But let us grasp the second part of the text and we will not be dismayed. By faith let us rejoice that we will yet reign in Christ Jesus, the woman's offspring.

JANUARY 2

The God of peace will soon crush Satan under your feet.

Romans 16:20

This promise follows yesterday's promise. It is clear that we are to be like our covenant Head, Jesus, not only in his being bruised in his heel, but also in his conquest of the evil one. Even under *our* feet is the old dragon to be bruised. The Roman believers were suffering from conflict in the church. But their God was "the God of peace," and he gave rest to their souls. The archenemy tripped up the feet of the unwary and deceived the hearts of the simple. But he would get the worst of it, for he would be trodden down by those whom he had troubled. This victory would not come to the people of God through their own skill or power, but God himself would bruise Satan. Though it would be under their feet, yet the bruising would be through the Lord alone.

Let us bravely tread upon the tempter! Not only lesser spirits, but the prince of darkness himself must fall before us. In unquestioning confidence in God, let us look for speedy victory. "Soon!" Happy word! *Soon* we will set our foot on the old serpent! What a joy to crush evil! What dishonor to Satan to have his head bruised by human feet! Let us by faith in Jesus tread the tempter down.

JANUARY 3

The land on which you lie I will give
to you and to your offspring.

Genesis 28:13

This promise is no one's private possession. It belongs not to one saint, but to all believers. If, my brother or sister, you can in faith lie down upon a promise and take your rest upon it, it is yours. Where Jacob came and stayed and rested, there he took possession. Stretching out his weary length upon the ground, with stones for his pillow, he little realized that he was entering into ownership of the land. Yet this is what happened. He saw in his dream that wonderful ladder which, for all true believers, unites earth and heaven. And surely where the foot of the ladder stood he must have a right to the soil, for otherwise he could not reach the divine stairway. All the promises of God are "Yes" and "Amen" in Christ Jesus. And, as he is ours, so every promise is ours if we lie down upon it in restful faith.

Come, weary one, use your Lord's words as your pillow. Lie down in peace. Dream only of him. Jesus is your ladder of light. See the angels coming and going on him between your soul and your God. And be sure that the promise is your own God-given inheritance. So it will not be robbery for you to take it for yourself, as if it had been spoken *especially to you.*

JANUARY 4

I will make you lie down in safety.

Hosea 2:18

Yes, *the saints are to have peace.* The passage from which this gracious word is taken speaks of peace "with the beasts of the field, the birds of the heavens, and the creeping things of the ground" (Hos. 2:18). This is peace with earthly enemies, mysterious evils, and little annoyances! Any of these might keep us from lying down, but none of them will do so. The Lord will utterly destroy those things that threaten his people: "I will abolish the bow, the sword, and war from the land" (v. 18). Peace will be profound indeed when all the instruments of discord are broken to pieces.

With this peace will come rest. "For he gives to his beloved sleep" (Ps. 127:2). Fully supplied and divinely quieted, believers lie down in calm repose.

This rest will be a safe one. It is one thing to lie down, but quite another to "lie down in safety." We are brought to the land of promise, the house of the Father, the chamber of love, and the heart of Christ: surely we may now "lie down in safety." It is safer for a believer to lie down in peace than to sit up and worry. "He makes me lie down in green pastures" (Ps. 23:1). We never rest till the Comforter makes us lie down.

JANUARY 5

I will strengthen you.

Isaiah 41:10

When called to serve or to suffer, we take stock of our strength. And we find it to be less than we thought and less than we need. But do not let our hearts sink within us while we have such a word as this to fall back on. For it guarantees us all that we can possibly need. God has strength omnipotent. That strength he can share with us, and his promise is that he will do so. He will be the food of our souls and the health of our hearts. And so he will give us strength. There is no telling how much power God can put into a person. When divine strength comes, human weakness is no longer a hindrance.

Do we not remember periods of labor and trial in which we received such special strength that we wondered at ourselves? In the midst of danger we were calm, under bereavement we were resigned, in slander we were self-contained, and in sickness we were patient. The fact is, God gives unexpected strength when unusual trials come upon us. We rise out of our feeble selves. Cowards play the man, foolish ones receive wisdom, and the silent receive words to speak at the very moment they need them. My own weakness makes me shrink, but God's promise makes me brave. Lord, "strengthen me according to your word" (Ps. 119:28).

JANUARY 6

I will help you.

Isaiah 41:10

Yesterday's promise secured us strength for what we have to do, but this promise guarantees us help in situations where we cannot act alone. The Lord says, "I will help you." Strength on the inside is supplemented by help from the outside. God can raise up for us allies in our warfare if it seems good in his sight. And, even if he does not send us human assistance, he himself will be at our side, and this is better still. Our Ally is better than legions of mortal helpers.

His help is timely: he is "a very present help in trouble" (Ps. 46:1). His help is very wise: he knows how to give each person help suited just for them. His help is most effective, though the help of people is empty. His help is more than help, for he bears all the burden and supplies all the need. "The LORD is on my side; I will not fear. What can man do to me?" (Ps. 118:6).

Because he has already been our help, we feel confidence in him for the present and the future. Our prayer is, "O LORD, be my helper!" (Ps. 30:10). And our experience is, "The Spirit helps us in our weakness" (Rom. 8:26). Our expectation is, "I lift up my eyes to the hills. From where does my help come? My help comes from the LORD" (Ps. 121:1–2). And our song will soon be, "You, LORD, have helped me" (Ps. 86:17).

JANUARY 7

You will see greater things than these.

John 1:50

This promise was spoken to a childlike believer who was ready to accept Jesus as the Son of God, the King of Israel, after just one convincing piece of argument. Those who are willing to see shall see. It is because we shut our eyes that we become so sadly blind.

We have seen much already. The Lord has shown us great and unsearchable things for which we praise his name. But there are greater truths in his Word, greater depths of experience, greater heights of fellowship, greater works of usefulness, greater discoveries of power and love and wisdom. These we are yet to see if we are willing to believe our Lord. The capacity to invent false doctrine is ruinous, but the power to see the truth is a blessing. Heaven will be opened to us, the way there will be made clear to us in the Son of Man, and the angelic movement between the upper and the lower kingdoms will be revealed to us. Let us keep our eyes open toward spiritual objects, and expect to see more and more. Let us believe that our lives will not drivel down into nothing. But instead let us believe that we will be always growing, seeing greater and still greater things, until we behold the Great God himself, and never again lose sight of him.

JANUARY 8

Blessed are the pure in heart, for they shall see God.

Matthew 5:8

Purity, even purity of heart, is the main thing to be aimed at. We need to be made clean on the inside through the Spirit and the Word, and then we will be clean on the outside by consecration and obedience. There is a close connection between the affections and the understanding. If we love evil, we cannot understand that which is good. If the heart is foul, the eye will be darkened. How can those who love unholy things see a holy God?

What a privilege it is to see God! A glimpse of him is heaven below! In Christ Jesus the pure in heart see the Father. We see him, his truth, his love, his purpose, his sovereignty, and his covenant character. Yes, we see God himself in Christ. But this is only apprehended as sin is kept out of the heart. Only those who aim at godliness can cry, "My eyes are ever toward the LORD" (Ps. 25:15). The desire of Moses, "Please show me your glory" (Ex. 33:18), can only be fulfilled in us as we purify ourselves from all iniquity. "We shall see him as he is. And everyone who thus hopes in him purifies himself as he is pure" (1 John 3:2–3). The enjoyment of present fellowship and the hope of this coming vision of God are compelling motives for purity of heart and life.

Lord, make us pure in heart that we may see you!

JANUARY 9

Whoever brings blessing will be enriched.

Proverbs 11:25

If I want my soul to flourish, I must not hoard up my stores, but must distribute to the poor. To be tight and miserly is the world's way to prosperity, but it is not God's way. For God says, "One gives freely, yet grows all the richer; another withholds what he should give, and only suffers want" (Prov. 11:24). Faith's way of gaining is giving. I must try this again and again. And I may expect that as much prosperity as will be good for me will come to me as a gracious reward for a generous course of action.

Of course, I may not be sure of growing rich. I will "be enriched," but not with more riches than my soul can bear. Too many riches might weigh me down, tethering my heart to the treasures of this world or tying me down so I am no longer nimble in the service of God. Just as too much food can lead to heart disease, so too many riches can lead to soul disease. We must be learn to be content with the earthly treasure which God in his wisdom allows us to enjoy and look forward to the heavenly treasure that awaits the children of God.

But there is a mental and spiritual wealth which I greatly desire. And these come as the result of generous thoughts toward my God, his church, and my fellow men. Let me not be stingy, lest I starve my heart. Let me be bountiful and generous; for in this way I will be like my Lord. He gave himself for me: Will I grudge him anything?

JANUARY 10

One who waters will himself be watered.

Proverbs 11:25

If I carefully consider others, God will consider me. In some way or other he will recompense me. Let me consider the poor, and the Lord will consider me. Let me look after little children, and the Lord will treat me as his child. Let me feed his flock, and he will feed me. Let me water his garden, and he will make my soul a watered garden. This is the Lord's own promise: may I fulfill the condition, and then may I expect its fulfillment.

I may care about myself until I grow morbid. I may watch over my own feelings until I feel nothing. I may lament my weakness until I grow almost too weak to lament. It would be far more profitable for me to become unselfish, and out of love to my Lord Jesus begin to care for the souls of those around me.

My water tank is getting very low. No fresh rain comes to fill it. So what should I do? I will open the outlet, and let its contents run out to water the withering plants around me. What do I see? My cistern seems to fill as it flows. A secret spring is at work! While all was stagnant, the fresh spring was sealed. But as my reserves flow out to water others, the Lord considers my needs. Hallelujah!

JANUARY 11

When I bring clouds over the earth and the bow is
seen in the clouds, I will remember my covenant.

Genesis 9:14–15

Just now clouds are plentiful enough, but we are not afraid that the world
will be destroyed by a deluge. We see the rainbow often enough to prevent
us having any such fears. The covenant that the Lord made with Noah
stands fast, and we have no doubts about it. Why, then, should we think
that the clouds of trouble, which now darken our sky, will end in our
destruction? Let us dismiss such groundless and dishonoring fears.

Faith always sees the bow of covenant promise whenever sense sees
the cloud of affliction. God has a bow with which he might shoot out his
arrows of destruction. But look! It is turned upward. It is a bow without
an arrow or a string. It is a bow hung up for show, no longer used for
war. It is a bow of many colors, expressing joy and delight. It is not a bow
blood red with slaughter or black with anger.

So let us be of good courage. God never darkens our sky so as to leave
us without a sign of his covenant. And, even if he did, we would trust
him, since he cannot change, or lie, or in any other way fail to keep his
covenant of peace. Until the waters go over the earth again, we will have
no reason for doubting our God.

JANUARY 12

For the Lord will not
cast off forever.

Lamentations 3:31

The Lord may cast away for a season, but not forever. A woman may leave off her favorite jewelry for a few days, but she will not forget it, nor throw it in the wastebasket. In the same way, the Lord will not cast away those whom he loves. For, "having loved his own who were in the world, he loved them to the end" (John 13:1). Some talk of our being "in grace" and "out of it," as if we were like rabbits that run in and out of their burrows. But, it is not so. The Lord's love is far more serious and enduring.

He chose us from eternity, and he will love us throughout eternity. Jesus loved us so much that he died for us, and we may therefore be sure that his love will never die. His honor is so wrapped up in the salvation of the believer that he can no more cast us off than he can cast off the robes of his office as the King of glory. No, no! The Lord Jesus, as a Head, never casts off the members of his body. As a Husband, he never casts off his bride.

Did you think you have been cast off? Why did you think such evil of the Lord who has betrothed you to himself? Cast off such thoughts, and never let them lodge in your soul again. "God has not rejected his people whom he foreknew" (Rom. 11:2). "He hates divorce" (Mal. 2:16 NKJV).

JANUARY 13

Whoever comes to me I will never cast out.

John 6:37

Has there ever been a case of our Lord's casting out a coming one? If there is, we would like to know about it! But there has been none, and there never will be. Among the lost souls in hell there is not one that can say, "I went to Jesus, and he refused me." It is not possible that you or I should be the first to whom Jesus will break his word. Let us not entertain so dark a suspicion.

Suppose we go to Jesus now about the evils of today. Of this we may be sure—he will not refuse to give us an audience or cast us out. Those of us who have often been to him, and those who have never gone before—let us go together, and we will see that he will not shut the door of his grace in the face of any one of us.

"This man receives sinners," but he repulses none (Luke 15:2). We come to him in weakness and sin, with trembling faith, small knowledge, and slender hope. But still he does not cast us out. We come by prayer, and those prayers are broken. We come with confession, and that confession is faulty. We come with praise, and that praise falls far short of his merits. And yet he receives us. We come diseased, polluted, worn out, and worthless. But still he does not cast us out.

Let us come again today to him who never casts us out.

JANUARY 14

Come to me, all who labor and are heavy
laden, and I will give you rest.

Matthew 11:28

We who are saved find rest in Jesus. Those who are not saved will receive rest if they come to him, for here he promises to "give" it. Nothing can be freer than a gift. Let us gladly accept what he gladly gives. You are not to buy it, nor to borrow it; but to receive it as a gift. Do you labor under the lash of ambition, covetousness, lust, or anxiety? He will set you free from this iron bondage and give you rest. You are "laden"—yes, "*heavy laden*" with sin, fear, care, remorse, and fear of death. But if you come to him, he will unload you. He carried the crushing mass of our sin, that we might no longer carry it. He made himself the great Burden-Bearer, that we might no longer bend under the enormous pressure of our heavy burdens.

Jesus gives rest. It is so. Will you believe it? Will you put it to the test? Will you do so at once? Come to Jesus by quitting every other hope, by thinking of him, believing God's testimony about him, and trusting everything with him. If you come to him in this way, the rest which he will give you will be deep, safe, holy, and everlasting. He gives a rest which grows into heaven. And he gives it *this* day to all who come to him.

JANUARY 15

For the needy shall not always be forgotten,
and the hope of the poor shall not perish forever.

Psalm 9:18

Poverty is a hard inheritance. But those who trust in the Lord are made rich by faith. They know that they are not forgotten by God. Though it may seem they are overlooked in his providential distribution of good things, they look to a time when all this will be put right. Lazarus will not always lie among the dogs at the rich man's gate, but he will have his reward at Abraham's side (Luke 16:21–22).

Even now the Lord remembers his poor but precious sons. "I am poor and needy, but the Lord takes thought for me," said one of old (Ps. 40:17). And so it is. The godly poor have great expectations. They expect the Lord to provide everything necessary for life and godliness (2 Pet. 1:3). They expect to see all things working for their good (Rom. 8:28). They expect to have all the closer fellowship with their Lord, for he had nowhere to lay his head (Luke 9:58). They expect to share in the glory of his second coming. This expectation cannot perish for it is laid up in Christ Jesus, who lives forever; and because he lives, it will live also. The poor saint sings many a song which the rich sinner cannot understand. Therefore, let us, when we have meager provisions below, think of the royal table above.

JANUARY 16

And it shall come to pass that everyone who calls
on the name of the LORD shall be saved.

Joel 2:32

Why don't I call on his name? Why do I run to this neighbor and that, when God is so near and will hear my faintest call? Why do I sit down and devise schemes and invent plans? Why not at once hand myself and my burden over to the Lord? Straight ahead is the best direction to run. So why don't I run at once to the living God? It is useless to look for deliverance anywhere else. But with God I shall find it. For here I have his royal "shall" to guarantee it—"it *shall* come to pass."

I need not ask whether I *may* call on him or not, for that word "everyone" is a very wide and comprehensive one. "Everyone" means *me*, for it means anybody and everybody who calls upon God. I will therefore follow the leading of the text and at once call upon the glorious Lord who has made such a large promise.

My case is urgent, and I do not see how I can be delivered. But the means of my deliverance is not my business. He who makes the promise will find ways and means of keeping it. It is my task to obey his commands; it is not mine to direct his plans. I am his servant, not his master. I call upon him, and he will deliver me.

JANUARY 17

He said, "But I will be with you."

Exodus 3:12

Of course, if the Lord sent Moses on an errand, he would not let him go alone. The tremendous risk it would involve, and the great power it would require, would render it ridiculous for God to send a poor, lone Hebrew to confront the mightiest king in all the world, and then leave him to himself. It could not be imagined that a wise God would match poor Moses with Pharaoh and the enormous forces of Egypt. Hence he says, "I will certainly be with you" (Ex. 3:12 NKJV), as if it were out of the question that he would send him alone.

In my case, also, the same rule will hold good. If I go on the Lord's errand, with a simple reliance upon his power and a single eye to his glory, it is certain that he will be with me. His sending me binds him to back me up. Is this not enough? What more can I want? If all the angels and archangels were with me, I might fail. But if *he* is with me, I must succeed.

But let me take care that I respond to this promise in a worthy way. Don't let me go timidly, halfheartedly, carelessly, or presumptuously. What type of person ought he to be who has God with him? In such company, I ought to play the man and, like Moses, go to Pharaoh without fear.

JANUARY 18

When his soul makes an offering for guilt,
he shall see his offspring.

Isaiah 53:10

Our Lord Jesus has not died in vain. His death was sacrificial: he died as our substitute, because death was the penalty of our sins. And, because his substitution was accepted by God, he has saved those for whom he made his soul a sacrifice. By death he became like the grain of wheat which produces a great harvest. There must be a succession of children for Jesus, for he is the "Everlasting Father" (Isa. 9:6). He will say, "Behold, I and the children God has given me" (Heb. 2:13).

A man is honored in his children, and Jesus has his quiver full of these arrows of the mighty (Ps. 127:5). A man is represented in his children, and so is Christ in Christians. In his seed a man's life seems to be prolonged and extended; and so the life of Jesus is continued in believers.

Jesus lives, for he sees his seed. He fixes his eye on us; he delights in us; he recognizes us as the fruit of his soul's labor. Let us be glad that our Lord does not fail to enjoy the result of his dreadful sacrifice, and that he will never cease to feast his eyes upon the harvest of his death. Those eyes, which once wept for us, are now viewing us with pleasure. Yes, he looks on those who are looking to him. Our eyes meet! What a joy is this!

JANUARY 19

If you confess with your mouth that Jesus is
Lord and believe in your heart that God raised
him from the dead, you will be saved.

Romans 10:9

There must be confession with the mouth. Have I made it? Have I openly pledged my faith in Jesus as the Savior whom God has raised from the dead? And have I done it in God's way? These are questions we must each honestly ask ourselves.

There must also be belief with the heart. Do I sincerely believe in the risen Lord Jesus? Do I trust in him as my sole hope of salvation? Is this trust from my heart? Let me answer before God.

If I can truly claim that I have both confessed Christ and believed in him, then *I am saved*. The text does not say it *may* be so, but it is plain as day, and clear as the sun in the heavens: "You will be saved." As a believer and a confessor, I may lay my hand on this promise and plead it before the Lord God at this moment, throughout life, in the hour of death, and at the day of judgment.

I must be saved from the guilt of sin, the power of sin, the punishment of sin, and ultimately from the very being of sin. God has said it: "You will be saved." I believe it. I will be saved. I am saved. Glory be to God forever and ever!

To the one who conquers I will grant to eat of the
tree of life, which is in the paradise of God.

Revelation 2:7

No man may turn his back in the day of battle or refuse to go to the holy
war. We must fight if we would reign, and we must carry on the warfare
until we overcome every enemy. Otherwise this promise is not for us,
since it is only for "the one who conquers." We are to overcome the false
prophets who have come into the world, and all the evils which accompany their teaching. We are to overcome our own faintness of heart and
our tendency to lose our first love. Read the whole of the Spirit's Word to
the church at Ephesus (Rev. 2:1–7).

If by grace we win the day, as we will if we truly follow our conquering Leader, then we will be admitted to the very center of the paradise of
God. We will be permitted to pass by the cherubim and his flaming sword
(Gen. 3:24), and come to that guarded tree from which, if a man eats, he
will live forever. We will thus escape that endless death that is the doom
of sin. Instead, we will gain everlasting life that is the seal of innocence,
the outgrowth of immortal principles of Godlike holiness.

Come, my heart, pluck up courage! To flee the conflict will be to lose
the joys of the new and better Eden. To fight until victory is to walk with
God in paradise.

JANUARY 21

The Egyptians shall know that I am the LORD.

Exodus 7:5

The ungodly world is hard to teach. Egypt does not know the Lord, and therefore dares to set up its idols. It even ventures to ask, "Who is the LORD?" (Ex. 5:2). Yet the Lord intends to break proud hearts, whether they choose or not. When his judgments thunder over their heads, darken their skies, destroy their harvests, and slay their sons, they begin to discern something of the Lord's power. There will again be such things done in the earth to bring skeptics to their knees. Let us not be dismayed because of their blasphemies, for the Lord can take care of his own name, and he will do so in a very effectual manner.

The salvation of his own people was another powerful means of making Egypt know that the God of Israel was the Lord, the living and true God. No Israelite died by any one of the ten plagues. None of the chosen seed were drowned in the Red Sea. In the same way, the salvation of the elect and the sure glorification of all true believers will make the most obstinate of God's enemies acknowledge that "the LORD, he is God" (1 Kings 18:39).

Oh, that his convincing power would go forth by his Holy Spirit in the preaching of the gospel until all nations bow at the name of Jesus and call him Lord!

JANUARY 22

Blessed is the one who considers the poor!
In the day of trouble the LORD delivers him.

Psalm 41:1

To think about the poor and let them lie on our hearts is a Christian man's duty. For Jesus placed them with us and near us when he said, "For you always have the poor with you" (Matt. 26:11).

Many give their money to the poor in a hurry, without thought. And many more give nothing at all. This precious promise belongs to those who *consider* the poor, look into their case, devise plans for their benefit, and considerately carry them out. We can do more by care than by cash, and most with the two together.

To those who consider the poor, the Lord promises his own consideration in times of distress. He will bring us out of trouble if we help others when they are in trouble. We will receive very special providential help if the Lord sees that we try to provide for others. We will have a time of trouble, however generous we may be. But if we are charitable, we may put in a claim for peculiar deliverance, and the Lord will not deny his own word and bond. Miserly curmudgeons may help themselves, but considerate and generous believers will be helped by the Lord. As you have done to others, so will the Lord do to you. So empty your pockets!

JANUARY 23

He shall lay his hand on the head of the burnt offering, and
it shall be accepted for him to make atonement for him.

Leviticus 1:4

If the bull becomes his sacrifice when the one who offers it lays his hand on it, how much more will Jesus become ours by the laying on of the hand of faith?

> My faith doth lay her hand
> on that dear head of thine,
> while like a penitent I stand,
> and there confess my sin.
>
> *Isaac Watts*

If a bull could be accepted to make atonement, how much more will the Lord Jesus be our full and all-sufficient propitiation? Some quarrel with the great truth of substitution. But as for us, it is our hope, our joy, our boast, our all. Jesus is accepted for us to make atonement for us, and we are "blessed . . . in Christ" (Eph. 1:3).

Let the reader take care at once to lay his hand on the Lord's completed sacrifice, that by accepting it he may obtain the benefit of it. If he has done so once, let him do it again. If he has never done so, let him put out his hand without a moment's delay. Jesus is yours now if you will have him. Lean on him; lean hard on him; and he is yours beyond all question. You are reconciled to God, your sins are blotted out, and you are the Lord's.

JANUARY 24

He will guard the feet of his faithful ones.

1 Samuel 2:9

The way is slippery, and our feet are feeble. But the Lord will keep our feet. If we give ourselves up by obedient faith to be his holy ones, he will himself be our guardian. Not only will he charge his angels to keep us (Ps. 91:11), but he himself will preserve our ways (Ps. 121:8).

He will keep our feet from falling, so that we do not defile our garments, wound our souls, and cause the enemy to blaspheme.

He will keep our feet from wandering, so that we do not enter paths of error, or ways of folly, or routes of the world's custom.

He will keep our feet from swelling through weariness, or blistering because of the roughness and length of the way.

He will keep our feet from wounding. Our shoes will be iron and brass, so that even though we tread on the edge of the sword, or on deadly serpents, we will not bleed or be poisoned.

He will also pluck our feet out of the net. We will not be entangled by the deceit of our malicious and crafty foes.

With such a promise as this, let us run without weariness and walk without fear. He who guards our feet will do so effectively.

JANUARY 25

He sings before men and says:
"I sinned and perverted what was right,
and it was not repaid to me.
He has redeemed my soul from going down into the pit,
and my life shall look upon the light."

Job 33:27–28

This is a word of truth, gathered from the experience of a man of God, and it is tantamount to a promise. What the Lord has done and is doing, he will continue to do while the world stands. The Lord will receive to his heart all who come to him with a sincere confession of their sin. In fact, he is always on the lookout to discover any that are in trouble because of their faults.

Can we not endorse the language used here? Have we not sinned—sinned personally so as to say, "I have sinned"? Sinned willfully, having perverted that which is right? Sinned so as to discover that there is no profit in it, but an eternal loss? Let us, then, go to God with this honest acknowledgment. He asks no more. We can do no less.

Let us plead his promise in the name of Jesus. He will deliver us from the pit of hell even though it yawns open before us. He will grant us life and light. Why should we despair? Why should we even doubt? The Lord does not mock humble souls. He means what he says. The guilty can be forgiven. Those who deserve execution can receive free pardon.

Lord, we confess, and we ask you to forgive!

JANUARY 26

For there is no enchantment against Jacob,
no divination against Israel.

Numbers 23:23

How this should cut out—root and branch—all silly, superstitious fears! Even if there were any truth in witchcraft and omens, they could not affect the people of the Lord. Those whom God blesses, devils cannot curse.

Ungodly men, like Balaam, may cunningly plot the overthrow of the Lord's Israel (Numbers 23). But despite all their secrecy and scheming, they are doomed to fail. Their powder is damp; the edge of their sword is blunted. They gather together, but since the Lord is not with them, they gather together in vain. We may sit still and let them weave their nets, for we will not be captured in them. Though they call in the aid of Satan and employ all his serpentlike craft, it will not profit them at all. Their spells will not work and their divination will deceive them. What a blessing this is! How it stills the heart! God's "Jacobs" wrestle with God (Gen. 32:22–32), but none will wrestle with them and overcome. God's "Israels" have power with God and overcome, but none will have power to overcome against them. We need not fear the fiend himself, nor any of those secret enemies whose words are full of deceit, and whose plans are deep and unfathomable. They cannot hurt those who trust in the living God. We defy the devil and all his legions!

JANUARY 27

And there you shall remember your ways and all your
deeds with which you have defiled yourselves, and you shall
loathe yourselves for all the evils that you have committed.

Ezekiel 20:43

When we are accepted by the Lord, and are standing in the place of favor and peace and safety, then we are led to repent of all our failures and wrongdoing toward our gracious God. So precious is repentance that we may call it a diamond of the highest quality. And repentance is sweetly promised to the people of God. It is one of the main ways their salvation results in their sanctification. The God who accepts repentance also gives repentance. And repentance is not bitter food. It is like "wafers made with honey" on which he feeds his people (Ex. 16:31).

A sense of blood-bought pardon and of undeserved mercy is the best means of dissolving a heart of stone. Are we feeling hard? Let us think of covenant love, and then we will leave sin, lament sin, and loathe sin. Yes, we will loathe ourselves for sinning against such infinite love. Let us come to God with this promise of penitence and ask him to help us to remember, repent, regret, and return. Oh, that we could enjoy the melting heat of holy sorrow! What a relief would a flood of tears be! Lord, smite the rock, or speak to the rock, and cause the waters to flow (Ex. 17:1–7)!

JANUARY 28

He will wipe away every tear from their eyes.

Revelation 21:4

Yes, we will come to this if we are believers. Sorrow will cease, and tears will be wiped away. This is the world of weeping, but it passes away. There will be a new heaven and a new earth, so says the first verse of this chapter. And therefore there will be nothing to weep over concerning humanity's fall into sin and its consequent miseries. Read the second verse, and note how it speaks of the bride and her marriage. The Lamb's wedding is a time for boundless pleasure, and tears would be out of place. The third verse says that God himself will dwell among men; and surely at his right hand there are pleasures forevermore, and tears can no longer flow (Ps. 16:11).

What will our state be when there is no more sorrow, no more crying, no more pain? It will be more glorious than we can as yet imagine. Eyes that are red with weeping, cease your scalding flow, for in a little while you will know no more tears! None can wipe tears away like the God of love, and he is coming to do it. "Weeping may tarry for the night, but joy comes with the morning" (Ps. 30:5).

Come, Lord, and do not delay; for now both men and women must weep!

JANUARY 29

Be careful to obey all these words that I command
you, that it may go well with you and with your
children after you forever, when you do what is good
and right in the sight of the LORD your God.

Deuteronomy 12:28

Though salvation is not by the works of the law, yet the blessings which are promised to obedience are not denied to the faithful servants of God. The curses our Lord took away when he was made a curse for us, but no clause promising blessing has been abolished.

We are to note and listen to the revealed will of the Lord, giving our attention not just to parts of it, but to "all these words." There must be no picking and choosing, but an impartial respect to all that God has commanded. This is the road of blessing for parents and their children. The Lord's blessing is on those he has chosen to the third and fourth generation. If they walk uprightly before him, he will make all men know that they are a seed which the Lord has blessed.

No blessing can come to us or ours through dishonesty or double dealing. The ways of worldly conformity and unholiness cannot bring good to us or ours. It will go well with us when we go well before God. If integrity does not make us prosper, cheating will not. That which gives pleasure to God will bring pleasure to us.

JANUARY 30

Behold, I am with you and will keep you wherever you go.

Genesis 28:15

Do we need journeying mercies? Here are choice ones—God's presence and preservation. In all places we need both of these, and in all places we will have them if we go at the call of duty and not merely according to our own fancy. Why should we regard moving to another country as a sorrowful necessity when it is laid on us by the divine will? In all lands the believer is equally a pilgrim and a stranger. And yet also in every region the Lord is his dwelling place, even as he has been to his saints in all generations. We may miss the protection of an earthly monarch, but when God says, "I will keep you," we are in no real danger. This is a blessed passport for a traveler and a heavenly escort for an emigrant.

Jacob had never left his father's house before. He had been a mother's boy and not an adventurer like his brother. Yet he went abroad, and God went with him. He had little luggage and no attendants. Yet no prince ever journeyed with a nobler bodyguard. Even while he slept in the open field, angels watched over him, and the Lord God spoke to him. If the Lord sends us, let us say with our Lord Jesus, "Rise, let us go from here" (John 14:31).

JANUARY 31

My God will hear me.

Micah 7:7

Friends may be unfaithful, but the Lord will not turn away from the gracious soul. On the contrary, he will hear all its desires. The prophet says, "Guard the doors of your mouth from her who lies in your arms. . . . A man's enemies are the men of his own house" (Mic. 7:5–6). This is a wretched state of affairs. But even in such a case, the best Friend remains true, and we may tell him all our grief.

Our wisdom is to look to the Lord and not to quarrel with men or women. If our loving appeals are disregarded by our own relatives, let us wait upon the God of our salvation, for he will hear us. He will hear us all the more because of the unkindness and oppression of others. We will soon have reason to cry, "Rejoice not over me, O my enemy" (Mic. 7:8).

Because God is the living God, he can hear. Because he is a loving God, he will hear. Because he is our covenant God, he has bound himself to hear us. If we can each one speak of him as "my God," we may with absolute certainty say, "My God will hear me." Come, then, oh, bleeding heart, and let your sorrows tell themselves out to the Lord your God! I will bow the knee in secret and inwardly whisper, "My God will hear me."

FEBRUARY

FEBRUARY 1

But for you who fear my name, the sun of
righteousness shall rise with healing in its wings.

Malachi 4:2

Fulfilled once in the first coming of our glorious Lord, and yet to have a fuller accomplishment in his second coming, this gracious word is also for daily use. Is it dark with the reader? Does the night deepen into a denser blackness? Still, let us not despair: the sun will yet rise. When the night is darkest, dawn is nearest.

The sun which will arise is not the common sort. It is *the* sun—the Sun of Righteousness, whose every ray is holiness. He who comes to cheer us comes in the way of justice as well as of mercy, comes to violate no law as he saves us. Jesus as much displays the holiness of God as his love. Our deliverance, when it comes, will be safe because it is righteous.

Our one point of inquiry should be: Do we fear the name of the Lord? Do we reverence the living God and walk in his ways? Then for us the night must be short. And when the morning comes, all the sickness and sorrow of our soul will be over forever. Light, warmth, joy, and clearness of vision will come, and healing of every disease and distress will follow after.

Has Jesus risen upon us? Let us sit in the sun. Has he hidden his face? Let us wait for his rising. He will shine forth as surely as the sun.

FEBRUARY 2

For you who fear my name, the sun of righteousness
shall rise with healing in its wings. You shall
go out leaping like calves from the stall.

Malachi 4:2

Yes, when the sun shines, the sick leave their bedrooms and walk out to breathe the fresh air. When the sun brings spring and summer, the cattle leave their stalls and seek pasture on the higher Alps. Even thus, when we have conscious fellowship with our Lord, we leave the stall of despondency and walk out into the fields of holy confidence. We ascend to the mountains of joy and feed on sweet pasture that grows nearer heaven than the provisions of men of the flesh.

To "go out" and "to grow" (Mal. 4:2 NKJV) is a double promise. Oh, my soul, be eager to enjoy both blessings! Why should you be a prisoner? Arise, and walk at liberty. Jesus says that his sheep "will go in and out and find pasture" (John 10:9). Go out, then, and feed in the rich meadows of boundless love.

Why remain a babe in grace? Grow up. Young calves grow fast, especially if they are "stall-fed" (NKJV). And you have the best care of your Redeemer. Grow, then, in grace and in the knowledge of your Lord and Savior. Be neither confined nor stunted. The sun of righteousness has risen upon you. Respond to his beams as the buds to the natural sun. Open your heart; expand and grow up into him in all things.

FEBRUARY 3

He who did not spare his own Son but gave him up for us all,
how will he not also with him graciously give us all things?

Romans 8:32

If this is not a promise in form, it is in fact. Indeed, it is more than one promise; it is a conglomerate of promises. It is a mass of rubies, and emeralds, and diamonds, with a nugget of gold for their setting. It is a question which can never be answered so as to cause us any anxiety of heart. What can the Lord deny us after giving us Jesus? If we need all things in heaven and earth, he will grant them to us. For if there had been a limit anywhere, he would have kept back his own Son.

What do I need today? I have only to ask for it. I may seek earnestly, but not as if I had to use pressure and extort an unwilling gift from the Lord's hand. For he will give *freely*. Of his own will, he gave us his own Son. Certainly no one would have proposed such a gift to him. No one would have ventured to ask for it. It would have been too presumptuous. He freely gave his Only-Begotten; and, oh, my soul, can you not then trust your heavenly Father to give you anything—to give you everything? Your poor prayer would have no force with Omnipotence if force were needed. But his love, like a spring, rises of itself and overflows for the supply of all your needs.

FEBRUARY 4

I will not leave you as orphans; I will come to you.

John 14:18

He left us, and yet we are not left orphans. He is our comfort, and he is gone, but we are not comfortless. Our comfort is that he will come to us, and this is consolation enough to sustain us through his prolonged absence. Jesus is already on his way. He says, "I come quickly" (Rev. 22:12 KJV). He rides posthaste toward us. He says, "I will come." And none can prevent his coming or put it back for a quarter of an hour. He specially says, "I will come *to you*," and so he will. His coming is specially to and for his own people. This is meant to be their present comfort while they mourn that the Bridegroom does not yet appear.

When we lose the joyful sense of his presence, we mourn. But we may not sorrow as if there were no hope. Our Lord in his discipline has hidden himself from us for a moment, but he will return in full favor. He leaves us in a sense, but only in a sense. When he withdraws, he leaves a pledge behind that he will return. Oh, Lord, come quickly! There is no life in this earthly existence if you are gone. We sigh for the return of your sweet smile. When will you come to us? We are sure you will appear. But be like a young deer. Make no delay, oh, our God!

FEBRUARY 5

And when I see the blood, I will pass over you.

Exodus 12:13

My own sight of the precious blood is for my comfort; but it is the Lord's sight of it that secures my safety. Even when I am unable to behold it, the Lord looks at it and passes over me because of it. If I am not so much at ease as I ought to be because my faith is dim, yet I am equally safe because the Lord's eye is not dim. And he sees the blood of the great Sacrifice with a steady gaze. What a joy is this!

The Lord sees the deep inner meaning, the infinite fullness of all that is meant by the death of his dear Son. He sees it with restful memory of justice satisfied, and all his matchless attributes glorified. He beheld creation in its progress and said, "It is very good" (Gen. 1:31). But what does he say of redemption in its completeness? What does he say of the obedience even to death of his well-beloved Son (Phil. 2:8)? None can tell his delight in Jesus, his contentment with the sweet savor which Jesus presented when he offered himself without spot to God.

Now rest we in calm security. We have God's Sacrifice and God's Word to create in us a sense of perfect security. He will, he must, pass over us because he spared not our glorious Substitute. Justice joins hands with love to provide everlasting salvation for all the ones sprinkled with blood.

FEBRUARY 6

And all these blessings shall come upon you and
overtake you, if you obey the voice of the LORD
your God. Blessed shall you be in the city.

Deuteronomy 28:2–3

The city is full of care, and he who has to go there from day to day finds
it to be a place of great wear and tear. It is full of noise, and movement,
and bustle, and suffering. Many are its temptations, losses, and worries.
But to go there with divine blessing takes off the edge of its difficulty. To
remain there with that blessing is to find pleasure in its duties and strength
equal to its demands.

A blessing in the city may not make us great, but it will keep us good.
It may not make us rich, but it will keep us honest. Whether we are
porters, or clerks, or managers, or merchants, or magistrates, the city
will afford us opportunities for usefulness. It is good fishing where there
are shoals of fish, and there is hope when we work for our Lord among
the thronging crowds. We might prefer the quiet of a country life, but if
called to the town, then we may certainly prefer it because there is room
for our energies.

Today let us expect good things because of this promise, and let our
care be to have an open ear to the voice of the Lord and a ready hand to
execute his will. Obedience brings the blessing. In keeping his commandments "there is great reward" (Ps. 19:11).

FEBRUARY 7

If you return to the Almighty you will be built up.

Job 22:23

Eliphaz, in these words, spoke a great truth which is the summary of many an inspired Scripture.

Reader, has sin pulled you down? Have you become like a ruin? Has the hand of the Lord gone out against you, so that in body you are impoverished and in Spirit you are broken down? Was it your own folly which brought upon you all this dilapidation?

Then the first thing to do is to return to the Lord. With deep repentance and sincere faith, find your way back from your backsliding. It is your duty, for you have turned away from him whom you professed to serve. It is your wisdom, for you cannot strive against him and prosper. It is your immediate necessity, for what he has done is nothing compared to what he may do in the way of discipline, since he is almighty to punish.

See what a promise invites you! You will be "built up." None but the Almighty can set up the fallen pillars and restore the tottering walls of your condition. But he can, and he will do it if you return to him. Do not delay. Your crushed mind may fail you if you go on to rebel. But hearty confession will ease you, and humble faith will console you. Do this, and all will be well.

FEBRUARY 8

I will uphold you with my righteous right hand.

Isaiah 41:10

Fear of falling is healthy. To be reckless is not a sign of wisdom. There are times when we feel that we will collapse unless we have a very special support. Here we have it. God's right hand is a grand thing to lean upon. Mind you, it is not only his hand, though it keeps heaven and earth in their places, but his *right* hand. It is his power united with skill; his power where it is most dexterous. And this is not all, for it is written, "I will uphold you with *my righteous* right hand." That hand which he uses to maintain his holiness and to execute his royal sentences—this will be stretched out to hold up his trusting ones. Fearful is our danger, but joyful is our security. The man whom God upholds, devils cannot throw down.

Weak may be our feet, but almighty is God's right hand. Rough may be the road, but Omnipotence is our upholding. We may boldly go forward. We will not fall. Let us lean continually where all things lean. God will not withdraw his strength, for his righteousness is there as well. He will be faithful to his promise, and faithful to his Son, and therefore faithful to us. How happy we ought to be! Are you happy today?

FEBRUARY 9

And I will put this third into the fire,
and refine them as one refines silver,
and test them as gold is tested.
They will call upon my name,
and I will answer them.
I will say, "They are my people";
and they will say, "The LORD is my God."

Zechariah 13:9

Grace transforms us into precious metal, and then the fire and the furnace of suffering follow as a necessary consequence. Are we alarmed by this? Would we sooner be considered worthless that we might be inactive, like the stones of the field? This would be to choose the worst option—like Esau, to take some stew and give up the covenant portion (Gen. 25:29–34). No, Lord, we will gladly be cast into the furnace rather than be cast out from your presence!

The fire only refines; it does not destroy. We are to be brought through the fire, not left in it. The Lord values his people as silver, and therefore he is at pains to purge away their dross. If we are wise, we will welcome the refining process rather than decline it. Our prayer will be that our alloy may be taken from us rather than that we should be withdrawn from the crucible.

Oh, Lord, you test us indeed! We are ready to melt under the fierceness of the flame. Still, this is your way, and your way is the best. Sustain us under the trial and complete the process of our purifying, and we will be yours forever and ever.

FEBRUARY 10

For you will be a witness for him to everyone
of what you have seen and heard.

Acts 22:15

Paul was chosen to see and hear the Lord speaking to him out of heaven. This divine election was a high privilege for him. But it was not intended to end with him. It was meant to have an influence on others; yes, on all people. It is to Paul that Europe owes the gospel at this hour.

It is ours in our measure to be witnesses of that which the Lord has revealed to us. And it is at our peril that we hide the precious revelation. First, we must see and hear, or we will have nothing to tell. But when we have done so, we must be eager to bear our testimony. It must be personal: "You will be." It must be for Christ: "You will be a witness for him." It must be constant and all-absorbing. We are to be this above all other things, and to the exclusion of many other matters. Our witness must not be to a select few who will gladly receive us, but "to everyone"—to all whom we can reach, young or old, rich or poor, good or bad. We must never be silent like those who are possessed by a dumb spirit. For the text before us is a command, and a promise, and we must not miss it: "*You will be a witness for him.*" "You will be my witnesses," says the Lord (Acts 1:8).

Lord, fulfill this word to me as well!

FEBRUARY 11

I will pour my Spirit upon your offspring,
and my blessing on your descendants.

Isaiah 44:3

Our dear children do not have the Spirit of God by nature, as we plainly see. We see much in them which makes us fear for their future, and this drives us to agonizing prayer. When a son becomes especially obstinate, we cry with Abraham, "Oh that Ishmael might live before you!" (Gen. 17:18). We would sooner see our daughters like Hannah than like princesses (1 Samuel 1–2). This verse should greatly encourage us. It comes after the words, "Fear not, O Jacob my servant," and it may well dispel our fears (Isa. 44:2).

The Lord will give his Spirit; will give him plentifully, pouring him out; will give him effectually, so that he will be a real and eternal blessing. Under this divine outpouring, our children will come forward, and "one will say, 'I am the LORD's,' another will call on the name of Jacob" (Isa. 44:5).

This is one of those promises about which we may ask the Lord. Should we not, at set times, in a distinct manner, pray for our offspring? We cannot give them new hearts, but the Holy Spirit can; and he is easily to be entreated. The great Father takes pleasure in the prayers of fathers and mothers. Have we any dear ones outside of the ark? Let us not rest till they are shut in with us by the Lord's own hand (Gen. 7:13–16).

FEBRUARY 12

The LORD said to Abram, after Lot had separated
from him, "Lift up your eyes and look from the
place where you are, northward and southward and
eastward and westward, for all the land that you see
I will give to you and to your offspring forever."

Genesis 13:14–15

A special blessing for a memorable occasion. Abram had settled a family dispute. He had said, "Let there be no strife between you and me . . . for we are kinsmen" (Gen. 13:8). And as a result, he received the blessing that belongs to peacemakers. The Lord and giver of peace delights to manifest his grace to those who seek peace and pursue it. If we desire closer communion with God, we must keep closer to the ways of peace.

Abram had behaved very generously to his kinsman, giving him his choice of the land. If we deny ourselves for peace's sake, the Lord will more than make it up to us. As far as the patriarch can see, he can claim, and we may do the like by faith. Abram had to wait for the actual possession, but the Lord bestowed the land upon him and his posterity. Boundless blessings belong to us by covenant gift. All things are ours. When we please the Lord, he makes us look everywhere and see all things as ours. Whether things present or things to come, all are ours. And we are Christ's, and Christ is God's.

FEBRUARY 13

Blessed shall you be in the field.

Deuteronomy 28:3

So was Isaac blessed when he walked there in the evening to meditate. How often has the Lord met us when we have been alone! The hedges and the trees can bear witness to our joy. We look for such blessing again.

So was Boaz blessed when he reaped his harvest and his workmen met him with blessings. May the Lord prosper all who drive the plow! Every farmer may urge this promise with God, if indeed he obeys the voice of the Lord God.

We go to the field to labor as father Adam did. And, since the curse fell on the soil through the sin of the first Adam, it is a great comfort to find a blessing through the second Adam, Jesus.

We go to the field for exercise, and we are happy in the belief that the Lord will bless that exercise and give us health that we will use to his glory.

We go to the field to study nature, and there is nothing in a knowledge of the visible creation that may not be sanctified to the highest uses by the divine blessing.

Last of all, we have to go to the field to bury our dead. Indeed, others will in their turn take us to be buried in the field. But we are blessed, whether weeping at the tomb or sleeping in it.

FEBRUARY 14

Steadfast love surrounds the one who trusts in the LORD.

Psalm 32:10

Oh, fair reward of trust! My Lord, grant it me to the full! Above all men, the one who trusts in the Lord feels himself to be a sinner. And, look, mercy is prepared for him. He knows that he deserves nothing, but mercy comes and provides for him on a generous scale. Oh, Lord, give me this mercy, even as I trust in you!

Observe, my soul, what a bodyguard you have! As a prince is surrounded by soldiers, so are you surrounded by steadfast love. Before and behind, and on all sides, ride these mounted guards of grace. We dwell in the center of the whole system of mercy, for we dwell in Christ Jesus.

Oh, my soul, what an atmosphere you breathe! As the air surrounds you, even so does the mercy of your Lord. To the wicked there are many sorrows, but to you there are so many mercies that your sorrows are not worth mentioning. David says, "Be glad in the LORD, and rejoice, O righteous, and shout for joy, all you upright in heart!" (Ps. 32:11). In obedience to this command, my heart will triumph in God and I will proclaim my gladness. As you have surrounded me with steadfast love, I will also surround your altars, oh, my God, with songs of thanksgiving!

FEBRUARY 15

The LORD has remembered us; he will bless us.

Psalm 115:12

I can set my seal to that first sentence. Can you? Yes, the Lord has thought of us, provided for us, comforted us, delivered us, and guided us. In all the movements of his providence he has been mindful of us, never overlooking our meager affairs. His *mind* has been *full* of us—that is the other form of the word "mindful" (KJV). This has been the case all along and without a single break. At special times, however, we have more clearly seen this remembering or mindfulness, and we should recall them at this moment with overflowing gratitude. Yes, yes, "the Lord has remembered us."

The next phrase is a logical inference of the former one. Since God is unchangeable, he will continue to be mindful of us in the future, just as he has been in the past. And his mindfulness is tantamount to blessing us. But we have here, not only the conclusion of reason, but the declaration of inspiration: we have it on the Holy Spirit's authority—"*he will bless us.*" This means great and unsearchable things. The very indistinctness of the promise indicates its infinite reach. He will bless us according to his own divine manner, and he will do so forever and ever. Therefore, let us each say, "Bless the LORD, O my soul!" (Ps. 103:1).

FEBRUARY 16

I will not execute my burning anger;
I will not again destroy Ephraim;
for I am God and not a man.

Hosea 11:9

Thus the Lord makes known the mercy by which he spares us. It may
be that you have greatly displeased God, and everything threatens your
speedy doom. Let the text keep you from despair. The Lord now invites
you to consider your ways, and confess your sins. If he had been man, he
would long ago have cut you off. If he were now to act in a human way,
it would be a word and a blow and then there would be an end of you.
But it is not so, "for as the heavens are higher than the earth, so are my
ways higher than your ways" (Isa. 55:9).

You rightly judge that he is angry, but he does not keep being angry
forever. If you turn from sin to Jesus, God will turn from wrath. Because
God is God, and not man, there is still forgiveness for you, even though
you may be up to your neck in iniquity. You have God to deal with, and
not a hard man, nor even a merely just man. No human being could
have patience with you. You would have wearied an angel, as you have
wearied your sorrowing father. But God is long-suffering. Come and
try him at once. Confess, believe, and turn from your evil way, and you
will be saved.

FEBRUARY 17

But you, take courage! Do not let your hands be
weak, for your work shall be rewarded.

2 Chronicles 15:7

God had done great things for King Asa and Judah, yet they were a feeble
people. Their feet were faltering in the ways of the Lord, and their hearts
were hesitant so that they had to be warned that the Lord would be with
them while they were with him, but that if they forsook him, he would
leave them. They were also reminded how badly their sister kingdom
had suffered in its rebellion, and how the Lord was gracious to it when
repentance was shown. The Lord's design was to confirm them in his way
and make them strong in righteousness. So ought it to be with us. God
deserves to be served with all the energy of which we are capable.

If the service of God is worth anything, it is worth everything. We will
find our best reward in the Lord's work if we do it with determined diligence. Our labor is not in vain in the Lord, and we know it. Halfhearted
work will bring no reward. But, when we throw our whole soul into the
cause, we will see prosperity.

This text was sent to me at a time when my life felt like a terrible
storm, and it suggested to me that I sail full steam ahead with the assurance of reaching port in safety with a glorious cargo.

FEBRUARY 18

He fulfills the desire of those who fear him;
he also hears their cry and saves them.

Psalm 145:19

His own Spirit has wrought this desire in us, and therefore he will answer it. It is his own life within us which prompts the cry, and therefore he will hear it. Those who fear him are men under the most holy influence, and, therefore, their desire is to glorify God and enjoy him forever. Like Daniel, they are men of desires, and the Lord will cause them to realize their aspirations.

Holy desires are grace in a seed, and the heavenly Gardener will cultivate them until they come to the full corn in the ear. God-fearing men desire to be holy, to be useful, to be a blessing to others, and so to honor their Lord. They desire supplies for their need, help under burdens, guidance in perplexity, deliverance in distress. Sometimes this desire is so strong, and their case so pressing, that they cry out in agony like little children in pain. And then the Lord works in the most comprehensive way, and does all that is needed, according to this Word: "and saves them."

Yes, if we fear God, we have nothing else to fear. If we cry to the Lord, our salvation is certain. Let the reader lay this text on his tongue and keep it in his mouth all the day, and it will be to him as "wafers made with honey" (Ex. 16:31).

FEBRUARY 19

Though I have afflicted you,
I will afflict you no more.

Nahum 1:12

There is a limit to affliction. God sends it, and God removes it. Do you sigh and say, "When will this end?" Remember that our sufferings will surely and finally end when this poor earthly life is over. Let us quietly wait, and patiently endure the will of the Lord until he comes.

Meanwhile, our Father in heaven takes away the rod of discipline when his design in using it is fully served. When he has whipped away our folly, there will be no more blows. Or, if the affliction is sent to test us that our graces may glorify God, it will end when the Lord has made us bear witness to his praise. We would not wish the affliction to depart until God has gotten out of us all the honor which we can possibly yield to him.

There may today be a great calm. Who knows how soon those raging waves will give way to a sea of glass (Rev. 15:2), and the seabirds sit on the gentle waves? After a period of threshing, the flail is hung up and the wheat rests in the barn. Before long we may be just as happy as now we are sorrowful. It is not hard for the Lord to turn night into day. He that sends the clouds can as easily clear the skies. So let us be of good cheer. Better days are ahead. Let us sing "Hallelujah" in anticipation.

FEBRUARY 20

The LORD will guide you continually.

Isaiah 58:11

What troubles you? Have you lost your way? Are you entangled in a dark wood, unable to find the path? Stand still and see the salvation of God. He knows the way, and he will direct you in it if you cry to him.

Every day brings its own perplexity. How sweet to feel that the guidance of the Lord is continual! If we choose our own way, or consult with flesh and blood, we cast away the Lord's guidance. But if we abstain from self-will, then he will direct every step of our road, every hour of the day, and every day of the year, and every year of our life. If we will be guided, we will be guided. If we will commit our way to the Lord, he will direct our course so that we will not get lost.

But notice to whom this promise is made. Read the previous verse: "if you pour yourself out for the hungry" (Isa. 58:10). We must feel for others and give them, not a few dry crusts, but the same things that we ourselves would wish to receive. If we show a tender care for our fellow creatures in their hour of need, then the Lord will attend to our necessities and make himself our continual Guide. Jesus is the Leader, not of misers, nor of those who oppress the poor, but of the kind and tenderhearted. Such persons are pilgrims who will never miss their way.

FEBRUARY 21

He will bless those who fear the LORD,
both the small and the great.

Psalm 115:13

This is a word of cheer to those who are of humble station and meager estate. Our God has a very gracious consideration for those of small property, small talent, small influence, small weight. God cares for the small things in creation and even regards sparrows in their lighting upon the ground. Nothing is too small to God, for he makes use of insignificant agents for the accomplishment of his purposes. Let the least important person seek from God a blessing on his littleness, and they will find their contracted sphere to be a happy one.

Among those who fear the Lord, there are little and great. Some are babes, and others are giants. But these are all blessed. Little faith is blessed faith. Trembling hope is blessed hope. Every grace of the Holy Spirit, even though it is only a bud, bears a blessing within it. Moreover, the Lord Jesus bought both the small and the great with the same precious blood, and he has engaged to preserve the lambs as well as the full-grown sheep. No mother overlooks her child because it is little; no, the smaller it is, the more tenderly does she nurse it. If there be any preference with the Lord, he does not arrange them as "great and small," but as "small and great."

FEBRUARY 22

And David said, "The LORD who delivered me from
the paw of the lion and from the paw of the bear
will deliver me from the hand of this Philistine."

1 Samuel 17:37

This is not a promise if we consider only the words, but it is truly a promise according to its sense. For David spoke a word which the Lord endorsed by making it true. He argued from past deliverances that he would receive help when he faced a new danger. In Jesus all the promises are "Yes" and "Amen" to the glory of God by us (2 Cor. 1:20), and so the Lord's former dealings with his believing people will be repeated.

Come, then, let us recall the Lord's former loving-kindnesses. We could not have hoped to be delivered previously by our own strength. Yet the Lord delivered us. Will he not save us again? We are sure he will. As David ran to meet his foe, so will we. The Lord has been with us, he is with us, and he has said, "I will never leave you nor forsake you" (Heb. 13:5). Why do we tremble? Was the past a dream? Think of the dead bear and lion. Who is this Philistine? True, he is not quite the same as a bear nor a lion. But then God *is* the same, and his honor is as much involved in the one case as in the other. He did not save us from the beasts of the forest to let a giant kill us. So let us be of good courage.

FEBRUARY 23

If you abide in me, and my words abide in you, ask
whatever you wish, and it will be done for you.

John 15:7

Of necessity we must be in Christ to live for him. And we must abide in
him to be able to claim the largesse of this promise from him. To abide
in Jesus is never to leave him for another love, or another object, but to
remain in living, loving, conscious, willing union with him. The branch is
not only always near the stem, but always receiving life and fruitfulness
from it. All true believers abide in Christ in a sense. But there is a higher
meaning, and this we must know before we can gain unlimited power at
the throne. "Ask whatever you wish" is for Enochs who walk with God
(Gen 5:24), for Johns who recline at the Lord's side (John 13:23), for
those whose union with Christ leads to constant communion.

The heart must remain in love. The mind must be rooted in faith. The
hope must be cemented to the Word. The whole person must be joined
to the Lord. Otherwise it would be dangerous to trust us with power in
prayer. The carte blanche can only be given to one whose very life can be
summed up as: "It is no longer I who live, but Christ who lives in me"
(Gal. 2:20). Oh, you who break your fellowship, what power you lose!
If you would be mighty in your pleadings before God, the Lord himself
must abide in you, and you in him.

FEBRUARY 24

If you abide in me, and my words abide in you,
ask whatever you wish, and it will be done for you.

John 15:7

Note well that we must hear Jesus speak if we expect him to hear us
speak. If we have no ear for Christ, he will have no ear for us. In proportion to what we hear will we be heard.

Moreover, what is heard must remain, must live in us; and must abide
in our character as a force and a power. We must receive the truths which
Jesus taught, the precepts which he issued, and the stirrings of his Spirit
within us. Otherwise we will have no power at the mercy seat.

Suppose our Lord's words are received, and abide in us; what a boundless field of privilege is opened up to us! We are to have our will in prayer,
because we have *already surrendered our will* to the Lord's command. In
this way Elijahs are trained to handle the keys of heaven and lock or loose
the clouds (James 5:17–18). One such man is worth a thousand common
Christians. Do we humbly desire to be intercessors for the church and
the world, and like the Reformer Martin Luther, to be able to have what
we will from the Lord? Then we must bow our ear to the voice of the
Well-Beloved, treasure up his words, and carefully obey them. You need
to "faithfully obey" if you want to pray effectually (Deut. 28:1 KJV).

FEBRUARY 25

You shall be called the priests of the LORD.

Isaiah 61:6

This literal promise to Israel belongs spiritually to the seed according to the Spirit, namely, to all believers. If we live up to our privileges, we will live for God so clearly and distinctly that people will see that we are set apart for holy service and will call us "the priests of the LORD." We may work or trade, as others do, and yet we may truly and completely be ministering servants of God. Our one occupation will be to present a perpetual sacrifice of prayer and praise and testimony and self-consecration to the living God by Jesus Christ.

Since this is our one aim, we may leave distracting concerns to those who have no higher calling. "Leave the dead to bury their own dead" (Luke 9:60). It is written, "Strangers shall stand and tend your flocks; foreigners shall be your plowmen and vinedressers" (Isa. 61:5). They can manage politics, puzzle out financial problems, discuss science, and settle the latest quibbles of criticism. But we will give ourselves to the service that befits those who, like the Lord Jesus, are ordained to a perpetual priesthood.

Accepting this honorable promise concerning our sacred duty, let us put on the priestly garments of holiness and minister before the Lord all day long.

FEBRUARY 26

Truthful lips endure forever,
but a lying tongue is but for a moment.

Proverbs 12:19

Truth wears well. Time tests it, and truly it endures trials well. If, then, I have spoken the truth, and have for the present to suffer for it, I must be content to wait. If also I believe the truth of God, and endeavor to declare it, I may meet with much opposition. But I need not fear, for ultimately the truth must prevail.

What a poor thing is the temporary triumph of falsehood! "A lying tongue is but for a moment!" It is like a fragile plant, which comes up in a night and dies in a night (Jonah 4:6–10). The faster its development, the more obvious its decay. On the other hand, how worthy of an immortal being is the guarantee and defense of that truth which can never change—the everlasting gospel. The gospel is established by the unchanging truth of an unchanging God! An old proverb says, "He who speaks truth shames the devil." Certainly he who speaks the truth of God will put to shame all the devils in hell and confound all the seed of the serpent that now hiss out their falsehoods.

Oh, my heart, take care that you are in everything on the side of truth, both in small things and great. But especially take care to be on the side of him by whom grace and truth have come among us (John 1:17)!

FEBRUARY 27

He is not afraid of bad news;
his heart is firm, trusting in the LORD.

Psalm 112:7

Suspense is dreadful. When we have no news from home, we are inclined to grow anxious. We cannot be persuaded that "no news is good news." Faith is the cure for this condition of sadness. The Lord by his Spirit settles the mind in holy tranquility, and all fear is gone for the future as well as for the present.

The firmness of heart of which the psalmist speaks is to be diligently sought. It is not believing this or that promise of the Lord, but the general condition of unstinting trust in our God. It is the confidence which we have that he himself will not harm us, nor will he let anyone else harm us. This constant confidence meets the unknown things of life as well as the known things. Let tomorrow be what it may, our God is the God of tomorrow. Whatever events may have happened, which to us are unknown, our Lord is God of the unknown as well as of the known. We are determined to trust the Lord, come what may. If the very worst should happen, our God is still the greatest and best. Therefore we will not fear, though the postman's knock should startle us or a message wake us at midnight. The Lord lives, and what can his children fear?

FEBRUARY 28

You knew that you yourselves had a better
possession and an abiding one.

Hebrews 10:34

This is good. Our substance here on earth is very insubstantial. There is no substance in it. But God has given us a promise of real estate in the land of glory. And that promise comes to our hearts with such full assurance of its certainty that we know in ourselves that we have an enduring possession there. Yes, we have it even now. They say, "A bird in the hand is worth two in the bush." But we have our bird in the bush and in the hand too. Even now, heaven is ours. We have the title deed of it, we have the guarantee of it, we have the firstfruits of it. The price of heaven has been paid, the promise of heaven has been given, and so it is ours in principle. This we know not only through the hearing of the ear, but *in ourselves*, as this verse says.

Should not the thought of this better possession on the other side of Jordan reconcile us to present losses? We may lose our spending money, but our treasure is safe. We have lost the shadows, but the substance remains, for our Savior lives, and the place that he has prepared for us abides. There is a better land, a better possession, a better promise. And all this comes to us by a better covenant. Therefore let us be in better spirits, and say to the Lord, "Every day I will bless you and praise your name forever and ever" (Ps. 145:2).

FEBRUARY 29

Surely goodness and mercy shall follow me
all the days of my life.

Psalm 23:6

A devout poet sings:

> Lord, when thou
> puttest in my time a day, as you dost now,
> unknown in other years, grant, I entreat,
> such grace illume it, that whate'er its phase
> it add to holiness, and lengthen praise!
>
> *Henry Hallam Tweedy*

This day only comes once every four years. Oh, that we could win a fourfold blessing on it! Up until now, goodness and mercy, like two guards, have followed us from day to day, bringing up the rear even as grace leads at the front. And, as this out-of-the-way day is one of the days of our life, the two guardian angels will be with us today as well. *Goodness* to supply our needs, and *mercy* to blot out our sins. These two will follow us every step of the way today, and every day till days will be no more. Therefore, let us serve the Lord on this peculiar day with a special consecration of heart. And let us sing his praises with more zest and sweetness than ever. Could we not today make an unusual offering to the cause of God or to the poor? With an inventive love, let us make this twenty-ninth of February a day to be remembered forever.

MARCH

MARCH 1

Hear the word of the LORD,
you who tremble at his word:
"Your brothers who hate you
and cast you out for my name's sake
have said, 'Let the LORD be glorified,
that we may see your joy';
but it is they who shall be put to shame."

Isaiah 66:5

Possibly this text may not apply to one in a thousand of the readers of this little book of promises. But the Lord cheers that one with such words as these. Let us pray for all who are cast out wrongfully from the company they love. May the Lord appear to their joy!

The text applies to truly gracious people who tremble at the word of the Lord. These people were hated of their brothers and eventually cast out because of their faithfulness and their holiness. This must have been very bitter to them. And all the more so because it was done in the name of religion. They were explicitly cast out with the aim of glorifying God. How much is done for the devil in the name of God! The use of the name of Jehovah to add venom to the bite of the old serpent is an example of his subtlety.

The appearing of the Lord for them is the hope of his persecuted people. He appears as the advocate and defender of his elect. And when he does so, it means a clear deliverance for the God-fearing and shame for their oppressors.

Oh, Lord, fulfill this word to those whom people are deriding!

MARCH 2

But when you give to the needy, do not let your
left hand know what your right hand is doing,
so that your giving may be in secret. And your
Father who sees in secret will reward you.

Matthew 6:3–4

No promise is made to those who give to the poor to be seen by others. They have their reward at once, and cannot expect to be paid twice.

Let us hide away our charity. Yes, let us hide it even from ourselves. Give so often and so much as a matter of course that you no more take note that you have helped the poor than that you have eaten your regular meals. Do your alms without even whispering to yourself, "How generous I am!" Do not in this way attempt to reward yourself. Leave the matter with God, who never fails to see, to record, and to reward. Blessed is the man who is busy in secret with his kindness. He finds a special joy in his unknown generosity. This is the bread which, eaten in secret, is sweeter than the banquets of kings. How can I indulge myself today with this delightful luxury? Let me have a real feast of divine tenderness and communion with my soul.

Now and in the future the Lord himself will personally ensure the secret giver of charity is rewarded. This will be in his own way and time— and he will choose the very best. How much this promise means, it will need eternity to reveal.

MARCH 3

For you will not abandon my soul to Sheol,
or let your holy one see corruption.

Psalm 16:10

This word is properly fulfilled in the Lord Jesus. But it applies also, in a different way, to all who are in him. Our soul will not be left separated from our body, and our body, though it see corruption, will rise again. The general meaning, rather than the specific application, is that to which we would call our readers' thoughts at this particular time.

Our spirits may descend very low until we seem to be plunged in the abyss of hell. But we will not be left there. We may feel like we are at death's door in heart, and soul, and consciousness. But we cannot remain there. The inner death of joy and hope in us may proceed a long way. But it cannot run to its full consequences so that we reach the utter corruption of black despair. We may be very low, but no lower than the Lord permits. We may stay in the lowest dungeon of doubt for a while, but we will not perish there. The star of hope is still in the sky when the night is blackest. The Lord will not forget us and hand us over to the enemy.

Let us rest in hope. Our dealings are with One whose mercy endures forever. Surely out of death, darkness, and despair we will yet arise to life, light, and liberty.

MARCH 4

Those who honor me I will honor.

1 Samuel 2:30

Do I make the honor of God the great aim of my life and the rule of my conduct? If so, he will honor me. I may for a while receive no honor from people, but God himself will give me honor in the most effective manner. In the end, being willing to be shamed for the sake of conscience will prove the surest way to honor.

Eli had not honored the Lord by ruling his household well, and his sons had not honored the Lord by behavior worthy of their sacred office (1 Sam. 2:12–36). Therefore the Lord did not honor them. Instead, he took the high-priesthood from their family and made young Samuel ruler in the land instead of any of their descendants. If I want my family ennobled, I must honor the Lord in all things. God may allow the wicked to win worldly honors. But the dignity which he himself gives—which is glory, honor, and immortality—he reserves for those who by holy obedience take care to honor *him*.

What can I do this day to honor the Lord? I will promote his glory by my spoken testimony and by my practical obedience. I will also honor him with my property and by offering to him some special service. Let me sit down and think how I can honor him since he will honor me.

MARCH 5

He blesses the dwelling of the righteous.

Proverbs 3:33

He who fears the Lord comes under divine protection in the same way the roof covers himself and his family. His home is a house of love, a school of holy training, and a place of heavenly light. In it there is a family altar where the name of the Lord is revered each day. Therefore the Lord blesses his dwelling. It may be a humble cottage or a lordly mansion; but the Lord's blessing comes because of the character of the inhabitant, and not because of the size of the building.

That house is most blest in which the master and mistress are God-fearing people. But a son or daughter or even a servant may also bring blessing on a whole household. The Lord often preserves, prospers, and provides for a family for the sake of one or two in it. God regards them as just, because his grace has made them so.

Beloved, let us have Jesus for our constant guest even as the sisters of Bethany had, and then we will be blessed indeed (Luke 10:38; John 12:1–2).

Let us see to it that in all things we are just—in our trade, in our judgment of others, in our treatment of neighbors, and in our own personal character. A just God cannot bless unjust transactions.

MARCH 6

In you the orphan finds mercy.

Hosea 14:3

This is an excellent reason for casting away all other confidences and relying upon the Lord alone. When a child is left without its natural protector, our God steps in and becomes his guardian. So also when a man has lost every object upon which he depends, he may cast himself upon the living God and find in him all that he needs. Orphans are cast on the fatherhood of God, and he provides for them. The writer of these pages knows what it is to hang on the bare arm of God. He willingly bears witness that no trust is so well warranted by facts, or so sure to be rewarded by results, as trust in the invisible but ever-living God.

Some children who have fathers are not much better off because of them. But the fatherless with God are rich. Better to have God and no other friend than all the patrons on the earth and no God. To be bereaved is painful, but as long as the Lord remains the fountain of mercy to us, we are not truly orphaned.

Let fatherless children plead this morning's gracious word, and let all who have lost visible support do the same.

Lord, let me find mercy in you! The more needy and helpless I am, the more confident is my appeal to your loving heart.

MARCH 7

The LORD sets the prisoners free.

Psalm 146:7

He has done it. Remember Joseph, Israel in Egypt, Manasseh, Jeremiah, Peter, and many others. He can do it still. He breaks the bars of brass with a word and snaps the chains of iron with a look. He is doing it. In a thousand places, troubled ones are coming into light and freedom. Jesus still proclaims the opening of the prison to those that are bound. At this moment doors are flying back and chains are dropping to the ground.

He will delight to set you free, dear friend, if at this time you are mourning because of sorrow, doubt, and fear. It will be a joy to Jesus to give you liberty. It will give him as great a pleasure to set you free as it will be a pleasure to you to be freed. No, you do not have to snap the iron restraint—the Lord himself will do it. Only trust him, and he will be your Liberator. Believe in him in spite of the stone walls or the manacles of iron. Satan cannot hold you, sin cannot enchain you, even despair cannot bind you, if you will now believe in the Lord Jesus and in the freeness of his grace and the fullness of his power to save.

Defy the enemy, and let the word now before you be your song of deliverance: "The LORD sets the prisoners free."

MARCH 8

Blessed shall be your basket and your kneading bowl.

Deuteronomy 28:5

Obedience brings a blessing on all the provisions which our work earns for us. That which quickly comes in and goes out, like fruit in the basket which is for immediate use, will be blest. And that which is stored by us for a longer period will equally receive a blessing.

Perhaps all we have is a basket-sized portion. There is a little for breakfast and a little ready for dinner as we leave for work in the morning. But this is good, for the blessing of God is promised to the basket. If we live from hand to mouth, getting each day's supply in the day, we are as well off as Israel. For when the Lord hosted his favored people, he only gave them a day's manna at a time (Ex. 16:19–21). What more did *they* need? What more do *we* need?

But if we have a whole "store" of food (Deut. 28:5 KJV), how much we need the Lord to bless it! For there is the care of getting, the care of keeping, the care of managing, the care of using. And so, unless the Lord bless it, these cares will eat into our hearts until our goods become our gods and our cares corrupt us.

Oh, Lord, bless our possessions. Enable us to use them for your glory. Help us to keep worldly things in their proper place, and may our savings never endanger the saving of our souls.

MARCH 9

But seek the welfare of the city where I have sent
you into exile, and pray to the LORD on its behalf,
for in its welfare you will find your welfare.

Jeremiah 29:7

According to this text, it should be the desire of all of us who have become the Lord's strangers and foreigners to promote the peace and prosperity of the people among whom we dwell (1 Pet. 2:11–12). Our nation and our city should especially be blessed by our constant intercession. An earnest prayer for your country and other countries is entirely appropriate in the mouth of every believer.

Let us eagerly pray for the great gift of peace, both at home and abroad. If conflict should cause bloodshed in our streets, or if a foreign battle should slay our brave soldiers, we will all lament the calamity. Therefore let us pray for peace and diligently promote those principles by which social classes at home and the different races abroad may be bound together in bonds of friendship.

We ourselves are promised quiet lives in connection with the peace of the nation (1 Tim. 2:1–2). This is truly desirable; for it means we can bring up our families in the fear of the Lord, and also preach the gospel without obstruction or hindrance.

Today let us be much in prayer for our country, confessing national sins, and asking for national pardon and blessing, for Jesus's sake.

MARCH 10

I have come into the world as light, so that whoever
believes in me may not remain in darkness.

John 12:46

This world is as dark as midnight. Jesus has come that by faith we may
have light. He has come so that we may no longer sit in the gloom that
covers all the rest of humanity.

"Whoever" is a very wide term—it means you and me. If we trust in
Jesus, we will no longer sit in the dark shadow of death but will enter the
warm light of a day that will never end. Why do we not come out into
the light at once?

A cloud may sometimes hover over us, but we will not remain in
darkness if we believe in Jesus. He has come to give us broad daylight,
and he has not come in vain. If we have faith, then we have the privilege
of sunlight—so let us enjoy it. From the night of natural depravity, of
ignorance, of doubt, of despair, of sin, of dread, Jesus has come to set us
free. And all believers will know that he no more comes in vain than the
sun rises and fails to scatter heat and light.

Shake off your depression, dear brother or sister. Do not remain in the
dark, but remain in the light. In Jesus is your hope, your joy, your heaven.
Look to him, and him alone, and you will rejoice as the birds rejoice at
sunrise and as the angels rejoice before the throne.

MARCH 11

This day the Lord will deliver you into my hand
. . . that all this assembly may know that the Lord
saves not with sword and spear. For the battle is the
Lord's, and he will give you into our hand.

1 Samuel 17:46–47

Let this point be certain: the battle is the Lord's, and we may be quite sure of the victory. And we may be sure of a victory that will best display the power of God. The Lord is too often forgotten by all people, even by the assemblies of Israel. And when there is an opportunity to make people see that the Great First Cause can achieve his purposes without the power of man, it is a priceless occasion which should not be missed. Even Israel looked too often to the sword and spear. It is a grand thing to have no sword in the hand of David, and yet for David to know that his God will overthrow a whole army of foreigners.

If we are indeed contending for truth and righteousness, let us not wait until we have talent, or wealth, or any other form of visible power at our disposal. Instead, with whatever stones we find in the brook and with our own usual sling, let us run to meet the enemy. If it were our own battle, we might not be confident. But if we are standing up for Jesus, and fighting in his strength alone, who can withstand us? Without a trace of hesitation, let us face the Philistines. For the Lord of Hosts is with us, and who can be against us?

MARCH 12

And of Zebulun he said,
"Rejoice, Zebulun, in your going out."
Deuteronomy 33:18

The blessings of the tribes are ours, for we are the true Israel who worships God in the spirit and has no confidence in the flesh (Phil. 3:3). Zebulun was to rejoice because the LORD would bless his "going out." We also see a promise for ourselves lying latent in this blessing. When we go out, we will look out for occasions of joy.

We go out to travel, and the providence of God is our convoy. We go out to emigrate, and the Lord is with us both on land and sea. We go out as missionaries, and Jesus says, "Behold, I am with you always, to the end of the age" (Matt. 28:20). We go out day by day to our work, and we may do so with pleasure, for God will be with us from morning until evening.

A fear sometimes creeps over us when starting out, for we know not what we may meet. But this blessing may serve us well as a word of good comfort. As we pack up for moving, let us put this verse into our traveling bag; let us drop it into our hearts and keep it there. Indeed, let us put it on our tongue to make us sing. Let us weigh anchor with a song or jump into the carriage with a psalm. Let us belong to the rejoicing tribe, and in our every movement praise the Lord with joyful hearts.

MARCH 13

Then I said, "Ah, Lord GOD! Behold, I do not know how
to speak, for I am only a youth." But the LORD said to me,
"Do not say, 'I am only a youth';
for to all to whom I send you, you shall go,
and whatever I command you, you shall speak."

Jeremiah 1:6–7

Jeremiah was young and naturally shrank from the great errand upon which he was sent by the Lord. But he who sent him would not have him say, "I am only a youth." What he was in himself must not be mentioned but forgotten when considering that he was chosen to speak for God. He did not have to think out and invent a message, nor to choose an audience. He was to speak what God commanded, and speak where God sent him. And this he would be enabled to do in strength not his own.

Is it not the same for some young preacher or teacher who may read these lines? God knows how young you are and how slender your knowledge and experience are. But if he chooses to send you, it is not for you to shrink from the heavenly call. God will magnify himself in your feebleness. If you were as old as Methuselah (Gen. 5:27), how much would your years help you? If you were as wise as Solomon, you might be equally as willful as he was. Keep to your message, and it will be your wisdom; follow your marching orders, and they will be your guide.

MARCH 14

As one whom his mother comforts,
so I will comfort you.

Isaiah 66:13

A mother's comfort! Ah, this is tenderness itself. How she enters into her child's grief! How she presses him to her chest and tries to take all his sorrow into her own heart! He can tell her everything, and she will sympathize as nobody else can. Of all comforters, a child loves his mother the best. It is true even for many full-grown men.

Does the Lord condescend to play the role of a mother? This is goodness indeed. We readily perceive how he is a father. But will he be like a mother as well? Does not this invite us to holy familiarity, to unreserved confidence, to sacred rest? When God himself becomes the Comforter, no anguish can long remain. Let us pour out our trouble, even if sobs and sighs should become the language we use. He will not despise us for our tears, just as our mother did not. He will consider our weakness as she did. He will put aside our faults, only in a surer, safer way than our mother could do. We will not try to bear our grief alone—that would be unkind to one so gentle and so kind.

If we begin the day with our loving God, we will finish it in the same company, since mothers do not grow weary of their children.

MARCH 15

Therefore say, "Thus says the Lord GOD: Though I removed
them far off among the nations, and though I scattered
them among the countries, yet I have been a sanctuary to
them for a while in the countries where they have gone."

Ezekiel 11:16

Banished from the public means of grace, we are not removed from the grace behind the means of grace. The Lord who places his people where they feel like exiles will himself be with them. He will be to them all that they could have had at home in the place of their sacred assemblies. Take this promise as your own if you are called to wander!

God is to his people a place of *refuge*. They find sanctuary with him from every adversary. He is their place of *worship* too. He is with them as he was with Jacob when he slept in the open field and woke, saying, "Surely the LORD is in this place" (Gen. 28:16). To them he will also be a sanctuary of *peace*, like the Most Holy Place, which was the noiseless abode of the Eternal. They will be kept from fear of evil.

God himself, in Christ Jesus, is the sanctuary of *mercy*. The ark of the covenant is the Lord Jesus, and Aaron's rod, the pot of manna, the tables of the law are in Christ our sanctuary. In God we find the shrine of *holiness* and of *communion*. What more do we need?

Oh, Lord, fulfill this promise and always be to us like a little sanctuary!

MARCH 16

What you have learned and received and
heard and seen in me—practice these things,
and the God of peace will be with you.

Philippians 4:9

It is good when a man can be profitably copied so minutely as Paul might have been. Oh, for grace to imitate him this day and every day!

If we, with the help of divine grace, put into practice the teaching of Paul, we may claim this promise. And what a promise it is! God, who loves peace, makes peace, and breathes peace, will be with us. "Peace will be with you" is a sweet blessing. But for the God of peace to be with us is far more. For in God we have the fountain as well as the streams, the sun as well as his beams. If the God of peace be with us, we will enjoy the peace of God that passes all understanding (Phil. 4:7), even though outward circumstances threaten to disturb us. If people quarrel, we are certain to be peacemakers, if the Maker of peace is with us.

It is in the way of truth that real peace is found. If we quit the faith or leave the path of righteousness under the notion of promoting peace, we will be greatly mistaken. First pure, then peaceable, is the order of wisdom and of fact. Let us keep to Paul's line, and we will have the God of peace with us as he was with the apostle.

MARCH 17

Do not be afraid of them,
for I am with you to deliver you,
declares the LORD.

Jeremiah 1:8

Whenever fear comes in and makes us falter, we are in danger of falling into sin. To be conceited is to be dreaded, but so is cowardice. "Dare to be a Daniel" (Philip B. Bliss). Our great Captain should be served by brave soldiers.

What a reason for bravery there is here! God is with those who are with him. God will never be absent when the hour of struggle comes. Do they threaten you? Who are you that you should be afraid of a man that will die? Will you lose your position? Your God whom you serve will find bread and water for his servants. Can you not trust him? Do they pour ridicule upon you? Will this break your bones or your heart? Bear it for Christ's sake and even rejoice because of it.

God is with the true, the just, the holy, to deliver them; and he will deliver you. Remember how Daniel came out of the lions' den, and the three holy children out of the furnace (Daniel 3, 6). Your case is not as desperate as theirs. But even if it were, the Lord would bear you through and make you more than a conqueror. Fear to fear. Be afraid to be afraid. Your worst enemy is within your own heart. Get to your knees and cry for help, and then rise up, saying, "I will trust, and will not be afraid" (Isa. 12:2).

MARCH 18

The prayer of the upright is acceptable to him.

Proverbs 15:8

This is as good as a promise, for it declares a present fact which will be the same throughout all ages. God takes great pleasure in the prayers of upright men. He even calls them his "delight" (Prov. 15:8 KJV). Our first concern is to be upright. Neither bending this way nor that, continue upright: not crooked with policy, nor prostrate by yielding to evil; be upright with strict integrity and straightforwardness. If we begin to shuffle and shift, we will be left to shift for ourselves. If we try crooked ways, we will find that we cannot pray. And if we pretend to do so, we will find our prayers shut out of heaven.

Are we acting in a straight line and thus following the Lord's revealed will? Then let us pray much and pray in faith. If our prayer is acceptable and God's delight, let us not withhold from him that which gives him pleasure. He does not consider the grammar of it, nor the metaphysics of it, nor the rhetoric of it. In all these, men might despise our prayer. But he, as a Father, takes pleasure in the lisping of his own babes, the stammering of his newborn sons and daughters. Should we not delight in prayer since the Lord delights in it? Let us make errands to the throne. The Lord finds us enough reasons for prayer, and we ought to thank him that it is so.

MARCH 19

The Lord bestows favor and honor.

Psalm 84:11

Divine favor, or grace, is what we need just now, and it is to be had freely. What can be freer than a gift? Today we will receive sustaining, strengthening, sanctifying, satisfying grace. He has given daily grace until now, and, as for the future, that grace is still sufficient. If we have only a little grace, the fault must lie in ourselves. For the Lord is not limited; neither is he slow to bestow it in abundance. We may ask for as much as we want and never fear a refusal. He gives liberally without rebuking us.

The Lord may not give gold, but he will give grace. He may not give gain, but he will give grace. He will certainly send us trials, but he will give grace in proportion to those trials. We may be called to labor and to suffer, but with the call there will come all the grace required.

What an "and" there is in the text—"*and* honor"! We do not need honor and glory yet, and we are not yet fit for it. But we will have it in due course. After we have eaten the bread of grace, we will drink the wine of glory. We must go through the holy (which is grace) to the holiest of all (which is glory). These words "and honor" or "and glory" (in the KJV) are enough to make a man dance for joy. A little while, and then glory forever!

MARCH 20

But if God so clothes the grass of the field, which today
is alive and tomorrow is thrown into the oven, will he
not much more clothe you, O you of little faith?

Matthew 6:30

Clothes are expensive, and poor believers may be anxious about where their next suit will come from. The soles are thin: How will we get new shoes? See how our thoughtful Lord has provided for this care. Our heavenly Father clothes the grass of the field with a splendor that even Solomon could not equal. Will he not also clothe his own children? We are sure he will. There may be many a patch and a darn, but apparel we will have.

A poor minister found his clothes nearly threadbare and so far gone that they would hardly hold together. But as a servant of the Lord, he expected his Master to find him his attire. It so happened that the writer on a visit to a friend was preaching in the good man's church, and it came into his mind to make a collection for him. So it was that God provided him with *a new suit of clothes*! We have seen many other cases in which those who have served the Lord have found him taking care of their wardrobe. He made us so that when we sinned we needed garments, and in mercy he supplied us with them. And those clothes which the Lord gave to our first parents were far better than those they had made for themselves (Gen. 3:7, 21).

MARCH 21

Then you will walk on your way securely,
and your foot will not stumble.

Proverbs 3:23

That is to say, if we follow the ways of wisdom and holiness, we will be kept in them. He who travels by daylight along the highway is under some protection. There is a way for every person, namely, their own proper calling in life. And if we devoutly walk along that way in the fear of God, he will preserve us from evil. We may not travel luxuriously, but we will walk safely. We may not be able to run like young people, but we will be able to walk like good people.

Our greatest danger lies in ourselves. Our feeble foot is sadly so prone to stumble. Let us ask for more moral strength so that our tendency to slip may be overcome. Some stumble because they do not see the stone in the way. Divine grace enables us to spot sin and so to avoid it. Let us plead this promise, and trust in him who upholds his chosen.

Alas! Our worst peril is our own carelessness. But the Lord Jesus has put us on our guard against this by saying, "Watch and pray" (Matt. 26:41).

Oh, for grace to walk this day without a single stumble! It is not enough that we do not actually fall. Our cry should be that we may not make the smallest slip with our feet, but may in the end adore him "who is able to keep you from stumbling" (Jude 24).

MARCH 22

God . . . gives grace to the humble.

James 4:6

Humble hearts seek grace, and therefore they get it. Humble hearts yield to the sweet influences of grace, and so it is bestowed on them with more and more largesse. Humble hearts lie in the valleys where streams of grace are flowing, and hence they drink of them. Humble hearts are grateful for grace and give the Lord the glory for it, and hence it is consistent with his honor to give it to them.

Come, dear reader, take a low place. Be little in your own esteem, that the Lord may make much of you. Perhaps the sigh breaks out, "I fear I am not humble." It may be that this is the language of true humility. Some are proud of being humble, and this is one of the very worst sorts of pride. We are needy, helpless, undeserving, hell-deserving creatures, and if we are not humble, we ought to be. Let us humble ourselves because of our sins against humility, and then the Lord will give us a taste of his favor. It is grace that makes us humble, and grace that finds in this humility an opportunity for pouring in more grace.

Let us go down that we may rise. Let us be poor in spirit that God may make us rich. Let us be humble that we may not need to be humbled, but may be exalted by the grace of God.

MARCH 23

I will lead the blind
in a way that they do not know.

Isaiah 42:16

Think of the infinitely glorious Lord acting as a guide to the blind! What boundless condescension does this imply! A blind man cannot find a way that he does not know. Even when he knows the road, it is hard for him to follow it. But a road that he has never known is quite out of the question for his unguided feet.

Now, we are by nature blind when it comes to the way of salvation. And yet the Lord leads us into it, and brings us to himself, and then opens our eyes.

As to the future, all of us are blind and cannot see an hour ahead us. But the Lord Jesus will lead us right up to our journey's end. Blessed be his name!

We cannot guess in which way deliverance can possibly come to us, but the Lord knows, and he will lead us until we have escaped every danger. Happy are those who place their hand in that of the great Guide, and leave their way and themselves entirely with him. He will bring them all the way. And when he has brought them home to glory and has opened their eyes to see the way by which he has led them, what a song of gratitude will they sing to their great Benefactor!

Lord, lead your poor blind child this day, for I do not know my way!

MARCH 24

But the Lord is faithful. He will establish you
and guard you against the evil one.

2 Thessalonians 3:3

People are often as devoid of reason as of faith. There are among us still "wicked and evil men" (2 Thess. 3:2 KJV). There is no use arguing with them or trying to be at peace with them. They are false at heart and deceitful in speech. Well, what of this? Will we worry ourselves about them? No, let us turn to the Lord, for he is faithful. No promise from his Word will ever be broken. He is neither unreasonable in his demands upon us nor unfaithful to our claims upon him. We have a faithful God. Let this be our joy.

He will establish us so that wicked men will not cause our downfall, and he will keep us so that none of the evils that now confront us will really do us damage. What a blessing for us that we do not need to contend with men but are allowed to shelter ourselves in the Lord Jesus. And he has the truest sympathy with us. There is one true heart, one faithful mind, one never-changing love—there let us rest. The Lord will fulfill the purpose of his grace to us, his servants, and we need not allow a shadow of a fear to fall upon our spirits. Nothing that people or devils can do can deprive us of divine protection and provision.

This day let us ask the Lord to establish, guard, and keep us.

MARCH 25

If you lie down, you will not be afraid;
when you lie down, your sleep will be sweet.

Proverbs 3:24

Is the reader likely to be confined to bed for a while by sickness? Let him go upstairs without distress with this promise on his heart: "If you lie down, you will not be afraid."

When we go to bed at night, let this word smooth our pillow. We cannot guard ourselves while we are sleeping, but the Lord will keep us through the night. Those who lie down under the protection of the Lord are as secure as kings and queens in their palaces, and a great deal more so. If, as we lay our bodies down, we also lay down all our cares and ambitions, we will get refreshment from our beds the like of which the anxious and covetous never find in theirs. Ill dreams will be banished. Or, even if they come, we will wipe out their impression, knowing that they are only dreams.

If we sleep in this way, we will do well. How sweetly Peter slept when even the angel's light did not wake him, and he needed a hard jog in the side to wake him up (Acts 12:7). And yet he was sentenced to die the next day. So it is that martyrs have slept before their burning. "For he gives to his beloved sleep" (Ps. 127:2).

To have sweet sleep we must have sweet lives, sweet tempers, sweet meditations, and sweet love.

MARCH 26

Blessed is the one who considers the poor. . . .
The LORD sustains him on his sickbed.

Psalm 41:1, 3

Remember that this is a promise to the man who considers the poor. Are you one of these? Then take the text home.

See how in the hour of sickness the God of the poor will bless the person who cares for the poor! The everlasting arms will support their soul as friendly hands and downy pillows support the body of the sick. How tender and sympathetic this image is; how close it brings our God to our infirmities and sicknesses! Whoever heard this said of the old heathen Jove, or of the gods of India or China? This is language unique to the God of Israel. He it is who deigns to become nurse and attendant upon good people. If he strikes with one hand, he sustains with the other. Oh, it is blessed fainting when one falls on the Lord's own breast and is carried there! Grace is the best of restoratives. Divine love is the safest stimulant for a languishing patient. It makes the soul as strong as a giant, even when the bones are breaking through the skin. There is no physician like the Lord, no tonic like his promise, no wine like his love.

If the reader has failed in his duty to the poor, let him see what he is losing and at once become their friend and helper.

MARCH 27

Draw near to God, and he will draw near to you.

James 4:8

The nearer we come to God, the more graciously will he reveal himself to us. When the prodigal comes to his father, his father runs to meet him (Luke 15:20). When the wandering dove returns to the ark, Noah puts out his hand to pull her in to him (Gen. 8:9). When the tender wife seeks her husband's company, he comes to her on wings of love. Come then, dear friend, let us draw near to God who so graciously awaits us; indeed, comes to meet us.

Did you ever notice that passage in Isaiah 58:9? There the Lord seems to put himself at the disposal of his people, saying to them, "Here I am." It's as if he is saying, "What do you want from me? What can I do for you? I am waiting to bless you."

How can we hesitate to draw close? God is near to forgive, to bless, to comfort, to help, to give life, and to deliver. Let the main point of our lives be to get near to God. This done, all is done. If we draw near to others, they may eventually grow weary of us and leave us. But if we seek the Lord alone, he will never change his mind. Instead, he will continue to come nearer and yet nearer to us in fuller and more joyful fellowship.

MARCH 28

The LORD will make you the head and not the tail.

Deuteronomy 28:13

If we obey the Lord, he will compel our adversaries to see that his blessing rests on us. Though this is a promise of the law, yet it still stands good to the people of God today. For Jesus has removed the curse, and he has established the blessing.

It is for saints to lead the way in society by holy influence. They are not to be the tail, dragged here and there by others. We must not yield to the spirit of the age, but compel the age to honor Christ. If the Lord is with us, we will not simply crave tolerance for religion, but we will seek to place it on the throne of society. Has not the Lord Jesus made his people priests? Surely they are to teach and must not be students of the philosophies of unbelievers. Are we not in Christ made kings to reign on the earth? How, then, can we be the servants of custom or the slaves of human opinion?

Have you, dear friend, taken up your true position for Jesus? Too many Christians are silent because they are diffident, even cowardly. Should we allow the name of the Lord Jesus to be kept in the background? Should our religion drag along like a tail? Should it not rather lead the way and be the ruling force with ourselves and others?

MARCH 29

I am with you, and no one will attack you to harm you.

Acts 18:10

As long as the Lord had work for Paul to do in Corinth, the fury of the mob was restrained. The opposition and blasphemies of the Jews could neither stop the preaching of the gospel nor the conversion of the hearers. God has power over the most violent minds. He makes the wrath of humanity praise him when it breaks out, but displays his goodness even more when he restrains it. And he can restrain it. "Because of the greatness of your arm, they are still as a stone, till your people, O LORD, pass by" (Ex. 15:16).

Do not, therefore, feel any fear of people when you know that you are doing your duty. Keep going straight ahead, as Jesus would have done, and those who oppose you will be like a bruised reed and smoking flax. Many times people have had reason to fear because they were themselves afraid. But an intrepid faith in God brushes fear aside like the cobwebs in a giant's path. No man can harm us unless the Lord permits. He who makes the devil himself to flee at a word can certainly control the devil's agents. Maybe they are already more afraid of you than you are of them. Therefore, press on, and where you expected to meet foes, you will find friends.

MARCH 30

Do not be anxious about anything, but in everything
by prayer and supplication with thanksgiving let your
requests be made known to God. And the peace of
God, which surpasses all understanding, will guard
your hearts and your minds in Christ Jesus.

Philippians 4:6–7

No care, but all prayer. No anxiety, but much joyful communion with God. Carry your desires to the Lord of your life, the guardian of your soul. Go to him with two portions of prayer, and one of fragrant praise. Do not pray doubtfully, but thankfully. Consider that you have your petitions, and therefore thank God for his grace. He is giving you grace; give him thanks. Hide nothing. Allow no need to lie festering in your heart: "Let your requests be made known." Do not run to people. Go only to your God, the Father of Jesus, who loves you in him.

This will bring you God's own peace. You will not be able to understand the peace which you will enjoy. It will enfold you in its infinite embrace. Heart and mind through Christ Jesus will be steeped in a sea of rest. Come life or death, poverty, pain, or slander, you will dwell in Jesus above every ruffling wind or darkening cloud. Will you not obey this dear command?

Yes, Lord, I believe you. But, I entreat you, "Help my unbelief" (Mark 9:24).

MARCH 31

Do not be afraid of sudden terror
or of the ruin of the wicked, when it comes,
for the LORD will be your confidence
and will keep your foot from being caught.

Proverbs 3:25–26

When God is active in judgment, he does not want his people to be alarmed. He has not come to harm but to defend the righteous.

He would have them display *courage*. We who enjoy the presence of God ought to show presence of mind. Since the Lord himself may suddenly come, we ought not to be surprised at anything sudden. Serenity under the rush and roar of unexpected evils is a precious gift of divine love.

The Lord would have his chosen people show *discrimination* so that they may see that the desolation of the wicked is not a real calamity to the universe. Sin alone is evil. The punishment that follows it is like a preserving salt to keep society from putrefying. We should be far more shocked at the sin that deserves hell, than at the hell which comes from sin.

So, too, should the Lord's people exhibit great *quietness* of spirit. Satan and his serpent-seed are full of all sorts of cunning. But those who walk with God will not be taken in by their deceitful snares. Go on, believer in Jesus, and let the Lord be your confidence.

APRIL

APRIL 1

It shall belong to those who walk on the way;
even if they are fools, they shall not go astray.

Isaiah 35:8

The way of holiness is so straight and plain that the simplest minds cannot go astray if they constantly follow it. The worldly wise have many twists and turns, and yet they make terrible blunders and generally miss their goal. Worldly policy is a poor, shortsighted thing, and when people choose it as their road, it leads them over dark mountains. Gracious minds know no better than to do as the Lord bids them. But this keeps them in the King's highway and under royal protection.

Let the reader never for a moment attempt to help himself out of a difficulty by a falsehood or by a questionable act. But let him keep in the middle of the high road of truth and integrity, and he will be following the best possible course. In our lives we must never map out our direction from those around us. Be just and fear not. Follow Jesus and do not pay attention to evil consequences. If the worst of ills could be avoided by wrongdoing, we should, in the very attempt to avoid ill, have fallen into an evil worse than any other ill could be. God's way must be the best way. Follow it even if people think you a fool, and you will be truly wise.

Lord, lead your servants in a plain path because of their enemies.

APRIL 2

Practice these things, immerse yourself in
them, so that all may see your progress.

1 Timothy 4:15

This is, practically, a promise that, by diligent meditation and the giving
of our whole mind to our work for the Lord, we will make a progress
that all can see. We profit by the Word of God not through hasty reading, but through deep meditation. Not by doing a great deal of work in a
halfhearted way, but by giving our best thought to what we attempt, we
will get real profit. "In all toil there is profit" (Prov. 14:23), but not in
fuss and hurry without true heart-energy.

If we divide ourselves between God and mammon, or Christ and self,
we will make no progress. We must give ourselves wholly to holy things,
or else we will be poor traders in heavenly business, and at our stock-
taking no profit will be shown.

Am I a minister? Let me be a minister wholly and not spend my energies upon secondary concerns. What have I to do with party politics or
vain amusements? Am I a Christian? Let me make my service of Jesus
my occupation, my lifework, my one pursuit. We must be in-and-in *with*
Jesus, and then out-and-out *for* Jesus. Otherwise we will make neither
progress nor profit, and neither the church nor the world will feel that
forceful influence that the Lord would have us exercise.

APRIL 3

Because your heart was penitent, and you humbled yourself before the LORD, when you heard how I spoke against this place and against its inhabitants, that they should become a desolation and a curse, and you have torn your clothes and wept before me, I also have heard you, declares the LORD.

2 Kings 22:19

Many despise warnings and perish. Happy is he who trembles at the Word of the Lord. Josiah did so, and he was spared the sight of the evil that the Lord determined to send upon Judah because of her great sins. Have you this tenderness? Do you practice this self-humiliation? Then you also will be spared in the day of evil. God sets a mark upon the people who sigh and cry because of the sin of the times. The destroying angel is commanded to keep his sword in its sheath until the elect of God are sheltered (1 Chron. 21:14–17). These are best known by their godly fear and their trembling at the Word of the Lord.

Are the times threatening? Do heresy and infidelity advance with great strides? Do you dread God's discipline upon this polluted nation? Well you may. Yet rest in this promise: "You shall be gathered to your grave in peace, and your eyes will not see all the disaster that I will bring upon this place" (2 Kings 22:20). Better still, the Lord himself may come, and then the days of our mourning will come to an end.

APRIL 4

And I will send hornets before you, which shall drive out the
Hivites, the Canaanites, and the Hittites from before you.
Exodus 23:28

What the hornets were, we need not consider. They were God's own army
that he sent before his people to sting their enemies and render Israel's
conquest easy. Our God, by his own chosen means, will fight for his
people and vex their foes before they come to the actual battle. Often he
confounds the adversaries of truth by methods in which reformers themselves have no hand. The air is full of mysterious influences which harass
Israel's foes. We read in the book of Revelation that "the earth came to
the help of the woman" (12:16).

Let us never fear. The stars in their courses fight against the enemies
of our souls. Often when we march to the conflict, we find no army with
which to contend. "The LORD will fight for you, and you have only to
be silent" (Ex. 14:14). God's hornets can do more than our weapons. We
could never dream of the victory being won by such means as the Lord
will use. We must obey our marching orders and go out to conquer the
nations for Jesus. And we will find that the Lord has gone before us and
prepared the way. So in the end we will joyfully confess, "His right hand
and his holy arm have worked salvation for him" (Ps. 98:1).

APRIL 5

You are my servant;
O Israel, you will not be forgotten by me.

Isaiah 44:21

Our Lord cannot so forget his servants as to cease to love them. He chose them not for a time, but forever. He knew what they would be like when he called them into the divine family. He blots out their sins like a cloud. And we may be sure that he will not throw them out for iniquities that he has blotted out. It would be blasphemy to imagine such a thing.

He will not forget them so as to cease to think of them. One forgetful moment on the part of our God would be our ruin. Therefore he says: "You will not be forgotten by me." People forget us. Those whom we have blessed turn against us. We have no lasting place in the fickle hearts of people. But God will never forget one of his true servants. He binds himself to us not by what we do for him, but by what he has done for us. We have been loved too long, and bought at too great a price, to be now forgotten. Jesus sees in us his soul's struggle, and that he can never forget. The Father sees in us the spouse of his Son, and the Spirit sees in us his own effective work. The Lord thinks about us. This day we will be assisted and sustained.

Oh, that the Lord may never be forgotten by us!

APRIL 6

And the LORD will be king over all the earth. On that
day the LORD will be one and his name one.

Zechariah 14:9

Blessed prospect! This is not the dream of an enthusiast but the declaration of the infallible Word. The Lord will be known among all people, and his gracious rule will be acknowledged by every tribe of man. Today it is far from being so. Where do any bow before the great King? How much rebellion there is! There are so many lords and so many gods on the earth! Even among professing Christians there are such diversities of ideas about him and his gospel! One day there will be one King, one Lord, and one name for the living God. Oh, Lord, hasten it! We daily cry, "Your kingdom come" (Matt. 6:10).

We will not discuss the question of *when* this will be, in case we lose the comfort of the certainty that it will be. Just as surely as the Holy Spirit spoke by his prophets, so surely will the whole earth be filled with the glory of the Lord. Jesus did not die in vain. The Spirit of God does not work in vain. The Father's eternal purposes will not be frustrated. Here, where Satan triumphed, Jesus will be crowned and the Lord God omnipotent will reign.

Let us go our way to our daily work and spiritual warfare made strong in faith.

APRIL 7

And all the peoples of the earth shall see that you are called
by the name of the Lord, and they shall be afraid of you.

Deuteronomy 28:10

Then we can have no reason to be afraid of *them*. Such fear would show a mean spirit and be a token of unbelief rather than of faith. God can make us so like himself that people are forced to see that we rightly bear his name and truly belong to the holy Lord. Oh, that we may obtain this grace that the Lord waits to give!

Be assured that ungodly people have a fear of true saints. They hate them, but they also fear them. Haman trembled because of Mordecai, even when he sought the good man's destruction (Est. 6:13). In fact, their hate often arises out of a dread that they are too proud to confess. Let us pursue the path of truth and uprightness without the slightest tremor. Fear is not for us, but for those who do harm and fight against the Lord of hosts. If indeed the name of the eternal God is upon us, we are secure. In ancient days a Roman citizen simply had to say, "I am a Roman," and he could claim the protection of all the legions of the vast empire. So every one who belongs to God has omnipotence as his guardian. God will sooner empty heaven of angels than leave a saint without defense. Be braver than lions when you contend for righteousness, for God is with you.

APRIL 8

The Lord stood by him and said, "Take courage,
for as you have testified to the facts about me in
Jerusalem, so you must testify also in Rome."

Acts 23:11

Are you a witness for the Lord, and right now are you in danger? Then remember that you are immortal until your work is done. If the Lord has more witness for you to bear, you will live to bear it. Who is he that can break the utensil that the Lord intends to use again?

If there is no more work for you to do for your Master, it cannot distress you that he is about to take you home and put you where you will be beyond the reach of adversaries. Your witness-bearing for Jesus is your chief concern, and you cannot be stopped in it until it is finished. Therefore be at peace. Cruel slander, wicked misrepresentation, desertion by friends, betrayal by those you trusted most, and whatever else may come cannot hinder the Lord's purpose for you. The Lord stands by you in the night of your sorrow, and he says, "You must still bear witness for me." Be calm; be filled with joy in the Lord.

If you do not need this promise just now, you may very soon. Treasure it up. Remember also to pray for missionaries and all those who are persecuted, that the Lord would preserve them until they complete their life's work.

APRIL 9

Great peace have those who love your law;
nothing can make them stumble.

Psalm 119:165

Yes, a true love for the great Book will bring us great peace from the great God and be a great protection to us. Let us live constantly in the company of the law of the Lord, and it will breed in our hearts a restfulness in a way nothing else can. The Holy Spirit acts as a Comforter through the Word and so spreads those good influences that calm the storms of the soul.

Nothing is a stumbling block to the person who has the Word of God dwelling in him richly. He takes up his daily cross, and it becomes a delight. For the fiery trial he is prepared. He does not consider trials strange, so as to be utterly cast down by them. He is neither tripped up by prosperity as so many are, nor crushed by adversity as others have been. For he lives beyond the changing circumstances of external life. When his Lord puts before him some great mystery of the faith—which makes others cry, "This is a hard saying; who can listen to it?" (John 6:60)—the believer accepts it without question. For his intellectual difficulties are overcome by his reverent awe of the law of the Lord that is to him the supreme authority to which he joyfully bows.

Lord, work in us this love, this peace, and this rest this day.

APRIL 10

And the LORD said to Moses, "Make a fiery
serpent and set it on a pole, and everyone who
is bitten, when he sees it, shall live."
Numbers 21:8

This is a glorious gospel type. Jesus, numbered with the transgressors,
hangs before us on the cross. A look to him will heal us of the serpent
bite of sin. It will heal us at once. "When he sees it, [he] shall live." Let
the reader who is mourning his sinfulness note the words: "Everyone who
. . . sees it, shall live." Every looker will find this true. I have found it so.
I looked to Jesus and lived at once. I know I did. Reader, if you look to
Jesus, you will live too. True, you are swelling with the venom, and you
see no hope. True, *there is no hope but this one source.* But this is not a
dubious cure: "Everyone who is bitten, when he sees it, shall live."

The bronze serpent was not lifted up as a curiosity to be gazed upon
by the healthy. It was specifically aimed at those who were "bitten." Jesus
died as a real Savior for real sinners. Whether the bite has made you a
drunkard or a thief or an unfaithful or a profane person, a look at the
great Savior will heal you of these diseases and make you live in holiness
and communion with God. Look and live.

APRIL 11

And no longer shall each one teach his neighbor and each his brother, saying, "Know the Lᴏʀᴅ," for they shall all know me, from the least of them to the greatest, declares the Lᴏʀᴅ.

Jeremiah 31:34

Truly, whatever else we do not know, we know the Lord. This day this promise is true in our experience, and it is not a little one. The least believer among us knows God in Christ Jesus. Not as fully as we desire, yet truly and really we know the Lord. We not only know doctrines about him, but we know *him*. He is our Father and our Friend. We are acquainted with him personally. We can say, "My Lord and my God" (John 20:28). We are on terms of close fellowship with God, and many a happy time do we spend in his holy company. We are no more strangers to our God, but the secret of the Lord is with us.

This is more than nature could have taught us. Flesh and blood have not revealed God to us. Christ Jesus has made known the Father to our hearts. If, then, the Lord has made us know himself, is not this the fountain of all saving knowledge? To know God is eternal life. As soon as we come into acquaintance with God, we have the evidence of being awakened to newness of life.

Oh, my soul, rejoice in this knowledge and bless your God all this day!

APRIL 12

For I will forgive their iniquity, and I will
remember their sin no more.

Jeremiah 31:34

When we know the Lord, we receive the forgiveness of sins. We know him as the God of Grace, passing over our transgressions. What a joyful discovery is this!

But how divinely is this promise worded: the Lord promises to remember our sins no more! Can God forget? He says he will, and he means what he says. He will regard us as though we had never sinned. The great atonement so effectively removed all sin that it no longer exists to the mind of God. The believer is now in Christ Jesus, as accepted as Adam in his innocence. Indeed more so, for he wears a divine righteousness, and the righteousness of Adam was only human.

The Great Lord will not remember our sins so as to punish them, or so as to love us one atom less because of them. As a debt when paid ceases to be a debt, even so does the Lord make a complete obliteration of the iniquity of his people.

When we are mourning over our transgressions and shortcomings—and this is our duty as long as we live—let us at the same time rejoice that they will never be mentioned against us. This makes us hate sin. God's free pardon makes us anxious never again to grieve him by disobedience.

APRIL 13

The Lord Jesus Christ . . . will transform our lowly
body to be like his glorious body, by the power that
enables him even to subject all things to himself.

Philippians 3:20–21

Often when we are racked with pain, and unable to think or worship, we feel that this indeed is our "lowly body" or "the body of our humiliation" (in the ASV). And when we are tempted by the passions that rise from the flesh, we do not think the word "vile" to be an exaggerated translation (Phil. 3:21 KJV). Our bodies humble us; and that is about the best thing they do for us. Oh, that we were duly lowly, because our bodies ally us with animals and even link us with the dust!

But our Savior, the Lord Jesus, will change all this. We will be reshaped with a body like his own body of glory. This will take place in all who believe in Jesus. By faith their souls have been transformed, and their bodies will undergo such a renewal that they will match their regenerated spirits. How soon this grand transformation will happen, we cannot tell. But the thought of it should help us bear the trials of today and all the woes of the flesh. In a little while, we will be like Jesus is now. No more aching brows, no more swollen limbs, no more dim eyes, and no more fainting hearts. The old person will be no more a bundle of infirmities, nor the sick person a mass of agony. "Like his glorious body." What an expression! Even our flesh will rest in hope of such a resurrection!

APRIL 14

He chose our heritage for us.

Psalm 47:4

Our enemies would grant us a very dreary allocation. But we are not left in their hands. The Lord will cause us to stand in our lot, and our place is appointed by his infinite wisdom. A wiser mind than our own arranges our destiny. The ordaining of all things is with God, and we are glad to have it so. We choose that God should choose for us. If we had our own way, we would let all things go God's way.

Being conscious of our own folly, we have no desire to rule our own destinies. We feel safer and more at ease when the Lord steers our vessel than we could possibly be if we chose to direct it according to our own judgment. Joyfully we leave the painful present and the unknown future with our Father, our Savior, our Comforter.

Oh, my soul, this day lay down your wishes at Jesus's feet! Perhaps you have recently been somewhat wayward and willful, eager to be and to do what is in your own mind. If so, dismiss your foolish self and place the reins in the Lord's hands. Say, "He shall choose." If others dispute the sovereignty of the Lord and instead glory in the free will of man, answer them, "He shall choose for me." It is my freest choice to let him choose. As a free agent, I elect that he should have absolute sway.

APRIL 15

The desire of the righteous will be granted.

Proverbs 10:24

Because it is a righteous desire, it is safe for God to grant it. It would be neither good for the individual, nor for society at large, if such a promise were made to the unrighteous. Let us keep the Lord's commands and he will rightfully have a regard for our desires.

When righteous people are left to desire unrighteous desires, they will not be granted to them. But then these are not their real desires; they are their wanderings or blunders. And it is just as well that they are refused. Their gracious desires will come before the Lord, and he will not say "no" to them.

Does the Lord deny us our requests for a time? Let the promise for today encourage us to ask again. Has he denied us completely? We will thank him still, for it always was our desire that he should deny us if he judged a denial to be best.

As to some things, we ask very boldly. Our chief desires are for holiness, usefulness, likeness to Christ, readiness for heaven. These are the desires of grace rather than of nature—the desires of the righteous man rather than of the mere man. God will not shortchange us in these things but will give us exceeding abundantly. "Delight yourself in the LORD, and he will give you the desires of your heart" (Ps. 37:4).

This day, my soul, ask largely!

APRIL 16

On that day there shall be inscribed on the
bells of the horses, "Holy to the LORD."

Zechariah 14:20

Happy day when all things will be consecrated and the horses' bells will
ring out, "Holy to the LORD"! That day has come to me. Do I not make
all things holy to God? These clothes, when I put them on or take them
off, will they not remind me of the righteousness of Christ Jesus, my Lord?
Will not my work be done as to the Lord? Oh, that today my clothes may
be vestments, my meals sacraments, my house a temple, my table an altar,
my speech incense, and myself a priest! Lord, fulfill your promise, and let
nothing be to me common or unclean.

Let me in faith expect this. Believing it is so, I will be helped to make
it so. Since I myself am the property of Jesus, my Lord may take an inventory of all I have, for it is all his. And I resolve to prove it is so by the use
to which I put it this day. From morning until evening I will organize everything by a happy and holy rule. My bells will ring with holiness. Why
should they not? Even my horses will have bells. Who has such a right to
music in the way the saints have? But all my bells, my music, my joy, will
be turned toward holiness and will ring out the name of "the blessed" or
"happy God" (1 Tim. 1:11).

APRIL 17

When a man's ways please the LORD,
he makes even his enemies to be at peace with him.

Proverbs 16:7

I must see that my ways please the Lord. Even then I will have enemies; and, perhaps, all the more certainly because I endeavor to do that which is right. But what a promise this is! The Lord will cause the wrath of man to bring him praise and mitigate it so that it will not distress me.

God can make an enemy to stop harming me, even though this was his intent. This he did with Laban, who pursued Jacob but did not dare to touch him (Gen. 31:24). Or he can subdue the wrath of the enemy and make him friendly, as he did with Esau. Esau met Jacob in a brotherly manner, though Jacob had dreaded that Esau would attack him and his family with the sword (Gen. 33:1–11). The Lord can also convert a furious adversary into a brother or sister in Christ and a fellow worker, as he did with Saul of Tarsus (Acts 9:1–19). Oh, that he would do this in every case where a persecuting spirit appears!

Happy is the person whose enemies are made to be to them what the lions were to Daniel in the den, quiet and companionable (Daniel 6)! When I meet death, which is called the last enemy (1 Cor. 15:26), I pray that I may be at peace. Only let my great care be to please the Lord in all things. Oh, for faith and holiness—for these are a pleasure to the Most High!

APRIL 18

I will be with you. I will not leave you or forsake you.

Joshua 1:5

This word to Joshua is often quoted. It is the basis of that New Testament word: "He has said, 'I will never leave you nor forsake you'" (Heb. 13:5).

Beloved, a life of warfare is before us, but the Lord of Hosts is with us. Are we called to lead a great but fickle people? This promise guarantees us all the wisdom and prudence that we will need. Have we to contend with cunning and powerful enemies? Here is strength and valor, prowess and victory. Have we a vast heritage to win? By this sign we will achieve our purpose: the Lord himself is with us.

It would be sad for us indeed if the Lord could fail us. But, as this can never be, the winds of uneasiness are laid to sleep in the caverns of divine faithfulness. Not even once will the Lord desert us. Whatever happens, he will be at our side. Friends drop from us, for their help is like an April shower. But God is faithful, Jesus is the same forever, and the Holy Spirit remains in us.

Come, my heart, be calm and hopeful today. Clouds may gather, but the Lord can blow them away. Since God will not fail me, my faith will not fail. And, as he will not forsake me, neither will I forsake him. Oh, for a restful faith!

APRIL 19

For thus says the Lord GOD: Behold, I, I myself will
search for my sheep and will seek them out.

Ezekiel 34:11

This he does first of all when his elect are like wandering sheep that do
not know the Shepherd or the fold. How wonderfully the Lord finds his
chosen! Jesus is great as a *seeking* Shepherd as well as a *saving* Shepherd.
Though many of those his Father gave him have gone as near to the gates
of hell as they well can, yet the Lord by searching and seeking discovers
them and draws near to them in grace. He has sought out us. So let us
have good hope for those who are laid on our hearts in prayer, for he will
find them out also.

The Lord repeats this process when any of his flock stray from the
pastures of truth and holiness. They may fall into gross error, sad sin,
and grievous hardness. But yet the Lord, who has become a guarantee
for them before his Father, will not let one of them go so far away as to
perish. He will by providence and grace pursue them into foreign lands,
into places of poverty, into dens of obscurity, into deeps of despair. He
will not lose one of all that the Father has given him (John 6:39). It is a
point of honor with Jesus to seek and to save all the flock without a single
exception. What a promise to plead, if at this point I am compelled to cry,
"I have gone astray like a lost sheep"!

APRIL 20

The righteous shall live by faith.

Romans 1:17

I will not die. I can believe, and I do believe, in the Lord my God. And this faith will keep me alive. I want to be numbered among those who in their lives are righteous. But if I were perfect, I would not try to live by my righteousness. I would cling to the work of the Lord Jesus. I would still live by faith in him and by nothing else. If I were to give my body to be burned for my Lord Jesus, even then I would not trust in my own courage and constancy, but still I would live by faith.

> Were I a martyr at the stake
> I'd plead my Savior's name;
> entreat a pardon for his sake,
> and urge no other claim.
>
> *Thomas Greene*

To live by faith is a far surer and happier thing than to live by feelings or by works. The branch, by living in the vine, lives a better life than it would live by itself, even if it were possible for it to live at all apart from the stem. To live by clinging to Jesus, by deriving all from him, is a sweet and sacred thing. If even the most just must live in this fashion, how much more must I who am a poor sinner! Lord, I believe. I must trust you wholly. What else can I do? Trusting you is my life. I feel it to be so. I will abide by this to the very end.

APRIL 21

Whoever is generous to the poor lends to the LORD,
and he will repay him for his deed.

Proverbs 19:17

We are to give to the poor out of compassion—not to be seen and applauded, much less to get influence over them. But out of pure sympathy and pity we must give them help.

We must not expect to get anything back from the poor, not even gratitude. But we should regard what we have done as a loan to the Lord. He undertakes the obligation. And, if we look to him in the matter, we must not look to the second party. What an honor the Lord bestows upon us when he condescends to borrow from us! That merchant is greatly favored who has the Lord on his books. It would seem a pity to have such a name down for a paltry pittance. Let us make it a heavy amount. The next needy man that comes this way, let us help him.

As for repayment, we can hardly expect it, and yet here is the Lord's promissory notes. Blessed be his name, his promise to pay is better than gold and silver. Are we running a little short through the depression of the times? We may venture humbly to present this bill at the bank of faith. Has any one of our readers been a bit of a miser toward the poor? Poor soul. May the Lord forgive them.

APRIL 22

The LORD opens the eyes of the blind.
The LORD lifts up those who are bowed down.

Psalm 146:8

Am I bowed down? Then let me urge this word of grace before the Lord. It is his way, his custom, his promise, his delight, to raise up those who are bowed down.

Is it a sense of sin, and a consequent depression of spirit, that now distresses me? Then the work of Jesus is, in this case, made and provided to raise me up into rest. Oh, Lord, raise me, for your mercy's sake!

Is it a sad bereavement or a great fall in circumstances? Here again the Comforter has committed himself to console. What a mercy for us that one person of the sacred Trinity should become the Comforter! This work will be done well, since such a glorious One has made it his particular care.

Some are so bowed down that only Jesus can free them from their infirmity. But he can, and he will, do it. He can raise us up to health, to hope, to happiness. He has often done so in former trials. And he is the same Savior, and will repeat his acts of loving kindness. We who are today bowed down and sorrowful, we will yet be set on high, and those who mock us now will be greatly ashamed. What an honor to be raised up by the Lord! It is worthwhile to be bowed down that we may experience his upraising power.

APRIL 23

He who has an ear, let him hear what the Spirit
says to the churches. The one who conquers
will not be hurt by the second death.

Revelation 2:11

The first death we must endure unless the Lord suddenly comes to his temple (Mal. 3:1). For this let us remain in readiness, awaiting it without fear, since Jesus has transformed death from a dreary cavern into a passage leading to glory.

The thing to be feared is not the first death but the second death—not the parting of the soul from the body but the final separation of the entire man from God. This is death indeed. This death kills all peace, joy, happiness, hope. When God is gone, all is gone. Such a death is far worse than ceasing to be. It is existence without the life that makes existence worth having.

Now, if by God's grace we fight on to the end, and conquer in the glorious war, no second death can lay its chill finger upon us. We will have no fear of death and hell, for we will receive a crown of life that does not fade away. How this nerves us for the fight! Eternal life is worth a life's battle. To escape the hurt of the second death is a thing worth struggling for throughout a lifetime.

Lord, give us faith so that we may overcome, and then grant us grace to remain unharmed, though sin and Satan dog our heels!

APRIL 24

Bring the full tithe into the storehouse, that there may be food
in my house. And thereby put me to the test, says the LORD
of hosts, if I will not open the windows of heaven for you
and pour down for you a blessing until there is no more need.

Malachi 3:10

Many read and plead this promise without noticing the condition on which the blessing is promised. We cannot expect heaven to be opened or blessing poured out unless we pay our dues to the Lord our God and to his cause. There would be no lack of funds for holy purposes if all professing Christians paid their fair share.

Many are poor because they rob God. Many churches, also, miss the outpourings of the Spirit because they starve their ministers. If there is no temporal provision for God's servants, we need not wonder why their ministry has only a little food in it for our souls. When missions pine for support, and the work of the Lord is hindered by an empty treasury, how can we look for a large amount of soul-prosperity?

Come, come! What have I given recently? Have I been mean toward my God? Have I shortchanged my Savior? This will never do. Let me give my Lord Jesus his tithe by helping the poor and aiding his work. And then I will prove his power to bless me on a large scale.

APRIL 25

The righteous who walks in his integrity—
blessed are his children after him!

Proverbs 20:7

Anxiety about our family is natural. But we will be wise if we turn it into care about our own character. If we walk before the Lord in integrity, we will do more to bless our descendants than if we bequeathed them large estates. A parent's holy life is a rich legacy for their sons and daughters.

The upright person leaves their heirs their example, and this in itself will be a gold mine of true wealth. How many people may trace their success in life to the example of their parents!

They also leave them their reputation. People think all the better of us as children of a person who could be trusted, the successors of a tradesman of excellent repute. Oh, that all young people were anxious to keep up the family name!

Above all, they leave their children their prayers and the blessing of a prayer-hearing God. These make our offspring favored among the children of men. God will save them even after we are dead. Oh, that they might be saved at once!

Our integrity may be God's means of saving our sons and daughters. If they see the truth of our religion proved by our lives, it may be that they will believe in Jesus for themselves.

Lord, fulfill this word to my household!

APRIL 26

So the LORD your God will bless you in all that you do.

Deuteronomy 15:18

An Israelite master was to give his slave freedom at the appointed time. And when he left his service, he was to start him in life with an abundant share. This was to be done wholeheartedly and joyfully. Then the Lord promised to bless this generous act. The spirit of this precept—and, indeed, the whole law of Christ—compels us to treat colleagues and tradesmen well. We ought to remember how the Lord has dealt with us, and that this means it absolutely necessary that we should deal graciously with others. It is fitting for the children of a gracious God to be generous. How can we expect our great Master to bless us in our business if we oppress those who serve us?

What a blessing is here set before those with a generous frame of mind! To be blessed in all that we do is to be blessed indeed. The Lord will send us this partly through prosperity, partly through contentment of mind, and partly through a sense of his favor, which is the best of all blessings. He can make us feel that we are under his special care and are surrounded by his particular love. This makes this earthly life a joyous prelude to the life to come. God's blessing is more than a fortune. It makes us rich and brings no sorrow in the process.

APRIL 27

The LORD will fulfill his purpose for me.

Psalm 138:8

He who has begun a work in my soul will carry on that work. The Lord is concerned about everything that concerns me. All that is now good in me, but not perfect, the Lord will watch over, and preserve, and carry out to completion (Phil. 1:6). This is a great comfort. I could not complete the work of grace myself. Of that I am quite sure, for I fail every day, and have only held on for as long as I have because the Lord has helped me. If the Lord were to leave me, all my past experience would count for nothing, and I would wander from the way. But the Lord will continue to bless me. He will perfect my faith, my love, my character, and my lifework. He will do this because he has begun a work in me. He gave me the concern I feel, and, in a measure, he has fulfilled my gracious aspirations. He never leaves a work unfinished. That would not be for his glory, nor would it be like him. He knows how to accomplish his gracious design. And, though my own evil nature, the world, and the devil all conspire to hinder him, I do not doubt his promise. He will perfect his purpose for me, and I will praise him forever.

Lord, let your gracious work make some advance this day!

APRIL 28

I will make my dwelling among them and walk among them,
and I will be their God,
and they shall be my people.

2 Corinthians 6:16

Here is a *mutual interest*. Each belongs to each. God is the inheritance of his people, and the chosen people are the inheritance of their God. The saints find in God their chief possession, and he reckons them to be his particular treasure. What a gold mine of comfort lies in this fact for each believer!

This happy condition of mutual interest leads to *mutual consideration*. God will always think of his own people, and they will always think of him. This day my God will perform all things for me. What can I do for him? My thoughts ought to run toward him, since he thinks about me. Let me make sure that it is so, and not be content with merely admitting that it ought to be so.

This, again, leads to *mutual fellowship*. God dwells in us, and we dwell in him. He walks with us, and we walk with God. What a happy communion this is!

Oh, for grace to treat the Lord as my God—to trust him and to serve him as his Godhead deserves! Oh, that I could love, worship, adore, and obey the Lord in spirit and in truth! This is my heart's desire. When I attain it, I will have found my heaven.

Lord, help me! Be my God by helping me to know you as my God, for Jesus's sake.

Do not say, "I will repay evil";
wait for the LORD, and he will deliver you.

Proverbs 20:22

Do not be hasty. Let anger cool down. Say nothing and do nothing to revenge yourself. You will be sure to act unwisely if you raise your fists and fight your own battles. And, certainly, you will not show the spirit of the Lord Jesus. It is nobler to forgive and let the offense pass. To let an injury fester in your heart, and to meditate on revenge, is to keep old wounds open and to make new ones. Better to forget and forgive.

But perhaps you say that you must do something or you will be a great loser. Then do what this morning's promise advises: "Wait for the LORD, and he will deliver you." This advice will not cost you money, but is worth far more. Be calm and quiet. Wait on the Lord. Tell him your grievance. Spread Rabshakeh's letter before the Lord (2 Kings 19:14), and this by itself will be an ease to your burdened mind. Besides, there is the promise, "He will deliver you." God will find a way of deliverance for you. How he will do it neither you nor I can guess, but do it he will. If the Lord saves you, this will be a good deal better than getting into petty quarrels and covering yourself with filth by wrestling with unclean people. Do not be angry anymore. Leave your case with the Judge of all.

APRIL 30

To the one who conquers I will give some of the
hidden manna, and I will give him a white stone,
with a new name written on the stone that no
one knows except the one who receives it.

Revelation 2:17

Beloved, be stirred up to persevere in the holy war, for the reward of victory is great. Today we eat heavenly food which falls around our camps: the food of the wilderness, the food which comes from heaven, the food which never fails the pilgrims to Canaan (Exodus 16). But there is reserved for us in Christ Jesus a still higher degree of spiritual life, and a food for that life which is, as yet, hidden from our experience. In the golden pot that was stored in the ark there was a portion of manna hidden away, which though kept for ages never grew stale (Ex. 16:33–34). No one ever saw it, for it was hidden in the ark of the covenant in the Most Holy Place. In the same way, the highest life of the believer is hidden with Christ in God (Col. 3:3). We will come to it soon. Being made victorious through the grace of our Lord Jesus, we will eat the King's meat and feed upon royal dainties. We will feed upon Jesus. He is our "hidden manna" as well as the manna of the wilderness. He is all in all to us in our highest as well as in our lowest estate. He helps us to fight, gives us the victory, and then he himself is our reward.

Lord, help me to overcome.

MAY

MAY 1

The mountains and the hills before you
shall break forth into singing,
and all the trees of the field shall clap their hands.

Isaiah 55:12

When sin is pardoned, our greatest sorrow ends and our truest pleasure begins. Such is the joy that the Lord gives his reconciled ones—it overflows and fills all nature with delight. The material world has latent music in it, and a renewed heart knows how to bring it out and make it vocal. Creation is the organ, and a gracious man finds out its keys, lays his hand on them, and wakes the whole system of the universe to the harmony of praise. Mountains and hills and other great objects are, as it were, the bass of the chorus; while the trees of the wood and everything that has life take up the tune of the melodious song.

When God's Word is made to prosper among us, and souls are saved, then everything seems full of song. When we hear the confessions of young believers and the testimonies of well-instructed saints, we are made so happy that we must praise the Lord. And then it seems as if rocks and hills, and woods and fields, echo our notes of joy, and the world turns into an orchestra.

Lord, on this happy May Day, lead me out into your tuneful world as rich in praise as a lark in full song.

MAY 2

The one who sows to the Spirit will
from the Spirit reap eternal life.

Galatians 6:8

Sowing looks like a losing business, for we put good corn into the ground,
never to see it anymore. Sowing to the Spirit seems a very fanciful, dreamy
business. For we deny ourselves and apparently get nothing for it. Yet if
we sow to the Spirit by studying how to live to God, seeking to obey the
will of God, and pouring ourselves out to promote his honor, we will
not sow in vain. Life will be our reward, even everlasting life. This we
enjoy here as we enter into the knowledge of God, communion with God,
and enjoyment of God. This life flows on like an ever-deepening, ever-
widening river, until it carries us to the ocean of infinite happiness, where
the life of God is ours forever and ever.

Today let us not sow to our flesh, for the harvest will be corruption,
since flesh always tends that way. But with holy self-conquest, let us live
for the highest, purest, and most spiritual ends. Let us seek to honor our
most holy Lord by obeying his most gracious Spirit. What a harvest will
that create when we reap life everlasting! What sheaves of endless joy will
be reaped! What a festival will that harvest be!

Lord, make us such reapers, for your Son's sake.

MAY 3

And when you hear the sound of marching in the tops of the balsam trees, then rouse yourself, for then the LORD has gone out before you to strike down the army of the Philistines.

2 Samuel 5:24

There are signs of the Lord's moving which should move us. The Spirit of God blows where he wishes, and we hear the sound (John 3:8). Then is the time for us to be more than ever astir. We must seize the golden opportunity and make the most of it that we can. It is ours to fight the Philistines at all times. But when the Lord himself goes out before us, then we should be specially valiant in the war.

The breeze stirred the tops of the trees, and David and his men took this for the signal for an onslaught, and at their advance the Lord himself struck down the Philistines (2 Sam. 5:22–25). Oh, that this day the Lord may give us an opening to speak for him with many of our friends! Let us be on the watch to use the hopeful opening when it comes. Who knows but this may be a day of good news, a season of soul-winning. Let us keep our ear open to hear the rustle of the wind, and our minds ready to obey the signal. Is not this promise, "Then the LORD has gone out before you," a sufficient encouragement to play your part with courage? Since the Lord goes before us, we dare not hold back.

MAY 4

Rejoice not over me, O my enemy;
when I fall, I shall rise;
when I sit in darkness,
the LORD will be a light to me.

Micah 7:8

This may express the feeling of a man or woman downtrodden and oppressed. Our enemy may put out our light for a season. There is sure hope for us in the Lord. If we are trusting in him, and holding fast to our integrity, our season of downcasting and darkness will soon be over. The insults of the foe are only for a moment. The Lord will soon turn their laughter into lament, and our sighing into singing.

What if the great enemy of souls should triumph over us for a while, as he has triumphed over better men than we are? Yet let us take heart, for we will overcome him before long. We will rise from our fall, for our God has not fallen, and he will lift us up. We will not remain in darkness, although for the moment we sit in it, for our Lord is the fountain of light, and he will soon bring us a joyful day. Let us not despair or even doubt. One turn of the wheel and the lowest will be at the top. Woe to those who laugh now, for they will mourn and weep when their boasting is turned into everlasting contempt. But blessed are all holy mourners, for they will be divinely comforted (Luke 6:21, 25).

MAY 5

Then the LORD your God will restore your fortunes and
have mercy on you, and he will gather you again from all
the peoples where the LORD your God has scattered you.

Deuteronomy 30:3

God's own people may sell themselves into captivity by sin. This is a very bitter fruit of an exceeding bitter root. What a bondage it is when the child of God is sold under sin, held in chains by Satan, deprived of his liberty, robbed of his power in prayer and his delight in the Lord! Let us watch to ensure we do not come into such bondage.

But if this has already happened to us, let us by no means despair. For we cannot be held in slavery forever. The Lord Jesus has paid too high a price for our redemption to leave us in the enemy's hand. The way to freedom is, "Return to the LORD your God" (Deut. 30:2). Where we first found salvation, we will find it again. At the foot of Christ's cross, confessing our sin, we will find pardon and deliverance. Moreover, the Lord would have us obey his voice according to all that he has commanded us. We must do this with all our heart and all our soul. And then our captivity will end.

Often depression of spirit and great misery of soul are removed as soon as we quit our idols and bow ourselves in obedience before the living God. We need not be captives. We may return to Zion's citizenship, and that quickly.

Lord, turn our captivity!

MAY 6

Let not your heart envy sinners,
but continue in the fear of the LORD all the day.
Surely there is a future,
and your hope will not be cut off.

Proverbs 23:17–18

When we see the wicked prosper, we are inclined to envy them. When we hear the noise of their laughter, and our own spirit is heavy, we half think that they have the best of it. This is foolish and sinful. If we knew them better, and especially if we remembered their final end, we should pity them.

The cure for envy lies in living under a constant sense of the divine presence, worshiping God and communing with him all the day long, however long the day may seem. True religion lifts the soul into a higher region, where the judgment becomes more clear and the desires are more elevated. The more of heaven there is in our lives, the less of earth we will covet. The fear of God casts out envy of men.

The death blow of envy is a calm consideration of the future. The wealth and glory of the ungodly are an empty show. This pompous appearance flashes out for an hour, and then is extinguished. What advantage is there for the prosperous sinner in his prosperity when judgment overtakes him? As for the godly man, his final end is peace and blessing, and no one can rob him of his joy. Therefore, let him let go of envy and be filled with sweet contentment.

MAY 7

None of the devoted things shall stick to your hand,
that the LORD may turn from the fierceness of his
anger and show you mercy and have compassion on
you and multiply you, as he swore to your fathers.

Deuteronomy 13:17

Israel must conquer idolatrous cities and devote all the spoils of victory to destruction. All that had been polluted by idolatry was to be treated a cursed thing to be burned with fire. Now, sin of all sorts must be treated by Christians in the same way. We must not allow a single evil habit to remain. Our warfare involves putting the knife into sins of all sorts and sizes, whether of the body, the mind, or the spirit. Giving up of evil is not an act that earns us mercy; instead, we regard it as a fruit of the grace of God, that we would not miss on any account.

When God causes us to have no mercy on our sins, then he has great mercy on us. When we are angry with evil, God is no more angry with us. When we multiply our efforts against iniquity, the Lord multiplies our blessings. The way of peace, of growth, of safety, of joy in Christ Jesus will be found by following out these words: "None of the devoted things shall stick to your hand."

Lord, purify me this day. Compassion, prosperity, increase, and joy will surely be given to those who put away sin with solemn resolve.

MAY 8

He said to them, "You go into the vineyard too." And
when evening came, the owner of the vineyard said to his
foreman, "Call the laborers and pay them their wages."

Matthew 20:7–8

Yes, there is work in Christ's vineyard for old bodies. It is the eleventh
hour, and yet he will let us work. What great grace is this! Surely every old
person ought to jump at this invitation! Nobody wants people advanced
in years as workers. They go from shop to shop, and employers look at
the elderly's gray hairs and shake their heads. But Jesus will engage old
people and give them good wages too! This is mercy indeed. Lord, help
the aged to enlist in your service without an hour's delay.

But will the Lord pay wages to worn-out old people? Do not doubt
it. He says he will give you "whatever is right" if you will work in his
field (Matt. 20:4 NKJV). He will surely give you grace here and glory
hereafter. He will grant present comfort and future rest; strength equal to
your day, and a vision of glory when the night of death comes. All these
the Lord Jesus will give as freely to the aged convert as to one who enters
his service in his youth.

Let me tell this to some unsaved old man or old woman, and ask the
Lord to bless it for Jesus's sake. Where can I find such persons? I will be
on the lookout for them and kindly tell them the news.

MAY 9

For our heart is glad in him,
because we trust in his holy name.

Psalm 33:21

The root of faith produces the flower of heart-joy. We may not rejoice straightaway, but joy comes in good time. We trust the Lord when we are sad, and in due course he answers our confidence so that our faith comes to fruition and we rejoice in the Lord. Doubt breeds distress, but trust brings joy in the long run.

The assurance expressed by the psalmist in this verse is really a promise held out in the hands of holy confidence. Oh, for grace to make it our own. If we do not rejoice at this moment, we will do so as surely as David's God is our God.

Let us meditate upon the Lord's holy name, that we may trust him the better and rejoice the more readily. His character is holy, just, true, gracious, faithful, and unchanging. Is not such a God to be trusted? He is all-wise, almighty, and present everywhere. Can we not cheerfully rely on him? Yes, we will do so at once and do so without reservation. Jehovah-Jireh will provide, Jehovah-Shalom will send peace, Jehovah-Tsidkenu will justify, Jehovah-Shammah will be forever near, and in Jehovah-Nissi we will conquer every foe. "Those who know your name put their trust in you" (Ps. 9:10); and all those that put their trust in you "rejoice" (Ps. 5:11).

MAY 10

So we can confidently say,
"The Lord is my helper;
I will not fear;
what can man do to me?"

Hebrews 13:6

Because God will never leave nor forsake us (Heb. 13:5), we may be well content with such things as we have. Since the Lord is ours, we cannot be left without a friend, a treasure, and a dwelling place. This assurance may make us feel quite independent of other people. Under such high patronage we do not feel tempted to cringe before our fellow men nor ask their permission to call our lives our own. Instead, what we say, we say boldly and defy contradiction.

The one who fears God has nothing else to fear. We should stand in such awe of the living Lord. For then all the threats that can be used by the proudest persecutor will have no more effect on us than the whistling of the wind. These days people cannot do as much against us as they could when the apostle wrote this verse. Torturing people on the rack and burning them at the stake is out of fashion. If the followers of false teachers try cruel mockery and scorn, we are not surprised, since the people of this world cannot love the children of heaven. What then? We must bear the world's scorn. It breaks no bones. God helping us, let us be bold. When the world rages, let it rage, but let us not fear it.

MAY 11

Raiders shall raid Gad,
but he shall raid at their heels.

Genesis 49:19

Some of us have been like the tribe of Gad. For a while our adversaries were too many for us. They came upon us like a troop of soldiers. Yes, and for the moment they overcame us. And they rejoiced greatly because of their temporary victory. But all they have done is prove that we are part of God's oppressed family here on earth. For, like Gad, Christ's people will be overcome by a troop. Being overcome in this way is very painful. And we would have despaired if we had not by faith believed the second line of Jacob's blessings, *"He shall overcome at the last"* (Gen. 49:19 KJV). "All's well that ends well," wrote William Shakespeare; and he spoke the truth. A war is to be judged, not by first successes or defeats, but by that which happens "at the last." Others may initiate conflict, like the raiders who attacked Gad. But God's people shall overcome in the end, like Gad chasing at the heels of their retreating foes. The Lord will give victory "at the last" to truth and righteousness. As John Bunyan says, that means forever, for nothing can come after the last.

What we need is patient perseverance in well-doing and calm confidence in our glorious Captain. Our Lord Jesus Christ would teach us his holy art of setting the face like a flint (Isa. 50:7), to press on with work or suffering until we can say, "It is finished" (John 19:30).

Hallelujah. Victory! Victory! We believe the promise. "He shall overcome at the last."

MAY 12

Whoever tends a fig tree will eat its fruit,
and he who guards his master will be honored.

Proverbs 27:18

He who tends the fig tree has figs for his pains, and he who serves a good master has honor as his reward. Truly the Lord Jesus is the very best of masters, and it is an honor to be allowed to do the least act for his sake. To serve some lords is to watch over a crab tree and eat the crab apples as one's wages. But to serve my Lord Jesus is to tend a fig tree of the sweetest figs. His service is in itself delight, continuance in it is promotion, success in it is blessing below, and the reward for it is glory above.

Our greatest honors will be gathered in the season when the figs will be ripe, that is, in the world to come. Angels who are already our servants will bear us home when our day's work is done. Heaven, where Jesus is, will be our honorable mansion, eternal bliss our honorable portion, and the Lord himself our honorable companion. Who can imagine the full meaning of this promise, "He who guards his master will be honored"?

Lord, help me to wait on my Master. Let me leave all idea of receiving honor until the hour when you yourself will honor me. May your Holy Spirit make me a humble worker who waits patiently!

MAY 13

And I will give him the morning star.

Revelation 2:28

Before day breaks and shadows flee away, what a blessing it is to see in Jesus "the morning star"! I remember reading in the newspapers an idle tale that the star of Bethlehem had again appeared. On inquiry we found that it was only "the morning star." But no great mistake had been made after all.

It is best to see Jesus as the sun. But when we cannot do so, the next best thing is to see him as that star which signals the coming of the day and shows that the eternal light is near. If today I am not all that I hope to be, yet I see Jesus, and that assures me that I will one day be like him (1 John 3:2). A sight of Jesus by faith is the pledge of seeing him in his glory and being transformed into his image. If at this hour I do not have all the light and joy I could desire, yet I will have it. For as surely as I see the morning star, I will see the day. The morning star is never far from the sun.

Come, my soul, has the Lord given you the morning star? Do you hold fast to that truth, grace, hope, and love that the Lord has given you? Then in this you have the dawn of coming glory. He that makes you overcome evil, and persevere in righteousness, has in this given you the morning star.

MAY 14

Come, let us return to the LORD;
for he has torn us, that he may heal us;
he has struck us down, and he will bind us up.

Hosea 6:1

It is the Lord's way to tear before he heals. This is the honest love of his heart and the sure surgery of his hand. He also bruises before he binds up, otherwise it would be uncertain work. The law comes before the gospel; the sense of need before the supply of it. Is the reader now under the convincing, crushing hand of the Spirit? Has he received the spirit of bondage again to fear? This is a salutary preliminary to real gospel healing and binding up.

Do not despair, dear heart, but come to the Lord with all your jagged wounds, black bruises, and running sores. He alone can heal, and he delights to do it. It is our Lord's ministry to bind up the brokenhearted, and he is gloriously at home at it. Let us not linger, but at once return to the Lord from whom we have gone astray. Let us show him our gaping wounds and beg him to recognize his own work and complete it. Will a surgeon make an incision and then leave his patient to bleed to death? Will the Lord pull down our old house and then refuse to build us a better one?

Oh, Lord, do you ever recklessly increase the misery of poor anxious souls? This is far from you.

MAY 15

I will protect him, because he knows my name.

Psalm 91:14

Does the Lord say this to me? Yes, if I know his name. Blessed be the Lord, I am no stranger to him. I have tried him and proved him and known him, and therefore I trust him. I know his name as a sin-hating God. For by his Spirit's convincing power I have been taught that he will never close his eyes to evil. But I also know him as the sin-pardoning God in Christ Jesus. For he has forgiven me all trespasses. His name is Faithfulness, and I know it. For he has never forsaken me, though my troubles have multiplied upon me.

This knowledge is a gift of grace, and the Lord makes it the reason why he grants another gift of grace: "I will set him on high" (Ps. 91:14 KJV). This is grace upon grace. Observe that if we climb on high, the position may be dangerous. But if the Lord "will protect" us there, it is safe. He may raise us to great usefulness, to an eminent position, to success in service, to leadership among workers, or to a father's place among the little ones. If he does not do this, he may set us high by close fellowship, clear insight, holy triumph, and gracious anticipation of eternal glory. When God sets us on high, Satan himself cannot pull us down. Oh, that this be the case for us all through this day!

MAY 16

Blessed are the merciful, for they shall receive mercy.

Matthew 5:7

It is not fitting that the person who will not forgive should be forgiven, nor that the person who will not give to the poor should have their own needs relieved. God will measure to us by our own measures. And those who have been hard masters and hard creditors will find that the Lord will deal in a hard way with them. "For judgment is without mercy to one who has shown no mercy" (James 2:13).

This day let us try to give and to forgive. Let us mind the two "bears"— "bear" and "forbear." Let us be kind and gentle and tender. Let us not put harsh constructions on men's conduct, nor drive hard bargains, nor pick foolish quarrels, nor be difficult to please. Surely we want to be blessed, and we also want to obtain mercy. So let us be merciful, that we may have mercy. Let us fulfill the condition, that we may earn the blessing. Is it not a pleasant duty to be kind? Is there not much more sweetness in it than in being angry and ungenerous? Why, there is a blessing in the act itself! Moreover, obtaining mercy is a rich reward. Only sovereign grace could suggest such a promise as this! We are merciful to our fellow mortals in pennies, and the Lord forgives us "all that debt" (Matt. 18:32).

MAY 17

The blameless will have a goodly inheritance.

Proverbs 28:10

The book of Proverbs is also a book of promises. Promises ought to be proverbs among the people of God. This is a very remarkable one. We normally think of our good things as ours for a limited period, but here we are told that we will have them as an enduring possession.

All the malice and cunning of our enemies cannot cause our destruction. They will fall into the pit which they have dug. Our inheritance is so guaranteed to us that we will not be kept from it, nor so lose our way as to miss it.

But what do we have now? We have a quiet conscience through the precious blood of Jesus. We have the love of God set on us beyond all change. We have power with God in prayer in every time of need. We have the providence of God to watch over us, the angels of God to minister to us, and, above all, the Spirit of God to dwell in us. In fact, all things are ours. "Whether . . . the present or the future—all are yours" (1 Cor. 3:22). Jesus is ours. Indeed, the divine Trinity in unity is ours. Hallelujah!

Let us not pine and whine, and stint and slave, since we possess good things. Let us live depending on our God and rejoice in him all the day. Help us, oh, Holy Spirit!

MAY 18

I will restore to you the years
that the swarming locust has eaten.

Joel 2:25

Yes, those wasted years over which we sigh will be restored to us. God can give us such plentiful grace that we will crowd into the remainder of our days enough service as to be some recompense for those years before we were born again that we mourn in humble penitence.

The locusts of backsliding, worldliness, and lukewarmness are now viewed by us as a terrible plague. Oh, that they had never come near us! The Lord in mercy has now taken them away, and we are full of zeal to serve him. Blessed be his name, for we can produce such harvests of spiritual graces as will make our former barrenness disappear. Through rich grace we can turn our bitter experience into profit by using it to warn others. We can become even more rooted in humility, childlike dependence, and penitent spirituality because of our former shortcomings. If we are more watchful, zealous, and tender, then we will gain from our lamentable losses. The wasted years, by a miracle of love, can be restored. Does it seem too great a blessing? Let us believe for it, and live for it, and we may yet realize it, just as Peter became all the more useful after his presumption was cured by his discovered weakness.

Lord, aid us by your grace.

MAY 19

Therefore thus says the LORD:
"If you return, I will restore you,
and you shall stand before me.
If you utter what is precious, and not what is worthless,
you shall be as my mouth."
Jeremiah 15:19

Poor Jeremiah! Yet why do we say so? The weeping prophet was one of the greatest servants of God, and honored by him above many. He was hated for speaking the truth. The word that was so sweet to him was bitter to his hearers, yet he was accepted by his Lord. He was commanded to remain faithful, and then the Lord would continue to speak through him. He was to deal boldly and truthfully with men, and perform the Lord's winnowing work upon those in his day who claimed to worship God. And then the Lord gave him this word, "You shall be as my mouth."

What an honor! Should not every preacher, indeed every believer, covet it? For God to speak by us, what a marvel! We will speak sure, pure truth; and we will speak it with power. Our word will not return empty (Isa. 55:11). It will be a blessing to those who receive it, and those who refuse it will do so at their peril. Our lips will feed many. We will arouse the sleeping and call the dead to life.

Oh, dear reader, pray that it may be so with all the servants sent by our Lord.

MAY 20

I will go before you
and level the exalted places,
I will break in pieces the doors of bronze
and cut through the bars of iron.

Isaiah 45:2

This promise was for Cyrus. But forever it is the heritage of all the Lord's own spiritual servants. If we go forward by faith, then our way will be cleared for us. Twists and turns of human craft and satanic subtlety will be straightened for us. We will not need to follow their devious windings. The doors of bronze will be broken, and the iron bars which fastened them will be cut in two. We will not need the battering ram nor the crowbar. The Lord himself will do the impossible for us, and the unexpected will be a fact.

Let us not sit down in cowardly fear. Let us press onward in the path of duty. For the Lord has said, "I will go before you." Ours is not to reason why; ours is simply to dare and dash forward. It is the Lord's work, and he will enable us to do it. All impediments must give way to him. Has he not said, "I will break in pieces the doors of bronze"? What can hinder his purpose or prevent his decrees? Those who serve God have infinite resources. The way is clear to faith though barred to human strength. When the Lord says, "I will," as he does twice in this promise, we dare not doubt.

MAY 21

If the clouds are full of rain,
they empty themselves on the earth.

Ecclesiastes 11:3

Why, then, do we dread the clouds which now darken our sky? True, for a while they hide the sun, but the sun is not snuffed out. He will shine out again before long. Meanwhile, those black clouds are filled with rain. And the blacker they are, the more likely they are to produce plentiful showers. How can we have rain without clouds?

Our troubles have always brought us blessings, and they always will. They are the dark chariots of bright grace. These clouds will empty themselves before long, and every tender herb will be the gladder for the shower. Our God may drench us with grief, but he will not drown us with wrath. No, he will refresh us with mercy. Our Lord's love letters often come to us in black-edged envelopes. His wagons rumble, but they are loaded with benefit. His rod of discipline blossoms with sweet flowers and nourishing fruits. Let us not worry about the clouds, but sing because May flowers are brought to us through the April clouds and showers.

Oh, Lord, the clouds are the dust of your feet! How near you are in the cloudy and dark day! Love beholds you, and is glad. Faith sees the clouds emptying themselves and making the little hills rejoice on every side.

MAY 22

Though I walk in the midst of trouble,
you preserve my life;
you stretch out your hand against the wrath of my enemies,
and your right hand delivers me.

Psalm 138:7

Is it wretched to walk in the midst of trouble? No, it is blessed walking, for there is a special promise for it. Give me a promise, and what is the trouble? What does my Lord teach me to say here? Why this: "You preserve my life." Indeed, do we not often find that trouble actually revives our souls like a breath of cold air when one is ready to faint? I will have more life, more energy, and more faith.

How angry are my enemies, and especially the archenemy! Will I stretch out my hand and fight my foes? No, my hand is better employed in doing service for my Lord. Besides, there is no need, for my God will use his far-reaching arm, and he will deal with them far better than I could if I were to try. "Vengeance is mine; I will repay, says the Lord" (Rom. 12:19). He will save me with his own right hand of power and wisdom. What more could I want?

Come, my heart, talk this promise over to yourself until you can use it as the song of your confidence, the solace of your loneliness. Pray to be revived and preserved, and leave the rest with the Lord, "who fulfills his purpose for me" (Ps. 57:2).

MAY 23

For he delivers the needy when he calls,
the poor and him who has no helper.

Psalm 72:12

The needy call out. What else can they do? Their cry is heard by God. What else need they do? Let the needy reader take to calling at once, for this will be his wisdom. Do not cry in the ears of friends, for even if they can help you, it is only because the Lord enables them. The quickest way is to go straight to God, and let your cry come before him. Straight forward makes the best runner: run to the Lord, and not to secondary causes.

"Alas!" you cry, "I have no friend or helper." So much the better, for you can rely on God in both capacities—as without supplies and without helpers. Make your double need your double plea. Even for temporal mercies you may wait on God, for he cares for his children in these temporary concerns. As for spiritual necessities, which are the heaviest of all, the Lord will hear your cry, and will deliver you and supply you.

Oh, poor friend, try your rich God. Oh, helpless one, lean on his help. He has never failed *me*, and I am sure he will never fail *you*. Come as a beggar, and God will not refuse you help. Come with no plea but his grace. Jesus is King; will he let you perish in need? What! How have you forgotten this?

MAY 24

One man of you puts to flight a thousand, since it is the
LORD your God who fights for you, just as he promised you.

Joshua 23:10

Why count heads? One man with God is a majority even if there are a thousand on the other side. Sometimes our helpers may be too many for God to work with them, as was the case with Gideon, who could do nothing until he had increased his forces by thinning out their numbers (Judges 7). But the Lord's forces are never too few in number. When God would found a nation, he called Abram alone and blessed him. When he would conquer proud Pharaoh, he used no armies, just Moses and Aaron. The "one-man ministry," as certain wise men call it, has been far more used by the Lord than trained bands with their officers. Did all the Israelites together slay as many as Samson on his own? Saul and his forces struck down their thousands, but David his ten thousands (1 Sam. 18:7).

The Lord can give the enemy long odds and still conquer him. If we have faith, we have God with us, and what then are multitudes of men? One shepherd's dog can drive before him a great flock of sheep. If the Lord has sent you, my friend, his strength will accomplish his divine purpose. Therefore, rely on the promise and be very courageous.

MAY 25

The LORD will open to you his good treasury.

Deuteronomy 28:12

This refers first to the rain. The Lord will give this in its season. But rain is also a symbol of heavenly refreshment that the Lord is ready to give to his people. Oh, for a copious shower to refresh the Lord's heritage!

We seem to think that God's treasury can only be opened by a great prophet like Elijah, but it is not so. For this promise is to all the faithful in Israel, and, indeed, to each one of them. Oh, believing friend, "the LORD will open to you his good treasury." You, too, may see heaven opened, and thrust in your hand and take out your share, yes, and a share for all the brothers and sisters around you. Ask what you will, and you will not be denied if you remain in Christ and his words remain in you (John 15:7).

As yet you have not known all your Lord's treasures. But he will open them up to your understanding. Certainly you have not yet enjoyed the fullness of his covenant riches. But he will direct your heart into his love and reveal Jesus in you. Only the Lord himself can do this for you; but here is his promise. And if you will diligently respond to his voice, and obey his will, his riches in glory by Christ Jesus will be yours.

MAY 26

You shall serve the LORD your God, and he
will bless your bread and your water.

Exodus 23:25

What a promise is this! To serve God is in itself a high delight. But what an added privilege to have the blessing of the Lord resting on us in all things! Our everyday things become blessed when we ourselves are consecrated to the Lord. Our Lord Jesus took bread and blessed it. And look, we also eat blessed bread. Jesus blessed water and made it wine. The water that we drink is far better to us than any of the wine with which men make merry. Every drop has a benediction in it. The divine blessing is on the man of God in everything, and it will remain with him at all times.

What if we have only bread and water! Yet it is blessed bread and water. Bread and water we will have. That is implied, for it must be there for God to bless it. "His bread will be given him; his water will be sure" (Isa. 33:16). With God at our table, we not only ask a blessing, but we have one. It is not only at the altar but at the table that he blesses us. He serves those well who serve him well. This table-blessing is not of debt, but an act of grace. Indeed, there is a triple grace: he grants us grace to serve him, by his grace feeds us with bread, and then in his grace blesses it.

For if these qualities are yours and are increasing,
they keep you from being ineffective or unfruitful
in the knowledge of our Lord Jesus Christ.

2 Peter 1:8

If we desire to glorify our Lord by being fruitful, we must have certain things in us. For nothing can come out of us which is not first of all within us. We must begin with faith, which is the foundation of all the virtues. And then we must diligently add to it virtue, knowledge, self-control, and steadfastness. With these we must have godliness and brotherly affection (2 Pet. 1:5–7). All these put together will most certainly cause us to produce, as the fruit of our lives, clusters of usefulness. We will not be mere idle knowers but real doers of the Word. These holy things must not only be in us but abound, or we will be barren. Fruit is the overflow of life, and we must be full before we can flow over.

We have noticed people with considerable abilities and opportunities who have never succeeded in doing real good in the conversion of souls. And after close observation, we have concluded that they lacked certain graces that are absolutely essential to fruit-bearing. For real usefulness, graces are better than gifts. As the person is, so is their work. If we would *do* better, we must *be* better. Let the text be a gentle hint to unfruitful people who profess faith, *and to myself also.*

MAY 28

But you said, "I will surely do you good."

Genesis 32:12

This is the sure way of succeeding with the Lord in prayer. We may humbly remind him what he has said. Our faithful God will never turn back from his word, nor will he leave it unfulfilled. Yet he loves to hear his people make requests to him, and to remind him of his promise. This is refreshing to their memories, reviving to their faith, and renewing to their hope. God's Word is given, not for his sake, but for ours. His purposes are settled, and he needs nothing to keep him to his plan to do his people good. But he gives the promise to strengthen and comfort us. This is why he wishes us to plead it, and say to him, "You said."

"I will surely do you good" is just the essence of all the Lord's gracious words. Lay a special stress on the word "surely." He will do us good, real good, lasting good, only good, every good. He will make us good, and this is to do us good in the very highest degree. He will treat us as he does his saints while we are here, and that is good. And he will soon take us to be with Jesus and all his chosen, and that is supremely good. With this promise in our hearts, we need not fear angry Esau nor anyone else (Gen. 32:11). If the Lord will do us good, who can do us harm?

MAY 29

And Jesus said to them, "Follow me, and I
will make you become fishers of men."

Mark 1:17

Only by following Jesus can we obtain our heart's desire and be really useful to our fellow men. Oh, how we long to be successful fishers for Jesus! We would sacrifice our lives to win souls. But we are tempted to try methods that Jesus would never have tried. Will we give into this suggestion of the enemy? If so, we may splash the water, but we will never take the fish. We must follow after Jesus if we want to succeed. Sensational methods, entertainment, and so forth—are these following Jesus? Can we imagine the Lord Jesus drawing a congregation by such means as are often used now? What is the result of such expediency? The result is nothing that Jesus will count up at the last great day.

We must keep to preaching as our Master did; for this is the means by which souls are saved. We must preach our Lord's doctrine, and proclaim a full and free gospel; for this is the net in which souls are taken. We must preach with his gentleness, boldness, and love; for this is the secret of success with human hearts. We must work under divine anointing, depending on the sacred Spirit. Thus, following Jesus, and not running ahead of him nor away from him, we will be fishers of men.

MAY 30

But I tell you, from now on you will see the
Son of Man seated at the right hand of Power
and coming on the clouds of heaven.

Matthew 26:64

Ah, Lord, you were in your lowest state when before your persecutors you were made to stand like a criminal! Yet the eyes of your faith could see beyond your present humiliation to your future glory. What words are these, "I tell you, from now on"! I want to imitate your holy foresight, and in the midst of poverty or sickness or slander also say, "I tell you, from now on." Instead of weakness, you have all power; instead of shame, all glory; instead of derision, all worship. Your cross has not dimmed the splendor of your crown; neither has the spit marred the beauty of your face. Instead, you are the more exalted and honored because of your sufferings.

So, Lord, I also would take courage from the hereafter. I will forget the present troubles in the future triumph. Help me by directing me toward your Father's love and your own patience, so that when I am mocked for your name, I may not be shaken. May I think more and more of the future, and, therefore, all the less of today. I will be with you soon and behold your glory. Therefore I am not ashamed, but say in my inner soul, "I tell you, from now on."

MAY 31

In the world you will have tribulation. But
take heart; I have overcome the world.

John 16:33

My Lord's words are true as to the tribulation. I have my share of it beyond all doubt. The threshing rod has not been hung away, nor can I hope that it will be as long as I lie on the threshing floor. How can I look to be at home in the enemy's country, joyful while in exile or comfortable in a wilderness? This is not my rest. This is the place of the furnace, and the forge, and the hammer. My experience tallies with my Lord's words.

I note how he exhorts me to "take heart." Sadly, I am far too inclined to be despondent. My spirit soon sinks when I am heavily tried. But I must not give way to this feeling. When my Lord bids me cheer up, I dare not be cast down.

What is the argument that he uses to encourage me? Why, it is his own victory. He says, "I have overcome the world." His battle was much more severe than mine. I have not yet resisted to the point of shedding blood (Heb. 12:4). Why do I despair of overcoming? Look, my soul, the enemy has been once overcome. I fight with a beaten foe. Oh, world, Jesus has already conquered you; and in me, by his grace, he will overcome you again. Therefore I take heart, and sing to my conquering Lord.

JUNE

JUNE 1

Cast your bread upon the waters,
for you will find it after many days.

Ecclesiastes 11:1

We must not expect to see an immediate reward for all the good we do. Nor must we always confine our efforts to places and persons that seem likely to produce a reward for our labors. Egyptians cast their seed on the waters of the flooded Nile, which might seem a sheer waste of corn. But in due time the water subsides, the rice or other grain sinks into the fertile mud, and rapidly a harvest is produced. Let us today do good to the ungrateful and the evil. Let us teach the careless and the obstinate. Unlikely waters may cover hopeful soil. Nowhere will our labor be in vain in the Lord.

It is ours to cast our bread on the waters; it remains with God to fulfill the promise, "You will find it." He will not let his promise fail. His good word that we have spoken will live, will be found, will be found by us. Perhaps not just yet, but someday we will reap what we have sown. We must exercise our patience; for perhaps the Lord may exercise it. "After many days," says the Scripture, and in many instances those days run into months and years. Yet the Word stands true. God's promise will keep. So let us be careful to keep the command and keep it this day.

JUNE 2

And now I will break his yoke from off you
and will burst your bonds apart.

Nahum 1:13

The Assyrian was allowed for a period to oppress the Lord's people, but there came a time for his power to be broken. In the same way, many a heart is held in bondage by Satan, and frets greatly under the yoke. Oh, that to such prisoners of hope the word of the Lord may come at once, according to the text: "Now I will break his yoke from off you and will burst your bonds apart"!

See, the Lord promises a deliverance in the present: "*Now* I will break his yoke from off you." Believe for immediate freedom, and according to your faith so will it be to you at this very hour. When God says "now," let no one say "tomorrow."

See how complete the rescue will be. For the yoke will not be removed, but broken; and the bonds are not to be untied, but burst apart. Here is a display of divine force which guarantees that the oppressor will not return. His yoke is broken, and we cannot again be bent down by its weight. His bonds are burst apart; they can hold us no longer. Oh, to believe in Jesus for complete and everlasting emancipation! "If the Son sets you free, you will be free indeed" (John 8:36).

Come, Lord, and set free your captives according to your word.

JUNE 3

GOD, the Lord, is my strength;
he makes my feet like the deer's;
he makes me tread on my high places.

Habakkuk 3:19

This confidence of the man of God is tantamount to a promise, for that which faith is persuaded of is the purpose of God. The prophet had to pass through the deep places of poverty and famine. But he went downhill without slipping, for the Lord gave him *standing*. In due course, he was called to the high places of the hills of conflict. And he was no more afraid to go up as he was to go down.

See, the Lord lent him *strength*. Indeed, the Lord himself was his strength. Think of that: the Almighty God himself becomes our strength!

Notice that the Lord also gave him *sure-footedness*. The deer leap over rock and crag, never missing their foothold. Our Lord will give us grace to follow the most difficult paths of duty without a stumble. He can prepare our foot for the crags, so that we will be at home where without God we should perish.

One of these days we will be called to higher places still. Up above we will climb, even to the mountain of God, the high places where the shining ones are gathered. Oh, what feet are the feet of faith, by which, following the Doe of the Dawn (Ps. 22:1), we will ascend the hill of the Lord (Ps. 24:3)!

JUNE 4

They shall be mine, says the LORD of hosts, in the
day when I make up my treasured possession.

Malachi 3:17

A day is coming in which the crown jewels of our great King will be counted, that it may be seen whether they match the inventory which his Father gave him. My soul, will you be among the precious things of Jesus? You are precious to him if he is precious to you. And you shall be his "in the day," if he is yours in this day.

In the days of Malachi, the chosen of the Lord were accustomed to God himself listening to their conversations (Mal. 3:16). He liked their talk so much that he took notes of it. Indeed, he made a book of it, which he lodged in his record office. Pleased with their conversation, he was also pleased with them.

Pause, my soul, and ask yourself: If Jesus were to listen to your talk, would he be pleased with it? Is it to his glory and to the edification of your brothers and sisters? Answer, my soul, and be sure you tell the truth.

But what an honor it will be for us poor creatures to be counted by the Lord as his crown jewels! This honor belongs to all the saints. Jesus not only says, "They are mine," but, "They shall be mine." He bought us, sought us, brought us in, and has so far wrought in us his image. Surely then, we will be fought for by him with all his might.

JUNE 5

But not a dog shall growl against any of the people of
Israel, either man or beast, that you may know that the
LORD makes a distinction between Egypt and Israel.

Exodus 11:7

What! Has God power over the tongues of dogs? Can he keep curs from barking? Yes, even this is true. He can even prevent an Egyptian dog from worrying one of the lambs of Israel's flock. Does God silence dogs, and doggish people, and the great dog at hell's gate? Then let us move on our way without fear.

Even if he lets dogs move their tongues, he can stop their teeth. They may make a dreadful noise and still do us no real harm. Yet how sweet is quiet! How delightful to move about among enemies and perceive that God ensures they are at peace with us! Like Daniel in the den of lions, we are unhurt amid destroyers (Daniel 6).

Oh, that today this word of the Lord to Israel might be true to me! Does the dog worry me? I will tell my Lord about him.

Lord, he does not care about my pleadings. But if you speak the word of power, then he must lie down. Give me peace, oh, my God, and let me see your hand so clearly in it that I may clearly spot the difference that your grace makes between me and the ungodly!

JUNE 6

The LORD has heard my plea;
the LORD accepts my prayer.

Psalm 6:9

The experience recorded here is mine. I can certify that God is true. In very wonderful ways he has answered the prayers of his servant many times over. Yes, and he is hearing my present request. He is not turning away his ear from me. Blessed be his holy name!

What then? Why, for certain the promise that lies sleeping in the psalmist's believing confidence is also mine. Let me grasp it by the hand of faith: "The LORD accepts my prayer." He will accept it, think of that, and grant it in the way and time that his loving wisdom judges to be best. I bring my poor prayer in my hand to the great King, and he gives me an audience, and graciously receives my petition. My enemies will not listen to me, but my Lord will. They ridicule my tearful prayers, but my Lord does not. My prayer reaches his ear and his heart.

What a reception this is for a poor sinner! We receive Jesus, and then the Lord receives us and our prayers for his Son's sake. Blessed be that dear name which franks our prayers so that they freely pass even within the golden gates.

Lord, teach me to pray, since you hear my prayers.

JUNE 7

I give them eternal life, and they will never perish,
and no one will snatch them out of my hand.

John 10:28

We believe in the eternal security of the saints. First, because they are Christ's. And he will never lose the sheep which he has bought with his blood and received from his Father.

Next, because he gives them eternal life. And if it be eternal, well then, it is eternal. And there can be no end to it, not unless there can be an end to hell, and heaven, and God. If spiritual life can die out, it is clearly not eternal life but temporary life. But the Lord speaks of eternal life, and that effectually rules out the possibility of an end.

Observe, further, that the Lord expressly says, "They will never perish." As long as words have a meaning, this secures believers from perishing. The most obstinate unbelief cannot force this meaning out of this sentence.

Then, to make the matter complete, he declares that his people are in his hand, and he defies all their enemies to snatch them out of it. Surely it is something impossible even for the fiend of hell. We must be safe in the grasp of an almighty Savior.

May we dismiss fleshly fear as well as fleshly confidence, and rest peacefully in the hollow of the Redeemer's hand.

JUNE 8

If any of you lacks wisdom, let him ask God, who gives generously to all without reproach, and it will be given him.

James 1:5

"If any of you lacks wisdom." There is no "if" in the matter, for I am sure I lack it. What do I know? How can I guide my own way? How can I direct others? Lord, I am a mass of folly, and wisdom I have none.

You say, "Let him ask God." Lord, I ask now. Here at your footstool I ask to be furnished with heavenly wisdom for this day's perplexities, yes, and for this day's simplicities. For I know I can do very stupid things, even in plain matters, unless you keep me out of mischief.

I thank you that all I have to do is to ask. What grace is this on your part, that I only have to pray in faith and you will give me wisdom! Here you promise me a generous education, and that, too, without an angry tutor or a scolding schoolmaster. This, too, you will give me without a fee—give it to a fool who lacks wisdom. Oh, Lord, I thank you for that positive and clear word, "It will be given him." I believe it. You will today enable your child to know the hidden wisdom that the worldly prudent never learn. "You guide me with your counsel, and afterward you will receive me to glory" (Ps. 73:24).

JUNE 9

But I will leave in your midst
a people humble and lowly.
They shall seek refuge in the name of the LORD.

Zephaniah 3:12

When true religion is ready to die out among the wealthy, it finds a home among the poor of this world, those who are rich in faith. The Lord has even now his faithful remnant. Am I one of them?

Perhaps it is because people are afflicted and poor that they learn to trust in the name of the Lord. He who has no money must see what he can do on trust. He whose own name is good for nothing in his own esteem acts wisely when he rests in another name, even that best of names, the name of the Lord. God will always have a trusting people, and they will be an afflicted and poor people. Even though the world thinks little of them, they are left in the midst of a nation as the channel of untold blessings to it. Here is the conserving salt that keeps in check the corruption that is in the world as a result of sinful desires.

Again the question comes home to each one of us, Am I one of them? Am I afflicted by the sin within me and around me? Am I poor in spirit, poor spiritually in my own judgment? Do I trust in the Lord? That is what matters. Jesus reveals the name, the character, the person of God. Am I trusting in him? If so, I am left in this world for a purpose.

Lord, help me to fulfill it.

JUNE 10

For they shall graze and lie down,
and none shall make them afraid.

Zephaniah 3:13

Yesterday we thought of the afflicted and poor people whom the Lord left to be a living seed in a dead world. The prophet says of such people that they will "do no injustice and speak no lies" (Zeph. 3:13). So that while they had neither rank nor riches to guard them, they were also quite unable to use those weapons upon which the wicked rely. They could neither defend themselves through sin nor through subtlety.

What then? Would they be destroyed? By no means! They will both graze and rest. They will not merely be free from danger, but also still the fear of evil. Sheep are very feeble creatures, and wolves are terrible enemies. Yet at this time sheep are more numerous than wolves, and the cause of the sheep is always winning, while the cause of the wolves is always declining. One day, flocks of sheep will cover the plains and not a wolf will be left. The fact is, sheep have a shepherd, and he gives them provisions, protection, and peace. "None"—which means not one, whether in human or diabolical form—"shall make them afraid." Who will terrify the Lord's flock when he is near? We lie down in green pastures, for Jesus himself is food and rest to our souls.

JUNE 11

Fear not, for you will not be ashamed.

Isaiah 54:4

We will not be ashamed of our *faith*. Carping critics may attack the Scriptures on which we ground our belief. But every year the Lord will make it more and more clear that in his Book there is no error, no exaggeration, and no omission. It is no discredit to be a simple believer. The faith that looks alone to Jesus is a crown of honor on any person's head, and better than a star on their breast.

We will not be ashamed of our *hope*. It will be just as the Lord has said. We will be fed, led, blessed, and rested. Our Lord will come, and then the days of our mourning will be over. How we will glory in the Lord, who first gave us living hope and then gave us that which we hoped for!

We will not be ashamed of our *love*. Jesus is to us "altogether lovely" (Song 5:16 KJV), and never ever will we have to blush because we have given our hearts to him. The sight of our glorious Well-Beloved will justify the most enthusiastic attachment to him. No one will blame the martyrs for dying for him. When the enemies of Christ are clothed with everlasting contempt, the lovers of Jesus will find themselves honored by all holy beings, because they chose the reproach of Christ rather than the treasures of Egypt (Heb. 11:26).

JUNE 12

So Israel lived in safety,
Jacob lived alone,
in a land of grain and wine,
whose heavens drop down dew.

Deuteronomy 33:28

The more we live alone, the more safe will we be. God would have his people separate from sinners. His call to them is, "Go out from their midst" (2 Cor. 6:17). A Christianized world is such a monstrosity that the Scriptures never contemplate it. And a worldly Christian is spiritually diseased. Those who compromise with Christ's enemies will be counted with them.

Our safety lies, not in doing deals with the enemy, but in living alone with our best Friend. If we do this, we will live in safety despite the sarcasms, the slanders, and the sneers of the world. We will be safe from the pernicious influence of its unbelief, its pride, its vanity, and its filth.

God also will make us live in safety alone on that day when sin will come on the nations in the form of wars and famines.

The Lord brought Abram from Ur of the Chaldeans, but Abram stopped halfway (Gen. 11:31). He had no blessing until, having set out to go to the land of Canaan, to the land of Canaan he came. He was safe alone even in the midst of foes. Lot was not safe in Sodom even though he had friends around him (Gen. 19:1–29). Our safety is in living apart with God.

JUNE 13

I, the LORD, am its keeper;
every moment I water it.
Lest anyone punish it,
I keep it night and day.

Isaiah 27:3

When the Lord himself speaks directly rather than through a prophet, the word has a particular weight to believing minds. It is the Lord himself who is the keeper of his own vineyard. He does not entrust it to anyone else. Instead, he makes it his own personal responsibility. Are they not well kept whom God himself keeps?

God will graciously water his vineyard, not only every day and every hour, but "every moment." How we ought to grow! How fresh and fruitful every plant should be! What rich clusters the vines should bear!

But troublemakers come—little foxes and the boar. Therefore the Lord himself is our Guardian, and he is so at all times, both "night and day." What, then, can harm us? Why are we afraid? He tends, he waters, and he guards. What more do we need?

Twice in this verse the Lord promises action, saying, "I water" and "I keep." What truth, what power, what love, what immutability we find in the great word of the Lord! Who can resist his will? If he says he will do something, what room is there for doubt? With his word, we can face all the hosts of sin, death, and hell.

Oh, Lord, since you say "I water" and "I keep," I will reply, "I praise you!"

JUNE 14

For the LORD will not forsake his people, for
his great name's sake, because it has pleased the
LORD to make you a people for himself.

1 Samuel 12:22

God's choice of his people is the reason for his remaining with them and not forsaking them. He chose them for his love, and he loves them because of his choice to love them. His own good pleasure is the source of their election, and his election is the reason his pleasure continues in them. It would dishonor his great name for him to forsake them, since it would either show that he made an error in his choice, or that he was fickle in his love. God's love has this glory, that it never changes, and this glory he will never tarnish.

By all the memories of the Lord's former loving kindnesses, let us rest assured that he will not forsake us. He has gone so far as to make us his people; he will not now undo the creation of his grace. He has not worked wonders for us so that he might leave us in the end. His Son, Jesus, has died for us, and we may be sure that he has not died in vain. Can he forsake those for whom he shed his blood? Because he has so far taken pleasure in choosing and in saving us, it will be his pleasure to keep blessing us. Our Lord Jesus is no changeable lover. Having loved his own, he loves them to the end (John 13:1).

JUNE 15

The Lord bless you from Zion!
May you see the prosperity of Jerusalem
all the days of your life!

Psalm 128:5

This is a promise to the God-fearing person who walks in the ways of holiness with earnest attention. He will have domestic blessing. His wife and children will be a source of great happiness at home. But then as a member of the church, he desires to see its cause prosper. For he is as much concerned for the Lord's family as for his own. When the Lord builds our family, it is fitting that we should desire to see the Lord's family being built. Our goods are not truly good unless we use them to promote the good of the Lord's chosen church.

Yes, you will get a blessing when you go up to the assemblies of Zion. You will be instructed, enlivened, and comforted, where prayer and praise ascend, and testimony is given to the Great Sacrifice. May the Lord continually "bless you from Zion."

Nor will you alone profit. The church itself will prosper. Believers will be multiplied. And their holy work will be crowned with success. Some gracious Christians have this promise fulfilled to them as long as they live. Sadly, when they die, the cause of Christ often flags. Let us be among those who bring good things to Jerusalem all their days.

Lord, in your mercy, make us such people! Amen.

JUNE 16

For to the one who has, more will be given,
and he will have an abundance.

Matthew 13:12

When the Lord has given a person grace, he will give them more. A little faith is a nest egg; more faith will come of it. But it must not be faith only in appearance; it must be real and true faith. How important it is to make our religion sure. We must not be those who profess much and possess nothing! For one of these days the very profession will be taken from us, if that is all we have (Matt. 13:12). The threat is as true as the promise.

Blessed be the Lord. It is his way, when he has made a start, to go on giving the graces of his Spirit. He gives until those who only had a little, and yet truly had that little, are made to have abundance. Oh, for that abundance! Abundance of grace is a thing to be coveted. It is good to *know* much, but better to *love* much. It would be delightful to have an abundance of skill to serve God, but it is better still to have abundance of faith to trust in the Lord for skills and everything else.

Lord, since you have given me a sense of sin, deepen my hatred of evil. Since you have caused me to trust Jesus, raise my faith to full assurance. Since you have made me to love you, cause me to be carried away with vehement affection for you!

JUNE 17

For the LORD your God is he who goes with you to fight
for you against your enemies, to give you the victory.

Deuteronomy 20:4

We have no enemies but the enemies of God. Our fights are not against human beings but against spiritual wickedness (Eph. 6:12). We war with the devil, and the blasphemy, error, and despair that he brings into the field of battle. We fight with all the armies of sin—impurity, drunkenness, oppression, infidelity, and ungodliness. With these we fight with all seriousness. But we do not fight with sword or spear; the weapons of our warfare are not earthly.

The Lord our God hates everything that is evil. And therefore he goes with us to fight for us in this campaign. He will save us, and he will give us grace to fight well and win the victory. We may be sure that, if we are on God's side, God is on our side. With such an impressive ally the outcome is not in the least degree of doubt. It is not that truth is mighty and must prevail. Rather, might lies with the Father who is almighty, with Jesus who has all power in heaven and in earth, and with the Holy Spirit who works his will among humanity.

Soldiers of Christ, put on your armor. Strike home in the name of the God of holiness, and by faith grasp his salvation. Do not let this day pass without striking a blow for Jesus and holiness.

JUNE 18

"Now I will arise," says the LORD,
"now I will lift myself up;
now I will be exalted."

Isaiah 33:10

When the enemy had laid the land waste as if it had been devoured by locusts, and the warriors who had defended the country sat down and wept, then the Lord came to the rescue (Isa. 33:1–4). When travelers ceased traveling the roads to Zion, and Bashan and Carmel were like vineyards whose fruit has failed (Isa. 33:7–9), then the Lord arose. God is exalted in the middle of an afflicted people, for they seek his face and trust him. He is still more exalted when, in answer to their cries, he lifts himself up to deliver them and overthrow their enemies.

Is it a day of sorrow with us? Let us expect to see the Lord glorified in our deliverance. Are we worn out through fervent prayer? Do we cry day and night to him? Then the time set for his grace is near. God will lift himself up at the right moment. He will arise at the time that will most display his glory. We wish for his glory more than we long for our own deliverance. Let the Lord be exalted, and our chief desire is obtained.

Lord, help us in such a way that we may see that you yourself are at work. May we magnify you in our inmost souls. Make all around us see what a good and great God you are.

JUNE 19

May my heart be blameless in your statutes,
that I may not be put to shame!
Psalm 119:80

We may regard this inspired prayer as containing within itself the assurance that those who keep close to the Word of God will never have reason to be ashamed of doing so.

Notice that the prayer is for blameless of heart (in the KJV). A sound creed is good, a sound judgment concerning it is better, but a sound heart toward the truth is best of all. We must love the truth, feel the truth, and obey the truth; otherwise we are not truly sound in God's statutes. Are there many in these evil days who are sound? Oh, that the writer and the reader may be two examples of a sound heart!

Many will be ashamed on the last great day, when all disputes will be decided. Then they will see the folly of their inventions and be filled with remorse because of their proud infidelity and willful defiance of the Lord. But he who believed what the Lord taught, and did what the Lord commanded, will stand justified in what he did. "Then the righteous will shine like the sun" (Matt. 13:43). People who have been greatly slandered and abused will find their shame turned into glory in that day.

Let us pray the prayer of our text, and we may be sure that its promise will be fulfilled to us. If the Lord makes us sound, he will keep us safe.

JUNE 20

Even though I walk through the valley
of the shadow of death,
I will fear no evil,
for you are with me;
your rod and your staff,
they comfort me.

Psalm 23:4

How sweetly these words describe a deathbed assurance. How many have repeated them in their last moments with intense delight!

But the verse is equally applicable to agonies of spirit in the midst of life. Some of us, like Paul, die daily through a tendency toward a gloom in our souls. In his allegorical story *The Pilgrim's Progress*, John Bunyan puts the Valley of the Shadow of Death far earlier in the pilgrimage than the river he must cross at the end of his journey to reach the celestial hills. Some of us have traveled the dark and dreadful "shadow of death" several times. And we can bear witness that the Lord alone enabled us to keep going through its wild thoughts, its mysterious horrors, and its terrible depressions. The Lord has sustained us and kept us above all real fear of evil even when our spirits were overwhelmed. We have been pressed and oppressed, but yet we lived. For we felt the presence of the great Shepherd, and were confident that his staff would prevent the foe from giving us any deadly wounds.

Should the present time be one darkened by the raven wings of great sorrow, let us glorify God by peacefully trusting in him.

JUNE 21

The Lord will sell Sisera into the hand of a woman.

Judges 4:9

Rather an unusual text, but there may be souls in the world that may have faith enough to grasp it. Barak the man, though called to war, had little stomach for the fight unless Deborah went with him. And so the Lord decided to make it a woman's war. By this means he rebuked the inaction of the man, and gained for himself more renown, and cast more shame on the enemies of his people.

The Lord can still use weaker means. Why not me? He may use people who are not normally called to great public enterprises. Why not you? The woman who slew the enemy of Israel was no amazon, but a wife who remained in her tent (Judg. 4:17–21). She was no orator, but a woman who milked the cows and made butter. May not the Lord use any one of us to accomplish his purpose? Somebody may come to the house today, even as Sisera came to Jael's tent. May it be our role, not to slay them, but to save them. Let us receive them with great kindness, and then bring out the blessed truth of salvation through the Lord Jesus, our great Substitute. Let us press home the command, "Believe and live." Who knows but some resolute sinner may be slain by the gospel today?

JUNE 22

The fear of the LORD prolongs life,
but the years of the wicked will be short.

Proverbs 10:27

There is no doubt about it. The fear of the Lord leads to virtuous habits, and these prevent the waste of life that often comes from sin and evil. The holy rest that springs from faith in the Lord Jesus also greatly helps people when they are ill. Every doctor rejoices to have a patient whose mind is fully at ease. Worry kills, but confidence in God is like healing medicine.

We therefore have all the conditions for long life. So, if it be really for our good, we will see a good old age. We will come to our graves like sheaves of corn in their season. Let us not be overcome with the sudden expectation of death the moment a finger starts aching. Instead, let us expect to carry on working for many days to come.

And what if we should soon be called to the heavenly realm? Certainly there would be nothing to deplore in such a summons, but everything to rejoice in. Living or dying, we are the Lord's. If we live, Jesus will be with us; if we die, we will be with Jesus.

The truest lengthening of life is to live while we live, wasting no time, but using every hour for the highest ends. May it be so today.

JUNE 23

Therefore thus says the LORD concerning the
king of Assyria: He shall not come into this city
or shoot an arrow there, or come before it with
a shield or cast up a siege mound against it.

2 Kings 19:32

And so it was that Sennacherib, the king of Assyria, did not defile the city. He had boasted loudly, but he could not carry out his threats. The Lord is able to stop the enemies of his people in the very act. When the lion has the lamb between his jaws, the great Shepherd of the sheep can rob him of his prey. Our extreme need only provides an opportunity for a grander display of divine power and wisdom.

In the case before us, the terrible foe did not put in an appearance before the city which he thirsted to destroy. No threatening arrow could he shoot over the walls, no besieging engines could he put to work to batter down the castles, and no banks could he throw up to shut in the inhabitants. Perhaps also in our case, the Lord will prevent our adversaries from doing us the least harm. Certainly he can alter their intentions, or render their intentions so futile that they gladly give them up. Let us trust in the Lord and keep his way, and he will take care of us. Indeed, he will fill us with wonder and praise as we see the perfection of his deliverance.

Let us not fear the enemy until he actually comes, and then let us trust in the Lord.

JUNE 24

And Amaziah said to the man of God, "But what shall we do about the hundred talents that I have given to the army of Israel?" The man of God answered, "The LORD is able to give you much more than this."

2 Chronicles 25:9

If you have made a mistake, bear the loss it causes. But do not act contrary to the will of the Lord. The Lord can give you much more than you are likely to lose. And if he does not, will you begin bargaining and haggling with God? The king of Judah had hired an army from idolatrous Israel, and then he was commanded to send home the fighting men because the Lord was not with them. He was willing to send away the army, but he begrudged paying the hundred talents for nothing. Oh, what shame! If the Lord will give the victory without the mercenaries, surely it was a good bargain to pay their wages and to be rid of them.

Be willing to lose money for the sake of conscience, for the sake of peace, for the sake of Christ. Rest assured that losses for the Lord are not losses. Even in this life they are more than recompensed. In some cases the Lord prevents any loss from happening. As for our immortal life, what we lose for Jesus now is invested in heaven. So do not worry at apparent disaster but listen to the whisper, "The LORD is able to give you much more than this."

JUNE 25

And he said to him, "Truly, truly, I say to you,
you will see heaven opened, and the angels of God
ascending and descending on the Son of Man."
John 1:51

Yes, to our faith this sight is still plain today. We do see heaven opened. Jesus himself has opened that kingdom to all believers. We gaze into the place of mystery and glory, for he has revealed it to us. We will enter it soon, for he is the Way.

Now we see the explanation of Jacob's ladder. Between earth and heaven there is a holy exchange: prayer ascends and answers come down along the way of Jesus, the Mediator. We see this ladder when we see our Lord. In him a stairway of light now illuminates a clear passage to the throne of the Most High. Let us use it, and by it send up the messengers of our prayers. We will live the angelic life ourselves if we run up to heaven in intercession, and lay hold of the blessings of the covenant, and then descend again to scatter those gifts among the sons of men.

This precious sight that Jacob only saw in a dream, we will turn into a bright reality. This very day we will be up and down the ladder each hour: climbing in fellowship with God, and coming down in labor to save our fellow men.

This is your promise, oh, Lord Jesus. Let us joyfully see it fulfilled.

JUNE 26

You also, be patient. Establish your hearts,
for the coming of the Lord is at hand.

James 5:8

The last word in the Song of Solomon is, "Make haste, my beloved" (8:14). And among the last words of the book of Revelation we read, "The Spirit and the Bride say, 'Come'"; to which the heavenly Bridegroom answers, "Surely I am coming soon" (22:17, 20). Love longs for the glorious appearing of the Lord and enjoys this sweet promise: "The coming of the Lord is at hand." This reassures our minds about the future. We look out with hope through this window.

This sacred "window of agate" lets in a flood of light on the present (Isa. 54:12 KJV) and gets us in shape for immediate work or suffering. Are we tried? Then the nearness of our joy whispers patience. Are we growing weary because we do not see the harvest of our seed sowing? Again this glorious truth cries to us, "Be patient." Do our many temptations cause us to waver? Then the assurance that before long the Lord will be here preaches to us from this text, "Establish your hearts." Be firm, be stable, be constant, be "steadfast, immovable, always abounding in the work of the Lord" (1 Cor. 15:58). Soon will you hear the silver trumpets that announce the coming of your King. Do not be in the least bit afraid. Hold the fort, for he is coming. Indeed, he may appear this very day.

JUNE 27

Surely the righteous shall give thanks to your name;
the upright shall dwell in your presence.

Psalm 140:13

Oh, that my heart may be upright, that I may always be able to bless the name of the Lord! He is so good to those that are good, that I would gladly be among them and feel myself full of thankfulness every day. Perhaps for a moment the righteous stagger when their integrity results in severe trial. But the day will certainly come when they will bless their God that they did not give in to evil suggestions or adopt a policy of expedience. In the long run, true men will thank the righteous God for leading them along the right way. Oh, that I may be among them!

What a promise is implied in this second clause, "The upright shall dwell in your presence"! They will stand accepted where others come only to be condemned. They will be the courtiers of the Great King, granted an audience whenever they desire it. They will be favored ones upon whom the Lord smiles, and with whom he graciously fellowships.

Lord, I covet this high honor, this precious privilege. It will be heaven on earth to me to enjoy it. In all things make me upright, that I may today, and tomorrow, and every day, stand in your heavenly presence. Then will I give thanks to your name forever. Amen.

JUNE 28

And the LORD turned to him and said, "Go
in this might of yours and save Israel from the
hand of Midian; do not I send you?"

Judges 6:14

The Lord turned to him. What a look the Lord gave to Gideon when he turned toward him! He "turned" him out of his discouragements into a holy bravery. If turning to the Lord saves us, what will his turning to us do? Lord, turn to me this day, and embolden me for its duties and conflicts.

What a word was this that the Lord spoke to Gideon! "Go." He must not hesitate. He might have answered, "What, go in all this weakness?" But the Lord ruled that word out by saying, "Go in this might of yours." The turning of the Lord had brought might to Gideon, and he had now nothing to do but use it and save Israel by striking the Midianites. It may be that the Lord has more to do by me than I ever dreamed of. If he has turned to me, then he has made me strong. Let me by faith exercise the power with which he has entrusted me. He never exhorts me to waste my time in this my might. Far from it. I must "go," because he strengthens me.

What a question the Lord puts to me just as he put it to Gideon! "Do not I send you?" Yes, Lord, you have sent me, and I will go in your strength. At your command I go, and, going, I am assured that you will conquer through me.

JUNE 29

Call to me and I will answer you, and will tell you
great and hidden things that you have not known.

Jeremiah 33:3

God encourages us to pray. They tell us that prayer is a pious exercise
which has no influence except on the mind engaged in it. We know better. Our experience gives the lie a thousand times over to this unbelieving
assertion. Here the Lord, the living God, distinctly promises to answer
the prayer of his servant. Let us call on him again and allow no doubt on
the question of whether he hears us and answers us. He that made the
ear, will he not hear? He that gave parents a love for their children, will
he not listen to the cries of his own sons and daughters?

God will answer his pleading people in their anguish. He has wonders
in store for them. What they have never seen, heard of, or dreamed of, he
will do for them. He will invent new blessings if needed. He will ransack
sea and land to feed them. He will send every angel out of heaven to assist
them, if their distress requires it. He will astound us with his grace and
make us feel that provision never came in this way before. All he asks of
us is that we will call on him. He cannot ask less of us. Let us cheerfully
present our prayers to him at once.

JUNE 30

Yet I will remember my covenant with you in the days of your
youth, and I will establish for you an everlasting covenant.

Ezekiel 16:60

Despite our sins, the Lord is still faithful in his love to us.

He looks back. See how he remembers our early days when he took us
into a covenant relationship with himself, and we gave ourselves over to
him. They were happy days! The Lord does not reproach us with them,
and charge us with being insincere. No, he looks to his covenant with us
rather than to our covenant with him. There was no hypocrisy in that
sacred contract, on his part at any rate. How gracious is the Lord to look
back in this way in love!

He looks forward also. He is resolved that the covenant will not fail. If
we do not stand by it, he does. He solemnly declares, "I will establish for
you an everlasting covenant." He has no intention of drawing back from
his promises. Blessed be his name, for he sees the sacred seal, "the blood
of the eternal covenant" (Heb. 13:20). And so he remembers our surety in
whom he ratified that covenant, even his own dear Son. And therefore he
rests in his covenant commitments. "He remains faithful—for he cannot
deny himself" (2 Tim. 2:13).

Oh, Lord, lay this precious word on my heart and help me feed on it
throughout this day!

JULY

JULY 1

God will be with you.

Genesis 48:21

Good old Jacob could no longer be with Joseph, for his hour had come to die. But he left his son without anxiety, for he said with confidence, "God will be with you." When our dearest relations or our most helpful friends are called home by death, we must console ourselves with the reflection that the Lord has not departed from us. He lives for us and remains with us forever.

If God be with us, we are in company that ennobles us, even though we are poor and despised. If God be with us, we have all-sufficient strength, for nothing can be too hard for the Lord. If God be with us, we are always safe, for no-one can harm those who walk under his shadow. Oh, what a joy we have here! Not only *is* God with us, but he *will* be with us. With us as individuals; with us as families; with us as churches. Is not the very name of Jesus, Immanuel, "God with us" (Matt. 1:23)? Is not this the best thing of all, that God is with us? Let us be bravely diligent and joyously hopeful. Our cause must prosper and the truth must win, for the Lord is with those who are with him.

Throughout this day may this sweet word be enjoyed by every believer. No greater happiness is possible.

JULY 2

For he gives to his beloved sleep.

Psalm 127:2

Ours is not a life of anxious care but of happy faith. Our heavenly Father will supply the needs of his own children, and he knows what we have need of before we ask him (Matt. 6:8). We may therefore go to our beds at the proper time and not wear ourselves out sitting up late to plot, and plan, and contrive. If we have learned to rely on our God, then we will not lie awake with fear gnawing at our hearts. Instead, we will leave our care with the Lord, our meditation of him will be sweet, and he will give us refreshing sleep.

To be the Lord's beloved is the highest possible honor. And he who has this honor may feel that ambition itself could desire no more, and therefore every selfish wish may go to sleep. What more is there, even in heaven, than the love of God? Rest then, oh, soul, for you have all things.

Yet we toss to and fro unless the Lord himself gives us, not only the reasons for rest, but rest itself. Yes, he does this. Jesus himself is our peace, our rest, our all. In his arms we sleep in perfect security, both in life and in death.

Sprinkled afresh with pardoning blood,
I lay me down to rest,
as in the embraces of my God,
or on my Savior's breast.

Isaac Watts

JULY 3

This is God,
our God forever and ever.
He will guide us forever.

Psalm 48:14

We need a guide. Sometimes we would give all that we have to be told exactly what to do and where to turn. We are willing to do right, but we do not know which out of two roads we are to follow. Oh, for a guide!

The Lord our God condescends to serve us as our guide. He knows the way, and will pilot us along it until we reach our journey's end in peace. Surely we do not desire more infallible direction. Let us place ourselves absolutely under his guidance, and we will never miss our way. Let us make him our God and we will find him our guide. If we follow his law, we will not miss the right road of life, provided we first learn to lean on him in every step that we take.

Our comfort is that, as he is our God forever and ever, he will never cease to be with us as our guide. "Forever" will he lead us through life and death, and then we will dwell with him eternally and never more go out. This promise of divine guidance involves lifelong security: salvation now, guidance up until our last moment, and then endless blessing. Should not each one seek this while they are young, rejoice in it in when they are middle-aged, and rest in it when they are old? This day let us look up for guidance before we venture outside.

JULY 4

Man shall not live by bread alone, but by every
word that comes from the mouth of God.

Matthew 4:4

We could live without bread if this was God's will, just as Jesus did for
forty days (Matt. 4:2). But we could not live without his Word. By that
Word we were created, and by it alone we keep existing. For he sustains
all things by the Word of his power (Heb. 1:3). Bread is a secondary
cause; the Lord himself is the first source of our sustenance. He can work
without the secondary cause as well as with it. And we must not tie him
down to one mode of operation. Let us not be too eager for what is visible, but let us look to the invisible God. We have heard believers say that
in deep poverty, when bread ran short, their appetites became shorter as
well. And to others, when ordinary supplies failed, the Lord sent unexpected help. But we must have the Word of the Lord. With this alone we
can withstand the devil. Take this from us, and our enemy will have us
in his power, for we will soon faint. Our souls need food, and there is no
food for them apart from the Word of the Lord. All the books and all the
preachers in the world cannot supply us a single meal. It is only the Word
from the mouth of God that can fill the mouth of a believer.

Lord, give us this bread forevermore. We prize it above the treats of
a royal feast.

JULY 5

But I will deliver you on that day, declares the
Lord, and you shall not be given into the hand
of the men of whom you are afraid.

Jeremiah 39:17

When the Lord's faithful people are suffering for him, they will have sweet messages of love from him. And sometimes they will have glad tidings for those who sympathize with them and help them. Ebed-melech was only a despised Ethiopian, but he was kind to Jeremiah (Jer. 38:7–13). And so the Lord sent him this special promise by the mouth of his prophet. Let us always remember God's persecuted servants, and he will reward us.

Ebed-melech was to be delivered from the men whose vengeance he feared. He was an outsider, but the Lord would take care of him. Thousands were slain by the Chaldeans, but this humble African could not be hurt. We, too, may be fearful of some great people who are bitter toward us. But if we have been faithful to the Lord's cause in the hour of persecution, then he will be faithful to us. After all, what can a man do without the Lord's permission? He puts a bit into the mouth of rage, and a bridle on the head of power. Let us fear the Lord, and we will have no one else to fear. No cup of cold water given to a despised prophet of God will be without its reward (Matt. 25:34–40). If we stand up for Jesus, Jesus will stand up for us.

JULY 6

For God so loved the world, that he gave
his only Son, that whoever believes in him
should not perish but have eternal life.

John 3:16

Of all the stars in the sky, the polestar is the most useful to the sailor. This text is a polestar, for it has guided more souls to salvation than any other scripture.

Several words in it shine with particular brilliance. Here we have *God's love*, with a "so" added to it that marks its measureless greatness. Then we have *God's gift* in all its freeness and greatness. This also is *God's Son*, that unique and priceless gift of love. God's generosity could never fully show itself until heaven's Only-Begotten had been sent to live and die for humanity. These three points are full of light.

Then there is *the simple requirement* of believing that graciously points to a way of salvation suited to guilty men. This is backed by *a wide description*—"whoever believes in him." Many have found room in "whoever" who would have felt themselves shut out by a narrower word. Then comes *the great promise*, that believers in Jesus will not perish but have eternal life. This is cheering to everyone who feels that they are ready to perish and who feels that they cannot save themselves. We believe in the Lord Jesus, and we have eternal life.

JULY 7

Sing for joy, O heavens, and exult, O earth;
break forth, O mountains, into singing!
For the LORD has comforted his people
and will have compassion on his afflicted.

Isaiah 49:13

So sweet are the comforts of the Lord that not only the saints themselves may sing of them, but even the heavens and the earth may take up the song. It takes something to make a mountain sing! And yet the prophet summons quite a choir of them. Lebanon, Sirion, and the high hills of Bashan and Moab—he wants to get them all singing because of the Lord's grace to his own Zion. We, too, can make mountains of difficulty, trial, mystery, and labor become occasions for praise to our God. "Break forth, O mountains, into singing!"

This word of promise, that our God will have mercy on his afflicted people, has a whole peal of bells connected to it. Hear their music: "Sing!" "Exult!" "Break forth . . . into singing!" The Lord wants his people to be happy because of his unfailing love. He does not want us to be sad and doubtful. He claims from us the worship of believing hearts. He cannot fail us. So why should we sigh or sulk as if he might do so? Oh, for a well-tuned harp! Oh, for voices like those of the cherubim before the throne!

JULY 8

The angel of the LORD encamps
around those who fear him, and delivers them.

Psalm 34:7

We cannot see the angels, but it is enough that they can see us. There is one great Angel of the Covenant, whom not having seen we love (1 Pet. 1:8). And his eye is always on us, both day and night. He has a host of holy ones under his command. And he ensures they watch over his saints and guard them from all ill. If devils do us mischief, shining ones do us service. Notice that the Lord of angels does not come and go. He does not pay us transient visits. But he and his armies encamp around us. Those whose trust is in the living God live in the headquarters of the army of salvation. This camp surrounds the faithful. So they cannot be attacked from any direction—unless the adversary can break through the battlements of the Lord of angels. We have a fixed protection, a permanent watch. Sentineled by the messengers of God, we will not be surprised by sudden assaults, nor swallowed up by overwhelming forces. Deliverance is promised in this verse—deliverance through the great Captain of our salvation. And that deliverance we will obtain again and again until our warfare is over and we exchange the field of conflict for the home of rest.

JULY 9

I will look with favor on the faithful in the land,
that they may dwell with me;
he who walks in the way that is blameless
shall minister to me.

Psalm 101:6

If David spoke in this way, we may be sure that the Son of David will be of the same mind. Jesus looks out for faithful people, and he fixes his eyes on them to observe them, to bring them forward, to encourage them, and to reward them. Let no true-hearted Christian think that they are overlooked. The King himself has his eye on you.

There are two results of this royal notification. First we read, "that they may dwell with me." Jesus brings the faithful into his house, he sets them in his palace, he makes them his companions, he delights in their company. We must be true to our Lord, and he will then reveal himself to us. When our faithfulness costs us most, it will be the best rewarded. The more furiously people reject us, the more joyfully will our Lord receive us.

Next, he says of the faithful person, "he shall minister to me." Jesus will use for his glory those who reject cunning tricks and are instead faithful to him, his Word, and his cross. These will be in his royal retinue, the honored servants of his Majesty. Fellowship and usefulness are the wages of faithfulness.

Lord, make me faithful that I may dwell with you and serve you.

JULY 10

You will arise and have pity on Zion;
it is the time to favor her;
the appointed time has come.
For your servants hold her stones dear
and have pity on her dust.

Psalm 102:13–14

Yes, our prayers for the church will be heard. The appointed time has come. We love the prayer meeting, and the Sunday school, and all the services of the Lord's church. Our hearts are bound to all the people of God. We can truly say, "There's not a lamb in all your flock I would disdain to feed; there's not a foe before whose face I'd fear your cause to plead" (Philip Doddridge).

If this is the general feeling, we will soon enjoy times of refreshing from the presence of the Lord. Our meetings will be filled, saints will be revived, and sinners will be converted. This can only come through the Lord's mercy. But it will come, and we are called to expect it. The time, the appointed time, is come. Let us stir ourselves. Let us love every stone of our Zion, even if it is falling down. Let us treasure up the least truth, the least ordinance, the least believer, even though some may despise them as only so much dust. When we favor Zion, God is about to favor her. When we take pleasure in the Lord's work, the Lord himself will take pleasure in it.

JULY 11

And everyone who lives and believes in me
shall never die. Do you believe this?
John 11:26

Yes, Lord, we believe it. We shall never die. Our soul may be separated from our body, and this is a kind of death. But our soul will never be separated from God, which is the true death—the death which was threatened for sin—the death penalty, which is the worst thing that can happen. We believe this with every confidence, for who will separate us from the love of God which is in Christ Jesus our Lord (Rom. 8:35, 39)? We are members of the body of Christ; will Christ lose parts of his body? We are married to Jesus; will he be bereaved and widowed? It is not possible.

There is a life within us which cannot be separated from God. For, yes, the Holy Spirit lives within us. So how then can we die? Jesus himself is our life. And therefore there is no dying for us, for he cannot die again. In him we died to sin once, and capital punishment cannot be executed a second time. Now we live, and live forever. The reward of righteousness is life everlasting, and we have nothing less than the righteousness of God. Therefore we can claim this very highest reward.

Living and believing, we believe that we will live and enjoy. Therefore we press forward with full assurance that our life is secure in our living Head.

JULY 12

The Lord knows how to rescue the godly
from trials, and to keep the unrighteous under
punishment until the day of judgment.

2 Peter 2:9

The godly are tempted and tried. It is not true faith that is never put to the test. But the godly are delivered out of their trials. And that deliverance does not come by chance, nor by secondary agencies, but from the Lord himself. He personally undertakes the role of delivering those who trust him. God loves the godly, or godlike, and he makes a point of knowing where they are and how they are.

Sometimes their way seems to be a labyrinth, and they cannot imagine how they will escape from threatening danger. What they do not know, their Lord knows. He knows whom to deliver, and when to deliver, and how to deliver. He delivers in the way that is most beneficial to the godly, most crushing to the tempter, and most glorifying to himself. We may leave the "how" with the Lord, and be content to rejoice in the fact that he will, in some way or other, bring his people through all the dangers, trials, and temptations of this mortal life, to his own right hand in glory.

Today it is not for me to pry into my Lord's secrets. Instead my role is patiently to wait on his timing, knowing this: that, though I know nothing, my heavenly Father knows all.

JULY 13

For I will surely save you, and you shall not fall by the
sword, but you shall have your life as a prize of war,
because you have put your trust in me, declares the LORD.

Jeremiah 39:18

Look at the protecting power of trust in God. The great men of Jerusalem fell by the sword, but poor Ebed-melech was secure, for his confidence was in the Lord (Jer. 39:15–18). Where else should a person trust but in his Maker? We are foolish when we prefer the creature to the Creator. Oh, that we could in all things live by faith. Then we would be delivered in every time of danger! No one ever trusted in the Lord in vain, and no one ever will.

The Lord says, "I will surely save you." Notice the divine "surely." Whatever else may be uncertain, God's care of believers is sure. God himself is the guardian of the gracious. Under his sacred wing there is safety, even when every danger is around. Can we accept this promise as sure? Then in our present emergency we will find that it stands fast. We hope to be delivered because we have friends, or because we are prudent, or because we can see hopeful signs. But none of these things are half as good as God's simple "because you have put your trust in me." Dear reader, try this way, and, trying it, you will keep to it all your life. It is as sweet as it is sure.

JULY 14

Cast your burden on the LORD,
and he will sustain you;
he will never permit
the righteous to be moved.

Psalm 55:22

It is a heavy burden, so roll it onto Omnipotence. It is your burden now, and it crushes you. But when the Lord takes it, he will make nothing of it. If you are still called to bear it, "he will sustain you." It will be on him, and not on you. You will be so upheld under it that the burden will be a blessing. Bring the Lord into the matter, and you will stand upright under that which in itself would weigh you down.

Our worst fear is that our trial should drive us from the path of duty. But this the Lord will never permit. If we are righteous before him, he will not let our affliction move us from our standing. In Jesus he accepts us as righteous, and in Jesus he will keep us so.

What about the present moment? Are you going out to this day's trial alone? Are your poor shoulders again to be chafed by the oppressive load? Don't be so foolish. Tell the Lord all about your grief, and leave it with him. Don't cast your burden down and then take it up again. Instead roll it onto the Lord and leave it there. Then you will walk around, a joyful and unburdened believer, singing the praises of your great Burden-bearer.

JULY 15

Blessed are those who mourn, for they shall be comforted.

Matthew 5:4

By the valley of weeping we come to Zion (Ps. 84:6–7). One would have thought mourning and being blessed were in opposition. But the infinitely wise Savior puts them together in this beatitude. What he has joined together, let no man put asunder. Mourning for sin—our own sins and the sins of others—is the Lord's seal set on his faithful ones. When the Spirit of grace is poured on the house of David, or any other house, they will mourn. By holy mourning we receive the best of our blessings, just as the rarest commodities come to us by water. Not only will the mourner be blessed at some future day, but Christ pronounces him blessed even now.

The Holy Spirit will surely comfort those hearts which mourn for sin. They shall be comforted by the application of the blood of Jesus, and by the cleansing power of the Holy Spirit. When they mourn over the abounding sin of their city and of their age, they shall be comforted by the assurance that God will glorify himself, however much people may rebel against him. They shall be comforted with the expectation that they will be completely freed from sin before long, and will soon be taken up to live forever in the glorious presence of their Lord.

JULY 16

I will save the lame.

Zephaniah 3:19

There are plenty of these lame ones, both male and female. You may meet a lame one twenty times in an hour. They are on the right road, and extremely anxious to run along it with diligence, but they are lame. And so they walk badly along it. On the heavenly road there are many cripples. It may be that they say in their hearts, "What will become of us? Sin will overtake us. Satan will throw us down." "Ready-to-halt" is our name and our nature. The Lord can never make good soldiers of us, nor even nimble messengers to go on his errands. Well, well! He will save us, and that is no small thing. He says, "I will save the lame." In saving us he will greatly glorify himself. Everybody will ask, "How came this lame woman to run the race and win the crown?" And then all the praise will be given to almighty grace.

Lord, though I limp in faith, in prayer, in praise, in service, and in patience, save me, I urge you! Only you can save such a cripple as I am. Lord, do not let me perish because I am among the furthest behind. But by your grace, gather up the slowest of your pilgrims—including me.

Look, God has said it will be so. And therefore, like Jacob prevailing in prayer, I go forward even though my sinew is damaged (Gen. 32:31–32).

JULY 17

The people who know their God shall
stand firm and take action.

Daniel 11:32

"The LORD is a man of war; the LORD is his name" (Ex. 15:3). Those who enlist under his banner will have a Commander who will train them for the conflict, and give them both vigor and valor. The times of which Daniel wrote were of the very worst kind. And it was promised that in those times the people of God would come out in their best colors. They would be strong and stout to confront the powerful adversary.

Oh, that we may know our God—his power, his faithfulness, his immutable love—and so may we be ready to risk everything on his behalf. He is one whose character excites our enthusiasm, and makes us willing to live and to die for him. Oh, that we may know our God by familiar fellowship with him. For then we will become like him, and will be prepared to stand up for truth and righteousness. He who comes out fresh from beholding the face of God will never fear the face of man. If we dwell with him, we will catch the heroic spirit. To us a world of enemies will be but as the drop of a bucket. A countless array of men, or even of devils, will seem as little to us as the nations are to God, and he counts them only as grasshoppers. Oh, to be valiant for truth in this day of falsehood.

JULY 18

Therefore, behold, I will allure her,
and bring her into the wilderness,
and speak tenderly to her.

Hosea 2:14

The goodness of God sees us allured by sin, and it resolves to try on us the more powerful allurements of love. Do we not remember when the Lover of our souls first cast a spell on us and charmed us away from the fascinations of the world? He will do this again and again whenever he sees that we are likely to be ensnared by evil.

He promises to draw us aside, for that is where he can deal with us best. And this place without distractions will not be a paradise, but a wilderness. For in such a place there is nothing to pull our attention away from our God. In the deserts of affliction the presence of the Lord becomes everything to us. We prize his company in adversity far more than we did when we sat with our friends under our own vine and fig tree (Mic. 4:4). Solitude and affliction bring people to themselves and to their heavenly Father more than any other means.

When allured and secluded in this way, the Lord has sweet things to say to us for our comfort. He does "speak tenderly" as the text says. Oh, that this promise might be translated into our experience! Allured by love, separated by trial, and comforted by the Spirit of truth, may we know the Lord and sing for joy!

JULY 19

Your bars shall be iron and bronze,
and as your days, so shall your strength be.

Deuteronomy 33:25

"Your shoes shall be iron and bronze; and as your days, so shall your strength be" (Deut. 33:25 KJV). Two things are provided here for the pilgrim: shoes and strength.

As for the shoes: they are needed for traveling along rough ways and for trampling on deadly foes. We will not go barefoot—that would not be fitting for princes of the blood royal. Our shoes will not be ordinary shoes, for we will have soles of durable metal. They will not wear out even if the journey is long and difficult. We will have protection proportionate to the necessities of the road and the battle. Therefore let us march boldly on, fearing no harm even though we tread on serpents or set our foot upon the dragon himself (Rom. 16:20).

As for the strength: it will continue as long as our days continue. And it will be proportionate to the stress and burden of those days. The words are few: "As your days, so shall your strength be." But the meaning is full. This day we may look out for trials and for work that will require energy. But we may just as confidently look for equal strength. This word given to Asher is given to us as well if we have the faith to appropriate it. Let us rise to the holy boldness that this word is calculated to create within the believing heart.

JULY 20

Christ . . . will appear a second time, not to deal with
sin but to save those who are eagerly waiting for him.

Hebrews 9:28

This is our hope. He to whom we have already looked when he first came to bear the sins of many will be revealed again to the sons of men. This is a happy prospect in itself. But that second appearing has certain particular marks that will make it exceedingly glorious.

Our Lord will bring an end to the business of sin. He has so taken it away from his people, and so effectively borne its penalty, that he will have nothing to do with it at his second coming. He will present no sin offering, for he will have utterly put sin away.

Our Lord will then complete the salvation of his people. They will be finally and perfectly saved. And they will in every respect enjoy the fullness of that salvation. He comes not to bear the result of our transgressions, but to bring the result of his obedience; not to remove our condemnation, but to perfect our salvation.

Our Lord appears only in this way to those who look for him. His character will seem very different to those whose eyes are blinded by self and sin. To them he will be a terrible Judge, and nothing more. We must first look *to* him, and then look *for* him. In both cases, our look will be life.

JULY 21

And those who are wise shall shine like the brightness
of the sky above; and those who turn many to
righteousness, like the stars forever and ever.

Daniel 12:3

Here is something to wake me up. This is worth living for. *To be wise* is
a noble thing in itself. Here it refers to a divine wisdom which only the
Lord himself can give. Oh, to know myself, my God, my Savior! May I
be so divinely taught that I may put into practice heavenly truth, and live
in the light of it! Is my life a wise one? Am I seeking that which I ought to
seek? Am I living as I will wish I had lived when I come to die? Only such
wisdom can secure for me the eternal brightness of sunlit skies.

To be a winner of souls is a glorious thing to be. I will need to be wise
if I am to turn even one person to righteousness; much more if I am to
turn many. Oh, for the knowledge of God, of people, of the Word, and of
Christ that will enable me to convert my contemporaries, and to convert
large numbers of them! I would give myself to this, and never rest until
I accomplish it. This will be better than winning stars at court. This will
make me a star, a shining star, a star shining forever and ever. More than
this, it will make me shine like many stars.

My soul, arouse yourself! Lord, empower me!

JULY 22

And I will betroth you to me forever. I will betroth
you to me in righteousness and in justice, in steadfast
love and in mercy. I will betroth you to me in
faithfulness. And you shall know the LORD.

Hosea 2:19–20

Betrothed to the Lord! What an honor and a joy! My soul, is Jesus indeed yours by his own condescending betrothal? Then, notice that it is forever. He will never break his engagement, much less sue for divorce against a soul joined to himself in marriage bonds.

Three times the Lord says, "I will betroth you." What words he heaps together to confirm the betrothal! Righteousness comes in to make the covenant legal—so none can forbid these lawful bans. Judgment sanctions the alliance with its decree—so none can see folly or error in the match. Steadfast love confirms that this is a love union, for without love, betrothal is bondage instead of blessing. Meanwhile, mercy smiles and even sings. Indeed, she multiplies herself into "mercies" because of the abounding grace of this holy union.

Faithfulness is the registrar, and records the marriage. And the Holy Spirit says "Amen" to it, as he promises to teach the betrothed heart all the holy knowledge needed for its high destiny. What a promise!

JULY 23

I will remember their sins and their lawless deeds no more.

Hebrews 10:17

According to this gracious covenant, the Lord treats his people as if they had never sinned. Practically, he forgets all their trespasses. Sins of all kinds he treats as if they had never been, as if they have been completely erased from his memory. Oh, miracle of grace! God does here that which in certain aspects is impossible to him. His mercy works miracles which far transcend all other miracles.

Our God ignores our sin now that the sacrifice of Jesus has ratified the covenant. We may rejoice in him without fear that he will be provoked to anger against us because of our iniquities. See, he places us among his children; he accepts us as righteous; he takes delight in us as if we were perfectly holy. He even puts us into places of trust. He makes us guardians of his honor, trustees of the crown jewels, stewards of the gospel. He counts us worthy and gives us a ministry. This is the highest and most special proof that he does not remember our sins. Even when we forgive an enemy, we are very slow to trust that enemy. We judge it to be imprudent so to do. But the Lord forgets our sins and treats us as if we had never erred.

Oh, my soul, what a promise is this! Believe it and be happy.

JULY 24

The one who conquers will be clothed thus in white garments.

Revelation 3:5

Warrior of the cross, fight on! Never rest until your victory is complete, for your eternal reward will prove worthy of a life of warfare.

See, here is perfect purity for you! A few in Sardis kept their garments undefiled, and their reward is to be spotless (Rev. 3:4). Perfect holiness is the prize of our high calling. Let us not miss it.

See, here is joy! You will wear party clothes like those people put on at wedding feasts. You will be clothed with gladness, and be made bright with rejoicing (Isa. 61:3). Painful struggles will end in peace of conscience and joy in the Lord.

See, here is victory! You will have your triumph. Palm and crown and white robe will be your reward. You will be treated as a conqueror and acknowledged as such by the Lord himself.

See, here is priestly array! You will stand before the Lord in the same clothing that the sons of Aaron wore. You will offer the sacrifices of thanksgiving and draw near to the Lord with the incense of praise.

Who would not fight for a Lord who gives such large honors to the very least of his faithful servants? Who would not be clothed in a fool's coat for Christ's sake, since Christ will robe us with glory?

JULY 25

But go your way till the end. And you shall rest and shall
stand in your allotted place at the end of the days.

Daniel 12:13

We cannot understand all the prophecies, and yet we regard them with
pleasure and not with dismay. There can be nothing in the Father's decree which should rightly alarm his child. Though the abomination that
causes desolation be set up (Dan. 12:11), the true believer will not be
defiled. Instead they will be purified, and made white, and tried. Though
the earth be burned up, no smell of fire will come on God's chosen (Dan.
3:27). Amid the crash of matter, and the wreck of worlds, the Lord will
preserve his own people.

Calmly resolute in duty, brave in conflict, patient in suffering, let us
go our way, keeping to the road. Let us neither deviate from it nor loiter
in it. The end will come; let us go our way until it does.

Rest will be ours. All other things swing backward and forward, but
our foundation stands sure. God rests in his love, and, therefore, we rest
in it. Our peace is, and ever will be, like a river. An allotted place in the
heavenly Canaan is ours, and we shall stand in it, come what may. The
God of Daniel will give a worthy share to all who dare to be decided for
truth and holiness, just as Daniel was. No den of lions will deprive us of
our sure inheritance (Daniel 6).

JULY 26

And in that day, declares the LORD, you will call me "My
Husband," and no longer will you call me "My Baal."
For I will remove the names of the Baals from her mouth,
and they shall be remembered by name no more.

Hosea 2:16–17

That day has come. We no longer view God as Baal, as our tyrant lord and
mighty master. For we are not under law but under grace. We now think
of the Lord our God as our beloved "Husband," our lord in love, our
next-of-kin, bound to us in a sacred relationship. We do not revere him
less, but we love him more. We do not serve him less obediently, but we
serve him for a higher and more endearing reason. We no longer tremble
under his whip, but rejoice in his love. The slave has changed into a child,
and the task into a pleasure.

Is it so for you, dear reader? Has grace cast out slavish fear and im-
planted family love? How happy are we in such an experience! Now we
call the Lord's Day a delight, and worship is never a weariness. Prayer is
now a privilege, and praise is a holiday. To obey is heaven, and to give to
the cause of God is a banquet. So it is that all things have become new.
Our mouth is filled with singing, and our heart with music. Blessed be
our heavenly Husband forever and forever.

JULY 27

I will give you the holy and sure blessings of David.

Acts 13:34

Nothing of man is sure, but everything of God is. In particular, covenant mercies are "sure blessings." It is just as David said: "He has made with me an everlasting covenant, ordered in all things and secure" (2 Sam. 23:5).

We are sure that the Lord meant his blessings. He did not speak empty words. There is substance and truth in every one of his promises. His blessings are blessings indeed. Even if a promise seems as if it must fall because of death, yet it never will, for the good Lord will make good his word.

We are sure that the Lord will give promised blessings on all his covenanted ones. What he has promised will come in due course to all the chosen of the Lord. They are sure to all God's people, from the least of them to the greatest of them.

We are sure that the Lord will continue his blessings to his people. He does not give and take. What he has granted us is the token of much more. That which we have not yet received is as sure as that which has already come. Therefore, let us wait before the Lord and be still. There is no justifiable reason for the least doubt. God's love, and word, and faithfulness are sure. Many things are questionable, but of the Lord we sing:

For his mercies shall endure,
Ever faithful, ever sure.

John Milton

JULY 28

Humble yourselves, therefore, under the mighty hand
of God so that at the proper time he may exalt you.

1 Peter 5:6

This is tantamount to a promise: if we will bow down, the Lord will lift
us up. Humility leads to honor. Submission is the way to exaltation. That
same hand of God that presses us down is waiting to raise us up when
we are prepared to bear the blessing. We stoop to conquer. Many cringe
before other people and yet miss out on the patronage they crave. But he
that humbles himself under the hand of God will not fail to be enriched,
uplifted, sustained, and comforted by the ever-gracious One. It is a habit
of the Lord to cast down the proud and lift up the lowly.

Yet there is a time for the Lord's work. We ought now to humble
ourselves, even at this present moment. And we should be committed to
keep on doing so, whether the Lord lays his afflicting hand on us or not.
When the Lord strikes, it is our special duty to accept the discipline with
profound submission. But as for the Lord's exaltation of us, that can
only come "at the proper time." And God is the best judge of that day
and hour. Do we cry out impatiently for the blessing? Would we wish for
untimely honor? What are we doing? Surely we are not truly humbled, or
we would wait with quiet submission. Let us wait in humility.

JULY 29

He has cleared away your enemies.

Zephaniah 3:15

What a clear out that was! Satan has lost his throne in our nature even as he lost his seat in heaven. Our Lord Jesus has destroyed the enemy's reigning power over us. He may worry us, but he cannot claim us as his own. His chains are no longer on our spirits. The Son has made us free, and we are free indeed (John 8:36).

The archenemy is still the accuser of our brothers (Rev. 12:10). But our Lord has even driven him from this position. Our Advocate silences our accuser. The Lord rebukes our enemies, and pleads the cause of our soul, so that no harm comes of all the devil's accusations.

As a tempter, the evil spirit still assaults us and insinuates himself into our minds. But there also is he cast from his former position of preeminence. He wriggles about like a serpent, but he cannot rule like a sovereign. He hurls in blasphemous thoughts when he has opportunity. But what a relief it is when he is told to be quiet and forced to slink off like a whipped dog!

Lord, do this for any who at this time are worried and wearied by Satan's barks. Clear away their enemy and be glorious in their eyes. You have cast him down, Lord; now cast him out. Oh, that you would banish him from the world!

JULY 30

I will see you again, and your hearts will rejoice.

John 16:22

Surely Jesus will come a second time. And then, when he sees us, and we see him, there will be rejoicing indeed. Oh, for that joyous return!

But this promise is being fulfilled daily in another sense. Our gracious Lord has many "agains" in his dealings with us. He gave us pardon, and yet he sees us again and repeats the absolving word as fresh sins cause us grief. He has revealed to us that we are accepted before God. And when our faith in that blessing grows a little dim, he comes to us again and again, and says, "Peace be with you" (John 20:19); and our hearts are glad.

Beloved, all our past mercies are tokens of future mercies. If Jesus has been with us, he will see us again. Do not look on any former favor as dead and buried to be mourned over. But regard it as a seed sown that will grow. It will push its head up from the dust and cry, "I will see you again." Are the times dark because Jesus is not with us as he used to be? Let us pluck up courage. For he will not be away long. His feet are like those of a roe deer or a young hart, and they will soon bring him to us. Therefore let us begin to be joyful, since he says to us even now, "I will see you again."

JULY 31

And call upon me in the day of trouble;
I will deliver you, and you shall glorify me.

Psalm 50:15

This is a promise indeed!

Here is an urgent situation: "the day of trouble." It is dark at noon on such a day. And every hour seems blacker than the one that came before it. Then this promise is in season. It is written for the cloudy day.

Here is gracious advice: "Call upon me." We ought not to need the exhortation. It should be our constant habit all day and every day. What a mercy to have the freedom to call on God! What wisdom to make good use of it! How foolish to go running about to men! The Lord invites us to lay our cases before him, and surely we should not hesitate to do so.

Here is reassuring encouragement: "I will deliver you." Whatever the trouble may be, the Lord makes no exceptions, but promises full, sure, happy deliverance. He himself will work out our deliverance by his own hand. We believe it, and the Lord honors faith.

Here is an ultimate result: "You shall glorify me." Ah, that we will do most abundantly. When he has delivered us, we will loudly praise him. And since he is sure to do so, let us begin to glorify him at once.

AUGUST

AUGUST 1

And I will establish my covenant between me and
you and your offspring after you throughout their
generations for an everlasting covenant, to be
God to you and to your offspring after you.

Genesis 17:7

Oh, Lord, you have made a covenant with me, your servant, in Christ
Jesus my Lord. And now, I ask you, let my children be included in its
gracious provisions. Permit me to believe this promise as made to me as
well as to Abraham. I know that my children are born in sin, and brought
forth in iniquity, just like other people (Ps. 51:5). Therefore I ask nothing
on the grounds of their birth, for I know well enough that "that which is
born of the flesh is flesh," and nothing more (John 3:6). Lord, make them
to be born under your covenant of grace by your Holy Spirit!

I pray for my descendants throughout all generations. Be their God
as you are my God. My highest honor is that you have permitted me to
serve you. May my offspring serve you in all the years to come. Oh, God
of Abraham, be the God of his Isaac! Oh, God of Hannah, accept her
Samuel!

If, Lord, you have favored me in my family, I ask you to remember
other households of your people which remain unblessed. Be the God
of all the families of Israel. Let not one of those who fear your name be
tried with a godless and wicked household, for your Son Jesus Christ's
sake. Amen.

AUGUST 2

Now therefore go, and I will be with your mouth
and teach you what you shall speak.
Exodus 4:12

Many a true servant of the Lord is "slow of speech" (Ex. 4:10). And, when called on to speak for his Lord, he is greatly concerned about spoiling a good cause by his bad advocacy. In such a case it is good to remember that the Lord made the tongue that is so slow, and we must take care not to blame our Maker. It may be that a slow tongue is not so great an evil as a fast one. A few words may be more of a blessing than floods of verbiage. It is also quite certain that real saving power does not lie in human rhetoric, with its figures of speech, and pretty phrases, and grand displays. Lack of fluency is not so great a lack as it looks.

If God is with our mouth and with our mind, we will have something better than the noisy gong of eloquence or the clanging cymbal of persuasion (1 Cor. 13:1). God's teaching is wisdom; his presence is power. Pharaoh had more reason to be afraid of stammering Moses than of the most fluent talker in Egypt. For what Moses said had power in it—he spoke plagues and deaths. If the Lord is with us in our natural weakness, we will be clothed with supernatural power. Therefore let us speak for Jesus boldly, just as we ought to speak.

AUGUST 3

But if a priest buys a slave as his property for
money, the slave may eat of it, and anyone
born in his house may eat of his food.

Leviticus 22:11

Foreigners, exiles, and servants when hired were not to eat of holy things. It is so in spiritual matters still. But two types of people were free to come to the sacred table: those who were bought with the priest's money, and those who were born into the priest's house. Bought and born—these were the two indisputable proofs of a right to holy things.

Bought. Our Great High Priest has bought with a price all those who put their trust in him. They are his absolute property—altogether the Lord's. They are given the same privileges as their owner, not for what they are in themselves, but for their owner's sake. And so "they shall eat of his meat." He has meat to eat about which the people of this world know nothing. "Because you belong to Christ" you will therefore share with your Lord (Mark 9:41).

Born. This is an equally sure way to privilege. If born in the Priest's house, we take our place with the rest of the family. Regeneration makes us fellow heirs, and part of the same body. And, therefore, the peace, the joy, the glory that the Father has given to Christ, Christ has given to us.

Redemption and regeneration have given us a double claim to the divine permit in this promise.

AUGUST 4

The LORD bless you and keep you.

Numbers 6:24

This first clause of the high priest's blessing is effectively a promise. The blessing that our Great High Priest pronounces on us is sure to come, for he speaks the mind of God.

What a joy to live under divine blessing! This adds a gracious flavor to all things. If we are blessed, then all our possessions and enjoyments are blessed. And, yes, our losses and crosses, even our disappointments, are blessed. God's blessing is deep, emphatic, effectual. A human blessing may begin and end in words. But the blessing of the Lord makes rich and sanctifies. The best wish we can have for our dearest friend is not "May you be prosperous," but "The Lord bless you."

It is equally delightful to be kept by God; kept by him, kept near him, kept in him. They are truly kept whom God keeps. They are preserved from evil, and reserved for boundless happiness. God's keeping goes with his blessing to establish it and cause it to endure.

The author of this little book desires that the rich blessing and sure keeping pronounced here may come on every reader who at this moment may be looking at these lines. Please breathe the text to God as a prayer for his servants.

AUGUST 5

The law of his God is in his heart;
his steps do not slip.

Psalm 37:31

Put the law into the heart, and the whole person is right. This is where the law should be. For then it lies, like the tables of stone in the ark, in the place appointed for it. In the head it puzzles, on the back it burdens, in the heart it upholds.

What a delightful choice of words is used here, "the law of his God"! When we know the Lord as our own God, his law becomes liberty to us. God has covenanted to be with us, and this makes us eager to obey his will and walk in his commands. Is the precept my Father's precept? Then I delight in it.

We are here guaranteed that obedient-hearted people will be sustained in every step that they take. They will do that which is right, and they will therefore do that which is wise. Holy action is always the most prudent, though it may not at the time seem that way. We are moving along the great high road of God's providence and grace when we keep to the way of his law. The Word of God has not misled a single soul yet. Its plain directions to walk humbly, justly, lovingly, and in the fear of the Lord are as much words of wisdom to make our way prosperous as rules of holiness to keep our garments clean. He walks surely who walks righteously.

AUGUST 6

See, the LORD your God has set the land before you.
Go up, take possession, as the LORD, the God of your
fathers, has told you. Do not fear or be dismayed.

Deuteronomy 1:21

There is a heritage of grace that we ought to be bold enough to win for our own possession. All that one believer has gained is free to another. We may be strong in faith, fervent in love, and abundant in labor. There is nothing to prevent it. Let us go up and take possession. The sweetest experience and the brightest grace are as much for us as for any of our brothers and sisters. The Lord has set it before us; no one can deny our right to it. So let us go up and possess it in his name.

The world also lies before us to be conquered for the Lord Jesus. We are not to leave any country or corner of it unsubdued. That slum near our house is before us, not to baffle our endeavors, but to submit to them. We only have to summon up enough courage to go forward, and we will win dark homes and hard hearts for Jesus. Let us never leave the people in a lane or alley to die because we have not enough faith in Jesus and his gospel to go up and possess the land. No spot is too dark, no person so godless, as to be beyond the power of grace. Cowardice, be gone! Faith marches to the conquest.

AUGUST 7

Only be strong and very courageous, being careful to do
according to all the law that Moses my servant commanded
you. Do not turn from it to the right hand or to the left,
that you may have good success wherever you go.

Joshua 1:7

Yes, the Lord will be with us in our holy war. But he demands that we
strictly follow his rules. Our victories will very much depend on obeying
him *with all our hearts*, throwing strength and courage into the actions
of our faith. If we are halfhearted, we cannot expect more than half a
blessing.

We must obey the Lord *with care and thoughtfulness*. "Being careful to do" is the phrase used, and it is full of meaning. It refers to every
part of the divine will. We must obey *with universal readiness*. Our rule
of conduct is "according to all the law." We may not pick and choose.
Instead, we must take the Lord's commands as they come, one and all.
In all this we must go on *with precision and consistency*. Ours is to be a
straightforward course, which bends neither to the right nor to the left.
We are not to err by being more rigid than the law; nor are we to turn to a
more free and easy way out of a lack of seriousness. With such obedience
there will come spiritual prosperity.

Oh, Lord, help us to see that this is so! We will not test your promise
in vain.

AUGUST 8

The Lord GOD helps me.

Isaiah 50:7

These are prophetic words spoken by the Messiah. They refer to the time of his obedience to death, when he gave his back to those who struck him, and his cheeks to those who plucked off his hair. He was confident in divine support, and trusted in the Lord.

Oh, my soul, your sorrows are like specks of dust on measuring scales compared with your Lord's sufferings! Can you not believe that the Lord God will help you? Your Lord was in a unique position. For, as the representative of sinful humanity—their substitute and sacrifice—it was necessary for the Father to leave him and cause him to experience a desertion of soul. No such necessity is laid on you. You are not bound to cry, "Why have you forsaken me?" (Mark 15:34). Even in this situation, your Savior still relied on God. Can you not do so as well? He died for you, and so made it impossible that you should be left alone. Therefore, be of good cheer.

In today's labors or trials say, "The Lord GOD helps me." Go out boldly. Set your face like a flint and resolve that no disgrace or shame will come near you (Isa. 50:7). If God helps, who can hinder? If you are sure of omnipotent aid, what can be too heavy for you? Begin the day joyfully, and let no shade of doubt come between you and the eternal sunshine.

AUGUST 9

Every branch in me that does not bear fruit he
takes away, and every branch that does bear
fruit he prunes, that it may bear more fruit.

John 15:2

This is a precious promise to one who lives for fruitfulness. At first it
seems to be a harsh prospect. Must the fruitful branch be pruned? Must
the knife cut even the best and most useful? No doubt this is so, for much
of our Lord's purging work is done through afflictions of one kind or another. It is not the evil but the good who have the promise of tribulation
in this life (John 16:33). But, then, the end makes more than full amends
for the painful nature of the means. If we may produce more fruit for our
Lord, then we will not mind the pruning and the loss of foliage.

Still, purging is sometimes achieved by the Word from trials. And this
takes away whatever appears rough in the flavor of the promise. We will
by the Word be made more gracious and more useful. The Lord who has
made us fruit-bearing to some degree will operate on us until we reach a
far higher degree of fertility. Is not this a great joy? Truly there is more
comfort in a promise of fruitfulness than if we had been granted riches
or health or honor.

Lord Jesus, speedily fulfill your gracious word to me and cause me to
abound in fruit to your praise!

AUGUST 10

The LORD makes poor and makes rich;
he brings low and he exalts.

1 Samuel 2:7

All my changes in fortune come from him who never changes. If I grow rich, I should see his hand in it, and I should praise him. Let me equally see his hand if I am made poor, and let me praise him just as heartily. When we go down in the world, it is of the Lord, and so we may take it patiently. When we rise in the world, it is of the Lord, and we may accept it thankfully. In either case, the Lord has done it, and it is well.

It seems that the Lord's way is to lower those whom he means to raise, and to strip those whom he intends to clothe. If this is his way, it is the wisest and best way. If I am now being brought low, I may well rejoice because I see in it the prelude to being lifted up. The more we are humbled by grace, the more we will be exalted in glory. That impoverishment which will be overruled for our enrichment is to be welcomed.

Oh, Lord, you have brought me low recently, and made me feel my insignificance and sin. It is not a pleasant experience, but I pray that you will make it a profitable one to me. Oh, that in this way you would prepare me to bear a greater weight of delight and of usefulness. And when I am ready for it, then grant it to me, for Christ's sake! Amen.

AUGUST 11

For God alone my soul waits in silence;
from him comes my salvation.

Psalm 62:1

Blessed posture—waiting truly and only on the Lord! May this be our condition all this day and every day. Waiting for his pleasure, waiting in his service, waiting in joyful expectation, waiting in prayer, and waiting content. When the soul waits in this way, it is in the best and truest condition of a creature before his Creator, a servant before his Master, a child before his Father. We cannot allow any dictating to God, nor complaining of him. We will permit no petulance and no distrust. At the same time, we practice no running before the cloud and no seeking others for help. Neither of these would be waiting on God. God, and God alone, is the expectation of our hearts.

Blessed assurance—from him salvation is coming! It is on the road. It will come from him and from no one else. He will have all the glory from it, for he alone can and will perform it. And he will surely perform it in his own time and way. He will save from doubt and suffering and slander and distress. Though we see no sign of it yet, we are satisfied to bide the Lord's time, for we have no reason to suspect his love and faithfulness. He will make sure work of it before long, and we will praise him at once for the coming mercy.

AUGUST 12

For you are my lamp, O Lord,
and my God lightens my darkness.

2 Samuel 22:29

Am I in the light? Then you, oh, Lord, are my lamp. Take you away, and my joy would be gone. But as long as you are with me, I can do without the torches of time and the candles of created comfort. What a light the presence of God casts on all things! We heard of a lighthouse that could be seen for twenty miles. But our Lord is not only a God at hand, but can be seen from far away, even in the enemy's country. Oh, Lord, I am as happy as an angel when your love fills my heart. You are all my desire.

Am I in the dark? Then you, oh, Lord, will lighten my darkness. Before long, things will change. Affairs may grow more and more dreary, and cloud may be piled on cloud. But if it grows so dark that I cannot see my own hand, still I will see the hand of the Lord. When I cannot find a light within me, or among my friends, or in the whole world, the Lord, who said "Let there be light" and there was light, can say the same again (Gen. 1:3). He will speak me into the sunshine yet. I will not die but live. The day is already breaking. This sweet text shines like a morning star. I will clap my hands for joy before long.

AUGUST 13

Before they call I will answer;
while they are yet speaking I will hear.

Isaiah 65:24

Quick work this! The Lord hears us before we call. And often he answers us in the same speedy manner. Foreseeing our needs, and our prayers, he so arranges providence that before the need actually arises, he has supplied it; before the trial assaults us, he has armed us against it. This is the promptness of omniscience, and we have often seen it exercised. Before we dreamed of the affliction that was coming, the strong consolation that was to sustain us through it had already arrived. What a prayer-answering God we have!

The second clause suggests the telephone. Though God be in heaven and we are on earth, yet he makes our word, like his own word, travel very swiftly. When we pray aright, we speak into the ear of God. Our gracious Mediator presents our petitions at once, and the great Father hears them and smiles upon them. Grand praying this! Who would not be much in prayer when he knows that he has the ear of the King of kings? This day I will pray in faith, not only believing that I will be heard, but that I am heard; not only that I will be answered, but that I have the answer already.

Holy Spirit, help me in this!

AUGUST 14

And I will afflict the offspring of David
because of this, but not forever.

1 Kings 11:39

In the family of grace there is discipline, and that discipline is severe enough to make it an evil and a bitter thing to sin. Solomon, turned aside by his foreign wives, had set up other gods and grievously provoked the God of his father, David. Therefore, ten parts out of twelve of the kingdom were torn away and set up as a rival state (1 Kings 11–12). This was a painful affliction on the house of David, and it came on that dynasty specifically from the hand of God as the result of their unholy conduct. The Lord will discipline his most beloved servants if they depart from full obedience to his laws. Perhaps at this very time such discipline is on us. Let us humbly cry, *oh, Lord, "let me know why you contend against me"* (Job 10:2).

What a sweet saving clause is this: "but not forever"! The punishment of sin is everlasting, but the fatherly discipline of a child of God is only for a limited period. The sickness, the poverty, the depression of spirit will pass away when they have had their intended effect. Remember, we are not under law but under grace. The rod may make us smart, but the sword will not make us die. Our present grief is meant to bring us to repentance, that we may not be destroyed with the wicked.

AUGUST 15

Whatever you ask in my name, this I will do,
that the Father may be glorified in the Son.

John 14:13

Not every believer has yet learned to pray in Christ's name. To ask not only for his sake, but in his name, as authorized by him, is a high order of prayer. We would not dare to ask for some things in that blessed name, for it would be a wretched defilement of it. But when the petition is so clearly right that we dare set the name of Jesus to it, then it must be granted.

Prayer is all the more sure to succeed because it is for the Father's glory through the Son. It glorifies his truth, his faithfulness, his power, his grace. The granting of prayer, when offered in the name of Jesus, reveals the Father's love to him, and the honor that he has put on him. The glory of Jesus and of the Father are so wrapped up together that the grace which magnifies the one, magnifies the other. The channel is made famous through the fullness of the fountain, and the fountain is honored through the channel by which it flows. If the answering of our prayers would dishonor our Lord, we would not pray. But if he would be glorified in what we request, then we will pray without ceasing in that dear name in which God and his people have a fellowship of delight.

AUGUST 16

Whoever conceals his transgressions will not prosper,
but he who confesses and forsakes them will obtain mercy.

Proverbs 28:13

Here is the way of mercy for a guilty and repenting sinner. He must stop the habit of covering sin. This is attempted by falsehood, which denies sin; by hypocrisy, which conceals it; by boasting, which justifies it; and by loud profession, which tries to make amends for it.

The sinner's business is to confess and forsake. The two must go together. Confession must be honestly made to the Lord himself. It must include within it acknowledgment of the wrong, a sense of its evil, and an abhorrence of it. We must not throw the fault on others, nor blame circumstances, nor plead natural weakness. We must make a clean breast of it, and plead guilty to the accusation. There can be no mercy until this is done.

Furthermore, we must forsake the evil. Having owned our fault, we must disown all present and future intent to remain in it. We cannot remain in rebellion and also dwell with the King's Majesty. We must quit the habit of evil, together with all places, companions, pursuits, and books that might lead us astray.

Not *because of* our confession, nor *because of* our reformation, do we find pardon. We find pardon by faith in the blood of Jesus. Yet confession and reformation are connected to true pardon.

AUGUST 17

He said, "Do not be afraid, for those who are with
us are more than those who are with them."

2 Kings 6:16

Horses and chariots, and a great army, surrounded the prophet in the
city of Dothan (2 Kings 6:8–23). His young servant was alarmed. How
could they escape from such a body of armed men? But the prophet had
eyes that his servant did not have, and he could see a greater host with
far superior weapons guarding him from all harm. Horses of fire are
mightier than horses of flesh, and chariots of fire are far more preferable
than chariots of iron.

It is the same at this time. The adversaries of truth are many, influ-
ential, learned, and cunning. And truth suffers as a result. Yet the man
of God has no reason for trepidation. Agencies, seen and unseen, of the
most potent kind, are on the side of righteousness. God has armies waiting in ambush that will reveal themselves in the time of need. The forces
that are on the side of the good and the true far outweigh the powers of
evil. Therefore let us keep our spirits up, and walk with the step of men
who possess a cheerful secret that has lifted them above all fear. We are
on the winning side. The battle may be harsh, but we know how it will
end. Faith, having God with her, is in a clear majority. "Those who are
with us are more than those who are with them."

AUGUST 18

If you seek him, he will be found by you.

1 Chronicles 28:9

We need our God; and he is to be had by those who seek him. He will not deny himself to any one of us if we personally seek his face. It is not, if you deserve him, or buy his favor, but merely if you "seek" him. Those who already know the Lord must go on seeking his face through prayer, through diligent service, and through holy gratitude. To such people he will not refuse his favor and fellowship. Those who have not yet known him so that their souls have found rest should at once start seeking, and never stop until they find him as their Savior, their Friend, their Father, and their God.

What strong assurance this promise gives to the seeker! "The one who seeks finds" (Matt. 7:8). You, yes *you*, if you seek your God, will find him. When you find him, you have found life, pardon, sanctification, preservation, and glory. Will you not seek, and carry on seeking, since you will not seek in vain? Dear friend, seek the Lord at once. Here is the place, and now is the time. Bend that stiff knee. Yes, bend that stiffer neck (Ex. 32:9) and cry out for God, for the living God. In the name of Jesus, seek cleansing and justification. You will not be refused. Here is David's testimony to his son Solomon, and it is the writer's personal witness to the reader. Believe it and act upon it, for Christ's sake.

AUGUST 19

Mankind will say, "Surely there is a reward for the righteous;
surely there is a God who judges on earth."

Psalm 58:11

God's judgments in this life are not always clearly to be seen, for in many cases one event happens in the same way to everyone. This is the state of probation, and not yet of punishment or reward. Yet at times God works terrible things in righteousness, and even the careless are compelled to acknowledge his hand.

Even in this life, righteousness has a kind of reward that it prefers above all others, namely, the smile of God, which creates a quiet conscience. Sometimes other compensations follow, for God will be in no one's debt. But, at the same time, the chief reward of the righteous lies in the life to come.

Meanwhile, on a large scale, we mark the presence of the great Ruler among the nations. He breaks in pieces oppressive thrones, and punishes guilty peoples. No one can study the history of the rise and fall of empires without perceiving that there is a power that tends toward righteousness. In the end it brings iniquity into its courtroom, and condemns it with unsparing justice. Sin will not go unpunished, and goodness will not remain unrewarded. The Judge of all the earth must do right. Therefore, let us fear him and no more dread the power of the wicked.

AUGUST 20

He will deliver you from six troubles;
in seven no evil shall touch you.

Job 5:19

In this Eliphaz spoke the truth of God. We may have as many troubles as the work days of the week, but the God who worked on those *six* days will work for us until our deliverance is complete. We will rest with him, and in him on our Sabbath. The rapid succession of trials is one of the hardest tests of faith. Before we have recovered from one blow, it is followed by another and another until we are staggering. Still, the equally quick succession of deliverances is extremely cheering. New songs are rung out on the anvil by the hammer of affliction until we see in the spiritual world the equivalent of "the Harmonious Blacksmith"—the music by George Frederick Handel said to be based on the sound of a blacksmith's hammer. Our confidence is that when the Lord makes our trials six, six they will be, and no more.

It may be that we have no day of rest for *seven* troubles come on us. What then? "In seven no evil shall touch you." Evil may roar at us, but it will be kept at more than arm's length, for it shall not even touch us. Its hot breath may distress us, but its little finger cannot be laid on us.

With minds prepared for action, we will meet the six or the seven troubles, and leave fear to those who have no Father, no Savior, and no Sanctifier.

AUGUST 21

For his anger is but for a moment,
and his favor is for a lifetime.
Weeping may tarry for the night,
but joy comes with the morning.

Psalm 30:5

A moment under our Father's anger seems a very long time. And yet it is but a moment after all. If we grieve his Spirit, we cannot see his smile. But he is a God who is ready to pardon, and he soon puts aside any memory of our faults. When we faint and are ready to die because of his frown, his favor puts new life into us.

This verse has another note that is like a semi-quaver. Our weeping night soon turns into joyous day. Brevity is the mark of mercy in the discipline of believers. The Lord does not love to use the rod on his chosen. He gives a blow or two, and it is all over. Yes, and the life and the joy, which follow the anger and the weeping, more than make amends for the salutary sorrow.

Come, my heart, begin your hallelujahs! Do not weep all through the night, but wipe your eyes in anticipation of the morning. These tears are like dew which bring as much good to us as the sunbeams of the morning. Tears clear the eyes for the sight of God in his grace, and make the vision of his favor more precious. A night of sorrow supplies those shades of the picture that bring out the highlights with distinctness. All is well.

AUGUST 22

Surely the wrath of man shall praise you;
the remnant of wrath you will put on like a belt.

Psalm 76:10

Wicked men will be wrathful. We must endure their anger as the badge of our calling, the token of our separation from them. If we were of the world, the world would love its own. Our comfort is that the wrath of man shall be made to bring glory to God. When in their wrath the wicked crucified the Son of God, they were unwittingly fulfilling the divine purpose. And in a thousand cases the willfulness of the ungodly is doing the same. They think they are free, but like convicts in chains, they are unconsciously working out the decrees of the Almighty.

The schemes of the wicked are overruled for their defeat. They act in a suicidal way, and baffle their own plots. Nothing will come of their wrath that can do us real harm. When they burned the martyrs, the smoke that blew from the stake made people more sick of papal power than anything else.

Meanwhile, the Lord has a muzzle and a chain for bears. He restrains the extremes of the enemy's wrath. He is like a miller who holds back the mass of the water in the stream, and what he does allow to flow, he uses to turn his wheel. Let us not sigh, but sing. All is well, however hard the wind blows.

AUGUST 23

I love those who love me,
and those who seek me diligently find me.

Proverbs 8:17

Wisdom loves her lovers, and seeks her seekers. He is already wise who seeks to be wise, and he has almost found wisdom who diligently seeks her. What is true of wisdom in general is especially true of wisdom embodied in our Lord Jesus. We are to love and to seek him, and in return, we will enjoy his love and find him himself.

Our business is to seek Jesus diligently. Happy are the young who seek diligently early in life—whose morning is spent with Jesus! It is never too soon to seek the Lord Jesus. Early seekers make certain finders. We should seek him *early with diligence.* Thriving tradesmen are early risers, and thriving saints seek Jesus eagerly. Those who find that Jesus enriches them will give their hearts to seek him. We must seek him *first, and so early.* Above all things: Jesus. Jesus first, and nothing else even as a bad second.

The blessing is that he will be found. He reveals himself more and more clearly to our search. He gives himself up more fully to our fellowship. Happy are those who seek the One who, when he is found, remains with them forever. He will be a treasure growing increasingly precious to their hearts and understandings.

Lord Jesus, I have found you. May I find you to an unutterable degree of joyous satisfaction.

AUGUST 24

For it is written,
"I will destroy the wisdom of the wise,
and the discernment of the discerning I will thwart."

1 Corinthians 1:19

This verse is a threat as far as the worldly wise are concerned. But to the simple believer it is a promise. Those who claim to be learned are forever trying to undermine the faith of the humble believer, but they fail in their attempts. Their arguments break down, their theories fall under their own weight, their deeply laid plots discover themselves before their purpose is accomplished. The old gospel is not extinct yet, nor will it be while the Lord lives. If it could have been exterminated, it would have perished from the earth long ago.

We cannot destroy the wisdom of the wise, nor need we attempt to do so, for the work is in far better hands. The Lord himself says, "I will," and he never resolves in vain. Twice he declares his purpose in this verse, and we may rest assured that he will not turn aside from it.

What clean work the Lord makes of philosophy and "modern thought" when he puts his hand to it! He brings the fine appearance down to nothing; he utterly destroys the wood, hay, and stubble. It is written that so it will be, and so will it be.

Lord, make short work of it. Amen, and amen.

AUGUST 25

I myself will be the shepherd of my sheep, and I myself
will make them lie down, declares the Lord God.

Ezekiel 34:15

"I will feed my flock" (Ezek. 34:15 KJV). Under the care of the divine
Shepherd, saints are fed in full. Theirs is not an empty, unsatisfying meal
of mere human "thought." Instead, the Lord feeds them on the solid,
substantial truth of divine revelation. There are real nutrients for the soul
in Scripture, brought home to the heart by the Holy Spirit. Jesus himself
is the true, life-sustaining Food of believers. Here our Great Shepherd
promises that such sacred nourishment and care will be given to us by
him himself. If, on the Lord's Day, our earthly shepherd is empty-handed,
the Lord is not.

When filled with holy truth, the mind rests. Those whom the Lord
shepherds are at peace. No dog will worry them, no wolf will devour
them, no restless tendencies will disturb them. They will lie down and di-
gest the food which they have enjoyed. The doctrines of grace are not only
sustaining but consoling. In them we have the means for building up and
lying down. If preachers do not give us rest, let us look to the Lord for it.

Today may the Lord cause us to feed in the pastures of the Word, and
make us to lie down in them. May no folly and no worry, but meditation
and peace, mark this day.

AUGUST 26

I will judge between sheep and sheep.

Ezekiel 34:22

Some are fat and flourishing, and therefore they are unkind to the feeble (Ezek. 34:20–21). This is a grievous sin, and causes much sorrow. Sometimes members of God's flock thrust with their side or shoulder, or push the diseased sheep with their horns. This is a sad offense in the assembly of professing believers. The Lord takes note of these proud and unkind deeds. And he is greatly angered by them, for he loves the weak.

Is the reader one of the despised? Are you in mourning, and a marked person because of their tender conscience? Do their brothers and sisters judge them harshly? Do not let them resent their conduct. Above all, do not let them push and thrust in return. Let them leave the matter in the Lord's hands. He is the Judge. Why should we wish to intrude on his role? He will decide much more righteously than we can. His time for judgment is the best, and we need not be in a hurry to hasten it.

Let the hard-hearted oppressor tremble. Even though they may now ride roughshod over others with impunity, all their proud speeches are noted, and for every one of them account must be given in the courtroom of the great Judge.

Patience, my soul! Patience! The Lord knows your grief. Your Jesus has pity on you!

AUGUST 27

I have chosen thee in the furnace of affliction.

Isaiah 48:10 KJV

This has been the motto on the wall of my bedroom for a long time, and in many ways it has also been written on my heart. It is no small thing to be "chosen" by God. God's choice makes chosen people choice people. Better to be the elect of God than the elect of a whole nation. So eminent is this privilege that whatever drawback may be joined to it, we very joyfully accept it, just as the Jews ate the bitter herbs for the sake of the Paschal Lamb. We choose the furnace, since God chooses us in it.

We are chosen as an afflicted people, and not as a prosperous people. We are not chosen in the palace, but in the furnace. In the furnace beauty is marred, fashion is destroyed, strength is melted, glory is consumed. And yet here eternal love reveals its secrets and declares its choice. So has it been in our case. In severest times of trial, God has made our calling and election plain to us, so that it is confirmed to us (2 Pet. 1:10). Then we have chosen the Lord to be our God, and he has shown that we are certainly his chosen. Therefore, if today the furnace is heated seven times hotter, we will not dread it. For the glorious Son of God will walk with us amid the glowing coals (Dan. 3:19–25).

AUGUST 28

But I call to God,
and the LORD will save me.

Psalm 55:16

Yes, I must and will pray. What else can I do? What more can I do? Betrayed, forsaken, grieved, baffled, oh, my Lord, I will call on you. My Ziklag is in ashes, and men speak of stoning me (1 Sam. 30:1–6). But I encourage my heart in the Lord, who will bear me through this trial as he has borne me through so many others. The Lord will save me. I am sure he will, and I declare my faith.

The Lord and no one else will save me. I desire no other helper, and would not trust in an arm of flesh even if I could. I will cry to him evening, and morning, and noon, and I will cry to no one else, for he is all-sufficient.

How he will save me I cannot guess. But he will do it, I know. He will do it in the best and surest way, and he will do it in the largest, truest, and fullest sense. Out of this trouble and all future troubles the great "I AM" will bring me as surely as he lives. And when death comes, and all the mysteries of eternity follow, still this will be true: "*The* LORD *will save me.*" This will be my song throughout this autumn day. Is it not like a ripe apple from the tree of life? I will feed on it. How sweet it is to my taste!

Their life shall be like a watered garden.

Jeremiah 31:12

Oh, to have one's soul under heavenly cultivation—no longer a wilderness, but a garden of the Lord! Enclosed from the wasteland, walled around by grace, planted by instruction, visited by love, weeded by heavenly discipline, and guarded by divine power, one's favored soul is prepared to produce fruit to the Lord.

But a garden may become parched for want of water. And then all its herbs wilt and are ready to die. Oh, my soul, how soon would this be the case were the Lord to leave you! In the East, a garden without water soon ceases to be a garden at all. Nothing can come to perfection, grow, or even live. When irrigation is kept up, the result is charming. Oh, to have one's soul watered by the Holy Spirit uniformly—every part of the garden having its own stream; plentifully—a sufficient refreshment coming to every tree and herb, however thirsty by nature it may be; continually— each hour bringing not only its heat but its refreshment; wisely—each plant receiving just what it needs. In a garden you can see by the vigorous growth where the water flows, and you can soon perceive when the Spirit of God comes.

Oh, Lord, water me this day and cause me to produce for you a full reward, for Jesus's sake. Amen.

AUGUST 30

For does not my house stand so with God?
For he has made with me an everlasting covenant,
ordered in all things and secure.
For will he not cause to prosper
all my help and my desire?

2 Samuel 23:5

This is not so much one promise as a collection of promises—a box of pearls. The covenant is the ark that contains all things. These are the last words of David, but they may be mine today.

Here is *a sigh*, for David makes this declaration of faith in the face of adversity. Things with me and mine are not the way I would wish. There are trials, cares, and sins. These make the pillow hard.

Here is *a solace*: "He has made with me an everlasting covenant." The Lord has pledged himself to me, and sealed the contract with the blood of Jesus. I am bound to my God, and my God to me.

This brings into prominence *a security*, since this covenant is everlasting, ordered in all things and secure. There is nothing to fear from the lapse of time, the failure at some forgotten point, or the natural uncertainty of things. The covenant is a solid foundation to build on for life or for death.

David feels *satisfaction*. He wants nothing more for salvation or pleasure. He is delivered, and he is delighted. This covenant is all a man can desire.

Oh, my soul, turn this day to your Lord Jesus, whom the great Lord has given to be a covenant to the people. Take him to be your all in all.

AUGUST 31

"But the word of the Lord remains forever."
And this word is the good news that was preached to you.

1 Peter 1:25

All human teaching and, indeed, all human beings, will pass away like the grass of the meadow (1 Pet. 1:24). But we are here assured that the word of the Lord is of a very different character, for it will endure forever.

We have here *a divine gospel*. For what word can endure forever except that which is spoken by the eternal God?

We have here *an ever-living gospel*. It is as full of vitality as when it first came from the lips of God. It is as strong to convince and convert, to regenerate and comfort, to sustain and sanctify as ever it was in its first days of wonder-working.

We have *an unchanging gospel*. Today the grass is green, but tomorrow it will be dry hay. In contrast, God's word is always the abiding truth of the immutable Lord. Opinions alter, but truth certified by God can no more change than the God who uttered it.

Here, then, we have *a gospel to rejoice in*. We have a word of the Lord on which we can lean all our weight. "Forever" includes life, death, judgment, and eternity.

Glory be to God in Christ Jesus for everlasting comfort. Feed on the word today, and all the days of your life.

SEPTEMBER

SEPTEMBER 1

If you keep my commandments, you will abide in my love.

John 15:10

These things cannot be separated—abiding in obedience and abiding in the love of Jesus. Only a life under the rule of Christ can prove that we are the objects of our Lord's delight. We must keep our Lord's command if we want to bask in his love. If we live in sin, we cannot live in the love of Christ. Without the holiness which pleases God, we cannot please Jesus. He who cares nothing for holiness knows nothing of the love of Jesus.

Conscious enjoyment of our Lord's love is a delicate thing. It is far more sensitive to sin and holiness than mercury is to cold and heat. When we are tender of heart, and careful in thought, lip, and life to honor our Lord Jesus, then we receive tokens of his love without number. If we desire to perpetuate such happiness, we must perpetuate holiness. The Lord Jesus will not hide his face from us unless we hide our face from him. Sin makes the cloud which darkens our Sun. If we are watchfully obedient and completely consecrated, we may walk in the light as God is in the light. We may be as certain of abiding in the love of Jesus as Jesus has of abiding in the love of the Father. Here is a sweet promise with a solemn "if."

Lord, let me have this "if" in my hand, for like a key, it opens this casket.

SEPTEMBER 2

Let us know; let us press on to know the LORD.

Hosea 6:3

Not all at once, but by degrees will we gain holy knowledge. Our business is to persevere and learn little by little. We need not despair, even though our progress may be slow, for we will eventually know. "Then shall we know, if we follow on to know the LORD" (Hos. 6:3 KJV). The Lord, who has become our Teacher, will not give us up, however slow to understand we are. For it is not to his honor to allow any degree of human folly to baffle his skill. The Lord delights to make the simple wise (Ps. 19:7).

Our duty is to keep to our main topic. We are to press on to know, not one particular doctrine or another, but the Lord himself. To know Father, Son, and Spirit, the triune God—this is life eternal. Let us keep to this, for in this way we will gain complete instruction. By pressing on to know the Lord, we learn healing after being torn, binding up after smiting, and life after death (Hos. 6:1–2). Experience is made complete when the heart follows the road of the almighty Lord.

My soul, keep close to Jesus, press on to know God in Jesus, and so you will come to the knowledge of Christ, which is the most excellent knowledge of all. The Holy Spirit will lead you into all truth (John 16:13). Is not this his gracious work? Rely on him to fulfill it.

SEPTEMBER 3

And you shall know that I am the LORD, when I open your
graves, and raise you from your graves, O my people.

Ezekiel 37:13

Indeed it must be so: those who receive life from the dead are sure to
recognize the hand of the Lord in such a resurrection. This is the greatest
and most remarkable of all changes that a person can undergo—to be
brought out of the grave of spiritual death and made to rejoice in the light
and liberty of spiritual life. No one could accomplish this except the living
God, the Lord and giver of life.

Ah, me! How well do I remember when I was lying in the valley full
of dry bones, as dry as any of them (Ezek. 37:1–14)! Blessed was the day
when free and sovereign grace sent the man of God to prophesy on me!
Glory be to God for the stirring which that word of faith caused among
the dry bones. More blessed still was that heavenly breath from the four
winds which made me live! Now I know the life-giving Spirit of the ever-
living Lord. Truly the Lord is the living God, for he made me live. My
new life, even with its longings and sorrows, is clear proof to me that the
Lord can kill and make alive. He is the only God. He is all that is great,
gracious, and glorious, and my enlivened soul adores him as the great
"I AM." All glory be to his sacred name! As long as I live, I will praise him.

SEPTEMBER 4

But I will have mercy on the house of Judah, and I will
save them by the LORD their God. I will not save them by
bow or by sword or by war or by horses or by horsemen.

Hosea 1:7

Precious word! The Lord himself will deliver his people in the greatness of
his mercy, but he will not do it by the ordinary means. People are slow to
render to God the glory due to his name. If they go to battle with sword
and bow, and win the victory, they ought to praise their God. Yet they do
not. Instead they begin to magnify their own right arm, and glory in their
horses and horsemen. For this reason our Lord often decides to save his
people without secondary means, that all the honor may be to himself
alone.

Look, then, my heart to the Lord alone, and not to people. Expect to
see God all the more clearly when there is no one else to look to. If I have
no friend, no adviser, no one at my back, let me nevertheless be confident.
I can feel that the Lord himself is on my side. Yes, let me be glad if he gives
victory without battle, as the text seems to imply. Why do I ask for horses
and horsemen if the Lord himself has mercy on me, and lifts up his arm
in my defense? Why do I need the bow or sword if God will save me? Let
me trust and not be afraid, from this day onward and forevermore. Amen.

SEPTEMBER 5

The LORD will be with you.

2 Chronicles 20:17

This was a great mercy for Jehoshaphat, because a great multitude had come to fight against him (2 Chronicles 20). And it will be a great mercy for me, because I have great need, and I have no might or wisdom. If the Lord is with me, it matters little who may desert me. If the Lord is with me, I will conquer in the battle of life. And the greater my trials, the more glorious will be my victory.

How can I be sure that the Lord is with me? He is certain to be with me if I am with him. If I trust in his faithfulness, believe his words, and obey his commands, I can be sure he is with me. If I am on Satan's side, then God is against me, and he cannot be otherwise. But if I live to honor God, then I may be sure that he will honor me.

I am quite sure that God is with me if Jesus is my sole and only Savior. If I have placed my soul in the hands of God's only begotten Son, then I may be sure that the Father will use all his power to preserve me, so that his Son may not be dishonored. Oh, for faith to take hold of the short but sweet text for today!

Oh, Lord, fulfill this word to your servant! Be with me in the house, in the street, in the field, in the shop, in company, and alone. And also be with all your people.

SEPTEMBER 6

Wait for the LORD;
be strong, and let your heart take courage;
wait for the LORD!

Psalm 27:14

Wait! Wait! Let your waiting be on the Lord! He is worth waiting for. He never disappoints the waiting soul.

While waiting, keep your spirits up. Expect a great deliverance, and be ready to praise God for it.

The promise which should cheer you is in the middle of the verse: "Let your heart take courage," or "He shall strengthen your heart" (Ps. 27:14 NKJV). This goes at once to the place where you need help. If the heart is sound, all the rest of the system will work well. The heart needs calming and cheering; and both of these will come if it is encouraged and strengthened. A forceful heart rests and rejoices, and pumps power throughout the whole person.

No one else can get at the heart, that secret repository of life, so as to pour strength into it. He alone who made it can make it strong. God is full of strength, and, therefore, he can impart it to those who need it. Oh, be brave, for the Lord will impart his strength to you, and you will be calm in tempests and glad in sorrow.

He who penned these lines can write as David did: "Wait, *I say*, on the LORD" (Ps. 27:14 KJV). I do indeed say it. I know by long and deep experience that it is good for me to wait on the Lord.

SEPTEMBER 7

And in the place where it was said to them,
"You are not my people," it shall be said to
them, "Children of the living God."

Hosea 1:10

Sovereign grace can make strangers into sons. And the Lord declares here his intent to deal in this way with rebels, and to ensure they know what he has done. Beloved reader, the Lord has done this in my case. Has he done this for you? Then let us join hands and hearts in praising his adorable name.

Some of us were so decidedly ungodly that the Lord's word most truly said to our conscience and heart, "You are not my people." In the house of God, and in our own homes, when we read the Bible, this was the voice of God's Spirit in our soul, "You are not my people." Truly a sad, condemning voice it was. But now, in the same places, from the same ministry and Scripture, we hear a voice which says, "You are children of the living God." Can we be grateful enough for this? Is it not wonderful? Does it not give us hope for others? Who is beyond the reach of almighty grace? How can we despair of anyone, since the Lord has brought about such a marvelous change in us?

He who has kept this one great promise will keep every other. Therefore let us go forward with songs of adoration and confidence.

SEPTEMBER 8

A bruised reed he will not break,
and a faintly burning wick he will not quench.

Isaiah 42:3

Then I may count on tender treatment from my Lord. Indeed, I feel myself to be at best as weak, as pliant, as worthless as a reed. Someone said, "You're worth nothing more than straw." And the speech, though unkind, was true. Sadly, I am worse than a reed when it grows by the river, for at least that can hold up its head. I am bruised; sorely, sadly bruised. There is no music in me now. There is a split that lets out all the melody. Ah, me! Yet Jesus will not break me. And if *he* will not do so, then I care little what others try to do. Oh, sweet and compassionate Lord, I nestle down beneath your protection and forget my bruises!

Truly I am also like the burning wick whose light is gone and only its smoke remains. I fear I am a nuisance rather than a benefit. My fears tell me that the devil has blown out my light and left me as an obnoxious smoke, and that my Lord will soon put an extinguisher on me. Yet I can see that, though the law of God might limit a flame, it contained no extinguishers. And Jesus will not quench me. Therefore I am hopeful.

Lord, kindle me anew, and cause me to shine out to your glory so that I extol your tenderness.

SEPTEMBER 9

Blessed is the one who fears the LORD always.

Proverbs 28:14

The fear of the Lord is the beginning and the foundation of all true religion. Without a solemn awe and reverence of God, there is no foothold for the more brightly shining virtues. He whose soul does not worship will never live in holiness.

Whoever feels a jealous fear of doing wrong will be happy. Holy fear looks not only before it leaps, but even before it moves. It is afraid of error, afraid of neglecting duty, afraid of committing sin. It fears bad company, loose talk, and questionable policy. This does not make a person wretched, but brings them happiness. The watchful guard is happier than the soldier who sleeps at his post. Whoever foresees evil and escapes it is happier than those who walk carelessly and are destroyed.

Fear of God is a quiet grace which leads a person along a good road, of which it is written, "No lion shall be there, nor shall any ravenous beast come up on it" (Isa. 35:9). Fear of the very appearance of evil is a purifying principle. It enables a person, through the power of the Holy Spirit, to keep their clothes undefiled by the world. In both senses, he that "fears . . . always" is made happy. Solomon had tried both worldliness and holy fear: in the one he found vanity (Eccles. 1:2), in the other happiness. Let us not repeat his test, but abide by his verdict.

SEPTEMBER 10

Blessed shall you be when you come in, and
blessed shall you be when you go out.

Deuteronomy 28:6

The blessings of the law are not canceled. Jesus confirmed the promise when he bore the penalty. If I keep the commands of my Lord, I may appropriate this promise without question.

This day I will "come in" to my house without fearing bad news, and I will "come in" to my room expecting to hear good news from my Lord (Matt. 6:6). I will not be afraid to "come in" to myself through self-examination, nor to "come in" to my affairs by a diligent inspection of my business. I have a good deal of work to do indoors, within my own soul. Oh, for a blessing on it all, the blessing of the Lord Jesus, who has promised to remain with me.

I must also "go out." Timidity makes me wish that I could stay indoors and never go into the sinful world again. But I must go out to do my calling, and I must go out that I may be helpful to my brothers and sisters, and useful to the ungodly. I must be a defender of the faith and an assailant of evil. Oh, for a blessing on my going out this day! Lord, let me go where you lead, on your errands, under your command, and in the power of your Spirit.

Lord Jesus, come in with me and be my guest. And then walk out with me and cause my heart to burn while you speak with me along the way (Luke 24:32).

SEPTEMBER 11

It is good for a man that he bear
the yoke in his youth.

Lamentations 3:27

This is as good as a promise. It has been good, it is good, and it will be good for me to bear the yoke.

Early in life I had to feel the weight of conviction, and ever since it has proved a soul-enriching burden. Would I have loved the gospel as much as I do if I had not learned by deep experience the need of salvation by grace? Jabez was more honorable than his brothers because his mother gave birth to him with sorrow (1 Chron. 4:9–10). And those who suffer much when being born to God make strong believers in sovereign grace.

The yoke of rebuke is tiresome, but it prepares a man for future honor. He is not fit to be a leader who has not run the gauntlet of contempt. Praise intoxicates if it is not preceded by abuse. Men who rise to eminence without a struggle usually fall into dishonor.

By no means are we to seek the yoke of affliction, disappointment, and excessive labor. But when the Lord lays it on us in our youth, it frequently develops a character that glorifies God and blesses the church.

Come, my soul, bow your neck and take up your cross. It was good for you when you were young, and it will not harm you now. For Jesus's sake, shoulder it cheerfully.

SEPTEMBER 12

Believe in the Lord Jesus, and you will be
saved, you and your household.

Acts 16:31

This gospel for a man with a sword at his throat is the gospel for me (Acts 16:27). This would suit me if I were dying, and it is all that I need while I am living. I look away from self, and sin, and any idea of personal merit. Instead, I trust the Lord Jesus as the Savior whom God has given. I believe in him, I rest on him, I accept him to be my all in all.

Lord, I am saved, and I will be saved for all eternity, for I believe in Jesus. Blessed be your name for this. May I daily prove by my life that I am saved from selfishness, worldliness, and every form of evil.

But those last words about my "household": Lord, I would not run away with half a promise when you give a whole one. I ask you to save all my family. Save my nearest and dearest. Convert the children, and the grandchildren if I have any. Be gracious to all who live under my roof or work for me. You make this promise to me personally if I believe in the Lord Jesus. I ask you to do what you have said.

I would go over in my prayer every day the names of all my brothers and sisters, parents, children, friends, relatives, servants, and give you no rest until that word is fulfilled, "and your household."

SEPTEMBER 13

So Israel lived in safety,
Jacob lived alone,
in a land of grain and wine,
whose heavens drop down dew.

Deuteronomy 33:28

What the dew in the East is to the world of nature, so is the influence of the Spirit in the realm of grace. How greatly do I need it! Without the Spirit of God I am a dry and withered thing. I droop, I fade, I die. How sweetly does this dew refresh me! When once I have been favored with it, I feel happy, lively, vigorous, and elevated. I want nothing more. The Holy Spirit brings me life and all that life requires. Everything else without the dew of the Spirit is less than nothing to me: I hear, I read, I pray, I sing, I go to the table of communion, and I find no blessing there until the Holy Spirit visits me. But when he spreads dew on me, every means of grace is sweet and profitable.

What a promise is this for me! His "heavens drop down dew." I will be visited with grace. I will not be left in my natural drought, or to the world's burning heat, or to the desert winds of satanic temptation. Oh, that I may at this very hour feel the gentle, silent, saturating dew of the Lord! Why should I not? He who has made me to live like the grass in the meadow will treat me as he treats the grass—he will refresh me from above. Grass cannot call for dew like I do. Surely the Lord who visits the unpraying plant will answer to his pleading child.

SEPTEMBER 14

Blessed is the man who remains steadfast under trial, for
when he has stood the test he will receive the crown of
life, which God has promised to those who love him.

James 1:12

Yes, he is blessed while he is enduring the trial. No eye can see this until it has been anointed with heavenly ointment. But he must endure it, and neither rebel against God nor turn aside from his integrity. He is blessed who has gone through the fire and has not been consumed as a counterfeit.

When the test is over, then comes the hallmark of divine approval—"the crown of life." It is as if the Lord said, "Let him live; he has been weighed in the balances and not found wanting" (adapting Dan. 5:27). *Life* is the reward—not mere being, but holy, happy, true existence, the realization of the divine purpose for us. Already a higher form of spiritual life and enjoyment crowns those who have safely passed through fiercest trials of faith and love.

The Lord has promised the crown of life to those who love him. Only lovers of the Lord will hold out in the hour of trial. The rest will either sink or sulk or slink back to the world. Come, my heart, do you love your Lord? Truly? Deeply? Wholly? Then that love will be tried. But "waters cannot quench love, neither can floods drown it" (Song 8:7).

Lord, let your love nourish mine to the end.

SEPTEMBER 15

Each will be like a hiding place from the wind,
a shelter from the storm.

Isaiah 32:2

Who this *man* is, we all know. Who could he be but the Second Man (1 Cor. 15:47), the Lord from heaven, the Man of sorrows (Isa. 53:3), the Son of Man? What a hiding place he has been to his people! He bears the full force of the wind himself, and so he shelters those who hide themselves in him. In this way we *have* escaped the wrath of God, and in this way we will escape the anger of men, the cares of this life, and the dread of death. Why do we stand in the wind when we may so readily and so surely get out of it by hiding behind our Lord? Let us today run to him and be at peace.

Often the force of the common wind of trouble rises and becomes a tempest, sweeping everything before it. Things which looked firm and stable rock in the blast. Many and great are the falls among our fleshly confidences. Our Lord Jesus, the glorious Man, is a shelter that is never blown down. In him we can watch the tempest sweeping by while we ourselves rest in delightful serenity.

This day let us just stow ourselves away in our hiding place and sit and sing under the protection of our shelter.

Blessed Jesus! Blessed Jesus! How we love you! Well we may, for you are a shelter for us in the time of storm.

SEPTEMBER 16

And whoever gives one of these little ones even a
cup of cold water because he is a disciple, truly, I say
to you, he will by no means lose his reward.

Matthew 10:42

Well, I can do as much as *that*. I can do a kind act toward the Lord's servant. The Lord knows I love them all and would count it an honor to wash their feet (John 13:1–17). For the sake of their Master, I love the disciples.

How gracious of the Lord to mention so insignificant an action—to give even a cup of cold water! This I can do, however poor. This I may do, however lowly. This I will do cheerfully. This, which seems so little, the Lord notices—notices when it is done to the least of his followers. Evidently it is not the cost, nor the skill, nor the quantity that he looks at, but the motive. What we do to a disciple, because he is a disciple, his Lord observes and rewards. He does not reward us for the merit of what we do, but according to the riches of his grace (Phil. 4:19).

I give a cup of cold water, and he gives me living water to drink. I give to one of his little ones, and he treats me as one of them. Jesus finds a reason to be generous to me in that which his grace has led me to do, and he says, "He shall by no means lose his reward."

SEPTEMBER 17

The righteous flourish like the palm tree
and grow like a cedar in Lebanon.

Psalm 92:12

These trees are not trained and pruned by people. Palms and cedars are "trees of the LORD," and it is by his care that they flourish (Ps. 104:16). It is the same with the saints of the Lord—they are under his own care. These trees are evergreen and are beautiful objects at all seasons of the year. Believers are not sometimes holy and sometimes ungodly. They stand in the beauty of the Lord in all weathers. Everywhere these trees are noteworthy. No one can gaze on a landscape with palms or cedars without his attention being fixed on these royal trees. The followers of Jesus are the observed of all observers. Like a city set on a hill, they cannot be hid.

The child of God flourishes like a palm tree, which pushes all its strength upward in one upright column without a single branch. It is a pillar with a glorious capital. It has no growth to the right or to the left, but sends all its force heavenward. It bears its fruit as near the sky as possible.

Lord, fulfill this picture in me.

The cedar braves all storms and grows near the eternal snows. The Lord himself fills it with a sap that keeps its heart warm and its boughs strong.

Lord, may it be so with me, I pray. Amen.

SEPTEMBER 18

Of Benjamin he said,
"The beloved of the LORD dwells in safety.
The High God surrounds him all day long,
and dwells between his shoulders."

Deuteronomy 33:12

Yes, there is no safety like that which comes from dwelling near to God. The Lord can find no surer or safer place for his most loved people. Oh, Lord, let me always remain under your shadow, close to your wounded side. Nearer and nearer I want to come to you, my Lord. And once I am especially near you, I want to remain there forever.

What a covering the Lord gives to his chosen! They will not be covered by a fine roof, or a bombproof shelter, or even an angel's wing, but by the Lord himself. Nothing can come at us when we are covered in this way. This covering the Lord will grant us all day long, however long the day.

Lord, let me remain today consciously beneath this canopy of love, this pavilion of sovereign power.

Does the third clause mean that the Lord in his temple will dwell among the mountains of Benjamin? Or that the Lord will be where Benjamin's burden is placed? Or does it mean that we are carried on the shoulders of the Eternal? In any case, the Lord is the support and strength of his saints.

Lord, let me ever enjoy your help, and then my arms will be sufficient for me.

SEPTEMBER 19

The LORD your God is in your midst,
a mighty one who will save;
he will rejoice over you with gladness;
he will quiet you by his love;
he will exult over you with loud singing.

Zephaniah 3:17

What a word is this! The Lord God in the center of his people, in all the majesty of his power! This presence alone is enough to inspire us with peace and hope. Treasures of boundless might are stored in our Lord, and he dwells in his church. Therefore may his people shout for joy.

We not only have his presence, but he is engaged in his chosen work of salvation. He "will save." He is always saving. He takes his name "Jesus" from it. Let us not fear any danger, for he is mighty to save.

Nor is this all. He remains always the same. He loves, he finds rest in loving, he will not cease to love. His love gives him joy. He even finds a theme for song in his beloved. This is so wonderful. When God made creation, he did not sing but simply said, "It is very good" (Gen. 1:31). But when he came to redemption, then the sacred Trinity felt a joy to be expressed in song. Think of it and be astonished! The Lord Jesus sings a marriage song over his chosen bride. She is to him his love, his joy, his rest, his song.

Oh, Lord Jesus, by your immeasurable love to us teach us to love you, to rejoice in you, and to sing to you our life-psalm.

SEPTEMBER 20

Your people will offer themselves freely
on the day of your power.
Psalm 110:3

Blessed be the God of grace that this is so! He has a people whom he has chosen from of old to be his special inheritance. By nature they have wills as stubborn as the rest of the wayward sons of Adam. But when the day of his power comes, and grace displays its omnipotence, then they become willing to repent, and to believe in Jesus. None are saved unwillingly, but the will is made sweetly to submit itself. What a wondrous power is this, which never violates the will and yet rules it! God does not break the lock, but he opens it by a master key that he alone can handle.

Now we are willing to be, to do, or to suffer as the Lord determines. If at any time we grow rebellious, he has simply to come to us with power, and straightaway we run in the way of his commands with all our hearts. May this be a day of power with me for some noble effort for the glory of God and the good of my fellow men!

Lord, I am willing. Can I hope that this is a day of your power? I am wholly at your disposal. I am willing, yes, eager, to be used by you for your holy purposes. Oh, Lord, let me not have to cry, "I have the desire to do what is right, but not the ability to carry it out" (Rom. 7:18). Instead, give me ability as you give me desire.

SEPTEMBER 21

Knowing that suffering produces endurance.

Romans 5:3

This is a promise in essence if not in form. We have need of endurance, and here we see the way to get it. It is only by enduring that we learn to endure, just as people learn to swim by swimming. You could not learn that skill on dry land. Nor can you learn endurance without suffering. Is it not worthwhile to suffer troubles for the sake of gaining that beautiful composure of mind that quietly accepts all the will of God?

Yet our text describes an extraordinary fact that is not natural, but supernatural. Trouble in and of itself produces petulance, unbelief, and rebellion. It is only by the sacred alchemy of grace that it produces in us endurance. We do not thresh the wheat to calm the dust. Yet the flail of suffering does this on God's floor. We do not toss a man about in order to give him rest. Yet this is how the Lord handles his children. Truly this is not the human way, but it greatly glorifies our all-wise God.

Oh, for grace to let my trials bless me! Why should I wish to prevent their gracious work?

Lord, I ask you to remove my affliction, but I beg you ten times more to remove my impatience. Precious Lord Jesus, with your cross engrave the image of your endurance on my heart.

SEPTEMBER 22

But there the LORD in majesty will be for us
a place of broad rivers and streams,
where no galley with oars can go,
nor majestic ship can pass.

Isaiah 33:21

The Lord will be to us the greatest good without any of the drawbacks that seem to accompany the best earthly things. If a city is blessed with broad rivers, it is liable to attack from galleys with oars and other ships of war. But when the Lord represents the abundance of his generosity through this picture, he takes care expressly to remove the fear that the metaphor might suggest. Blessed be his perfect love!

Lord, if you send me wealth like broad rivers, do not let the "galley with oars" come up in the shape of worldliness or pride. If you grant me abundant health and happiness, do not let the "majestic ship" of fleshly ease come sailing up the flowing flood. If I have success in holy service, as broad as the German Rhine, yet let me never find the galley of self-conceit and self-confidence floating on the waves of my usefulness. Should I be so supremely happy as I enjoy the light of your face year after year, do not let me ever despise your weak saints, nor allow the vain notion of my own perfection to sail up the broad rivers of my full assurance. Lord, give me that blessing which makes rich without adding sorrow or sin (Prov. 10:22).

SEPTEMBER 23

For behold, I will command,
and shake the house of Israel among all the nations
as one shakes with a sieve,
but no pebble shall fall to the earth.

Amos 9:9

The shaking process is going on still. Wherever we go, we are still being winnowed and sifted. In every country God's people are being tried "as one shakes with a sieve." Sometimes the devil holds the sieve, and tosses us up and down at a great rate, with the earnest desire of getting rid of us forever. Unbelief is not slow to agitate our heart and mind with its restless fears. The world lends a willing hand in the process, and shakes us to the right and to the left with great vigor. Worst of all, the church, so largely unfaithful as it is, comes in to give a more furious force to the sifting process.

Well, well! Let it go on. So it is that the chaff is separated from the wheat. So it is that the wheat is delivered from dust and chaff. And how great is the mercy which comes to us in the text: "but no pebble shall fall to the earth"! Everything that is good, true, and gracious will be preserved. Not one of the least of believers will be lost; neither will any believer lose anything worth calling a loss. We will be so kept in the shaking that it will be a real gain to us through Christ Jesus.

SEPTEMBER 24

And wherever the river goes, every living creature that
swarms will live, and there will be very many fish.

Ezekiel 47:9

The living waters in the prophet's vision flowed into the Dead Sea and
carried life with them, even into that stagnant lake. Where grace goes,
spiritual life is the immediate and the everlasting consequence. Grace
proceeds sovereignly according to the will of God, just as a river in all
its windings follows its own sweet will. And wherever it goes, it does not
wait for life to come to it, but it creates life by its own life-giving flow.
Oh, that it would pour along our streets and flood our slums! Oh, that it
would come into my house and rise until every room were made to swim
with it!

Lord, let the living water flow to my family and my friends, and do not
let it pass me by. I hope I have drunk of it already. But I desire to bathe in
it; yes, to swim in it. Oh, my Savior, I need more abundant life. Come to
me, I pray, until every part of my nature is vividly energetic and intensely
active. Living God, I pray, fill me with your own life. I am a poor, dry
stick. Come and make me live so that, like Aaron's rod, I bud and blossom
and produce fruit to your glory (Num. 17:8). Give me life, for the sake
of my Lord Jesus. Amen.

SEPTEMBER 25

If the LORD had meant to kill us, he would not
have accepted a burnt offering and a grain offering
at our hands, or shown us all these things, or
now announced to us such things as these.

Judges 13:23

This is a sort of promise deduced by logic. It is an inference reasonably drawn from ascertained facts. It was not likely that the Lord had revealed to Manoah and his wife that a son would be born to them, and yet also had it in his heart to destroy them (Judges 13). The wife reasoned well, and we will do well if we follow her line of argument.

The Father has accepted the great sacrifice of Calvary and has declared himself pleased with it. How can he now mean to kill us? Why a substitute if the sinner must still perish? The accepted sacrifice of Jesus puts an end to fear.

The Lord has shown us our election, our adoption, our union to Christ, our marriage to the Well-Beloved. How can he now destroy us? The promises are loaded with blessings which require us to be preserved for eternal life. It is not possible for the Lord to cast us away and also fulfill his covenant. The past assures us, and the future reassures us. We will not die, but live. For we have seen Jesus, and in him we have seen the Father through the illumination of the Holy Spirit. Because of this life-giving sight, we must live forever.

SEPTEMBER 26

Behold, a people dwelling alone,
and not counting itself among the nations!
Numbers 23:9

Who would want to dwell among the nations and be counted with them? Why, even the so-called church is in such a state that to follow the Lord fully within it is very difficult. There is such a mingling and mixing that one often sighs for "a lodge in some vast wilderness" (William Cowper).

It is certain that the Lord wants his people to follow a separate path to that of the world, and to come out decidedly and distinctly from it (Rev. 18:4). We are set apart by the divine decree, purchase, and calling. And our experience has made us very different from people of the world. Therefore John Bunyan describes in *The Pilgrim's Progress*: our place is not in their Vanity Fair, nor in their City of Destruction, but on the narrow way along which all true pilgrims must follow their Lord.

This may not only reconcile us to the world's cold shoulder and sneers, but even cause us to accept them with pleasure as part of our covenant share. Our names are not in the same book, we are not of the same seed, we are not heading for the same place, nor are we trusting the same guide. Therefore it is good not to be counted among them. As long as we are found in the number of the redeemed, we are content to be odd and solitary to the end of the chapter.

SEPTEMBER 27

For it is you who light my lamp,
the LORD my God lightens my darkness.

Psalm 18:28

It may be that my soul sits in darkness. And if this darkness is spiritual darkness, then no human power can bring me light. Blessed be God! He can lighten my darkness, and at once light my lamp. Even though I may be surrounded by a darkness that can be felt (Ex. 10:21), yet he can break the gloom and immediately make it bright around me.

The mercy is that if he lights the lamp, no one can blow it out. Nor will it go out for lack of fuel, or burn itself out through the passage of time. The lights which the Lord kindled in the beginning are still shining. The Lord's lamps may need trimming, but he does not blow them out.

Let me, then, like the nightingale, sing in the dark. Expectation will supply me with music, and hope will pitch the tune. Soon I will rejoice in a lamp of God's light. I am dull and dreary just now. Perhaps it is the weather, or bodily weakness, or the surprise of a sudden trouble. But whatever has caused the darkness, it is God alone who will bring the light. My eyes look to him alone. I will soon have the lamps of the Lord shining around me. And, in the future in his own good time, I will be where they need no lamp, not even the light of the sun (Rev. 22:5). Hallelujah!

SEPTEMBER 28

So then, there remains a Sabbath rest for the people of God.

Hebrews 4:9

God has provided a Sabbath, and some must enter into it. Those to whom it was first preached did not enter because of their unbelief. Therefore that Sabbath remains for the people of God. David sang of it (Heb. 4:7). But he had to sing in a minor key, for Israel refused the rest of God. Joshua could not give it, nor Canaan yield it (v. 8). So it remains for believers.

Come, then, let us strive to enter into this rest (v. 11). Let us give up the weary toil of sin and self. Let us cease from all confidence, even in those works of which it might be said, "They are very good." Have we any like this? Even so, let us cease from our own works, just as God did from his. Now let us find comfort in the finished work of our Lord Jesus. Everything is completely done. Justice demands no more. Great peace is our inheritance in Christ Jesus.

As to matters of providence, the work of grace in the soul, and the work of the Lord in the souls of others—let us cast these burdens on the Lord and rest in him (Ps. 55:22). When the Lord gives us a yoke to bear, he does so that, by taking it up, we may find rest (Matt. 11:29). By faith we labor to enter into the rest of God, and we renounce all rest in self-satisfaction or laziness. Jesus himself is perfect rest, and we are filled to the brim in him.

SEPTEMBER 29

He will glorify me, for he will take what
is mine and declare it to you.

John 16:14

The Holy Spirit himself cannot glorify the Lord Jesus better than by showing us Christ's own things. Jesus is his own best commendation. There is no adorning him except with his own gold.

The Comforter shows us that which he has received from our Lord Jesus. We never see anything correctly until he reveals it. He has a way of opening our minds, and of opening the Scriptures. By this double process he displays our Lord to us. There is a great deal of skill involved in presenting an issue, and that skill belongs in the highest degree to the Spirit of truth. He shows us the realities themselves. This is a great privilege, as those who have enjoyed the holy vision know.

Let us seek the illumination of the Spirit—not to gratify our curiosity or even to bring us personal comfort, so much as to glorify the Lord Jesus. Oh, to have worthy ideas from him! Groveling notions dishonor our precious Lord. Oh, to have such vivid impressions of his person and work and glory that we may with heart and soul cry out to his praise! Where there is a heart enriched by the Holy Spirit's teaching, there will be a Savior glorified beyond expression.

Come, Holy Spirit, heavenly light, and show us Jesus our Lord!

SEPTEMBER 30

Open your mouth wide, and I will fill it.

Psalm 81:10

What an encouragement to pray! Our human notions lead us to ask small things because what we deserve is so small. But the Lord wants us to request great blessings. Prayer should be as simple a matter as opening our mouths. It should be a natural, unconstrained utterance. When a man is earnest he opens his mouth wide, and our text urges us to be fervent in our requests.

Yet it also means that we are to be bold before God, and ask many and large blessings from his hand. Read the whole verse, and see the argument: "I am the LORD your God, who brought you up out of the land of Egypt. Open your mouth wide, and I will fill it." Because the Lord has given us so much, he invites us to ask for more; yes, to expect more.

See how the little birds in their nests seem to be all mouth when the mother comes to feed them. Let it be the same with us. Let us take in grace at every door. Let us drink it in like a sponge sucks up the water in which it lies. God is ready to fill us if only we are ready to be filled. Let our needs make us open our mouths. Let our weakness cause us to open our mouths and pant. Yes, and let our alarm make us open our mouths with a child's cry. The opened mouth will be filled by the Lord himself.

So may it be for us, oh, Lord, today.

OCTOBER

OCTOBER 1

He provides food for those who fear him;
he remembers his covenant forever.

Psalm 111:5

Those who fear God need not fear being in need. Through all these long years the Lord has always found food for his own children, whether they have been in the wilderness, or by the brook Cherith (1 Kings 17:3), or in captivity, or in the midst of famine. So far the Lord has given us day by day our daily bread, and we do not doubt that he will continue to feed us until we have no more need.

As to the higher and greater blessings of the covenant of grace, he will never stop supplying them as our situation demands. He remembers that he made the covenant, and never acts as if he regretted it. He remembers it when we provoke him to destroy us. He remembers to love us, keep us, and comfort us, just as he committed to doing. He remembers every dot and comma of his commitments, never allowing one of his words to fall to the ground.

We sadly forget our God, but he graciously remembers us. He cannot forget his Son who is the Guarantee of the covenant, nor his Holy Spirit who actively carries out the covenant, nor his own honor which is bound up with the covenant. Hence God's firm foundation stands (2 Tim. 2:19), and no believer will lose their divine inheritance, which is theirs by a covenant of salt (Num. 18:19; 2 Chron. 13:5).

OCTOBER 2

And Joseph said to his brothers, "I am about to die, but
God will visit you and bring you up out of this land to the
land that he swore to Abraham, to Isaac, and to Jacob."

Genesis 50:24

Joseph had been an incarnate providence to his brothers. All our Josephs
die, and a thousand comforts die with them. Egypt was never the same,
for Israel after Joseph was dead. And the world cannot again be to us
what it was when our loved ones were alive.

But see how the pain of that sad death was alleviated! They had a
promise that the living God would *visit them*. A visit from the Lord! What
a favor! What a comfort! What a heaven below!

Oh, Lord, visit us this day, though we are "not worthy to have you
come under [our] roof" (Matt. 8:8).

But more was promised. The Lord would bring them out. They would
find a cold welcome in Egypt once Joseph was dead. Indeed, it would
become to them a house of slavery. But it was not to be so forever. They
would come out of it through divine deliverance, and march to the land
of promise. We will not weep here forever. We will be called home to the
glory land to join our dear ones. "Therefore encourage one another with
these words" (1 Thess. 4:18).

OCTOBER 3

As for me, I shall behold your face in righteousness;
when I awake, I shall be satisfied with your likeness.

Psalm 17:15

The portion of others fills their bodies and enriches their children, but the portion of the believer is of another sort. People of the world have their treasure in this world, but people of the world to come look higher and further.

Our possession is twofold. We have God's *presence* here and his *likeness* to come. Here we look on the face of the Lord in righteousness, for we are justified in Christ Jesus. Oh, the joy of looking on the face of a reconciled God! The glory of God in the face of Jesus Christ produces for us heaven below, and it will be the heaven of heavens for us above.

But seeing does not complete it. For we are to be changed into that which we gaze upon (1 John 3:2). We will sleep for a while and then wake up to find ourselves like mirrors that reflect the beauties of our Lord. Faith sees God with a transforming look (2 Cor. 3:18). The heart receives the image of Jesus into its own depths, until the character of Jesus is imprinted on the soul. This is satisfaction. To see God and to be like him—what more can I desire? David's assured confidence is here by the Holy Spirit made to be the Lord's promise. I believe it. I expect it.

Lord, grant it. Amen.

OCTOBER 4

And I, when I am lifted up from the earth,
will draw all people to myself.

John 12:32

Come, Christian workers, and be encouraged. You fear that you cannot draw a congregation. Try preaching a crucified, risen, and ascended Savior. For this is the greatest "draw" that has ever been seen. What drew you to Christ but Christ? What draws you to him now but his own blessed self? If you have been drawn to religion by anything else, you will soon be drawn away from it. But Jesus has held you, and will hold you to the end. Why, then, doubt his power to draw others? Go with the name of Jesus to those who have so far been stubborn, and see if it does not draw them.

No sort of person is beyond this drawing power. Old and young, rich and poor, ignorant and learned, depraved or amiable—all people will feel the attractive force. Jesus is the one magnet. Let us not think of any other. Music will not draw to Jesus, neither will eloquence, logic, ceremonies, or noise. Jesus himself must draw people to himself. And Jesus is quite equal to the work in every case. Do not be tempted by the latest claims. Instead, as workers for the Lord, work in his own way, and draw with the Lord's own cords. Draw to Christ, and draw by Christ, for then Christ will draw by you.

OCTOBER 5

Then the remnant of Jacob shall be
in the midst of many peoples
like dew from the LORD,
like showers on the grass,
which delay not for a man
nor wait for the children of man.

Micah 5:7

If this was true of the literal Israel, it is much more true of the spiritual Israel, the believing people of God. When saints are what they should be, they are an incalculable blessing to those among whom they are scattered.

They are like the dew, for in a quiet, unobtrusive manner they refresh those around them. Silently but effectually they minister to the life, growth, and joy of those who dwell with them. Coming fresh from heaven, glistening like diamonds in the sun, gracious men and women care for the weak and insignificant until each blade of grass has its own drop of dew. Though they are little as individuals, they are, when united, all-sufficient for the purposes of love that the Lord fulfills through them. Dewdrops accomplish the refreshing of broad acres.

Lord, make us like the dew!

Godly people are like showers that come at God's command without human leave and license. They work for God whether people desire it or not. They no more ask human permission than the rain does.

Lord, make us boldly active and generous in your service wherever we find ourselves.

OCTOBER 6

When the Spirit of truth comes, he will
guide you into all the truth.

John 16:13

Truth is like a vast cave into which we desire to enter, but we are not able to negotiate it alone. At the entrance it is clear and bright. But if we want to go further and explore its inner recesses, we must have a guide or we will lose ourselves. The Holy Spirit, who knows all truth perfectly, is the appointed guide of all true believers. He conducts them as they are able to bear it, from one inner chamber to another, so that they see the deep things of God, and his secret is made plain to them.

What a promise this is for the humbly inquiring mind! We desire to know the truth, and to enter into it. We are conscious of our own tendency to error, and we feel the urgent need of a guide. We rejoice that the Holy Spirit has come and dwells among us. He condescends to act as a guide to us, and we gladly accept his leadership. We want to learn "all . . . truth" so that we are not one-sided and unbalanced. We do not want to be willingly ignorant of any part of revelation in case we should miss blessing as a result, or incur sin. The Spirit of God has come that he may guide us into all truth. Let us with obedient hearts listen to his words and follow his lead.

OCTOBER 7

He is going before you to Galilee. There
you will see him, just as he told you.

Mark 16:7

Where he arranged to meet his disciples, there he would be at the due time. Jesus keeps his rendezvous. If he promises to meet us at the mercy seat, in public worship, or in the ordinances, we may depend on him to be there. We may wickedly stay away from the appointed meeting place, but he never does. He says, "Where two or three are gathered in my name, there am I" (Matt. 18:20). He does not say, "There I will be," but, "There I am already."

Jesus is always first in fellowship: "He is going before you." His heart is with his people, his delight is in them, he is never slow to meet them. In all fellowship, he goes before us.

But he reveals himself to those who come after him: "There you will see him." Joyful sight! We do not care whether we see the greatest of mere men. But to see *him* is to be filled with joy and peace. And we will see him, for he promises to come to those who believe in him, and to reveal himself to them. Rest assured that this will happen, for he does everything according to his word of promise: "Just as he told you." Catch those last words, and be assured that, to the end, he will do for you "just as he told you."

OCTOBER 8

You shall no more be termed Forsaken.

Isaiah 62:4

"Forsaken" is a dreary word. It sounds like a funeral bell. It records the sharpest sorrows and prophesies the direst ills. An abyss of misery yawns in that word "Forsaken." Forsaken by one who pledged his honor! Forsaken by a friend so long tried and trusted! Forsaken by a dear relative! Forsaken by father and mother! Forsaken by all! This is true sorrow, and yet it may be endured patiently if the Lord will take us up.

But how must it feel to be forsaken by God? Think of that bitterest of cries, "My God, my God, why have you forsaken me?" (Ps. 22:1). Have we ever in any degree tasted the wormwood and the gall of "Forsaken" in that sense (Lam. 3:19)? If so, let us beg our Lord to save us from any repetition of such an unspeakable sorrow. Oh, that such darkness may never return! People in malice said of a saint, "God has forsaken him; pursue and seize him" (Ps. 71:11). But it was always false. The Lord's loving favor will compel our cruel foes to eat their own words, or, at least, to hold their tongues.

The reverse of all this is that superlative word *Hephzibah* (Isa. 62:4 KJV)—"My Delight Is in Her" (Isa. 62:4). This turns weeping into dancing. Let those who dreamed that they were forsaken hear the Lord say, "I will never leave you nor forsake you" (Heb. 13:5).

OCTOBER 9

And the priest shall put some of the blood on the horns
of the altar of fragrant incense before the LORD.

Leviticus 4:7

The altar of incense is the place where saints present their prayers and praises. And it is delightful to think of it as sprinkled with the blood of the great sacrifice. This is what makes all our worship acceptable with the Lord. He sees the blood of his own Son, and therefore accepts our worship.

It is good for us to fix our eyes on the blood of the one offering for sin. Sin mingles with even our holy things, and our best repentance, faith, prayer, and thanksgiving could not be received by God were it not for the merit of the atoning sacrifice. Many sneer at "the blood." But to us it is the foundation of comfort and hope. What is on the horns of the altar is meant to be prominently before our eyes when we draw near to God. The blood gives strength to prayer, and so it is on the altar's horns. It is "before the LORD," and therefore it ought to be before us. It is on the altar before we bring the incense. It is there to sanctify our offerings and gifts.

Come, let us pray with confidence, since the victim is offered, the merit has been pleaded, the blood is within the temple curtain, and so the prayers of believers must be fragrant before the Lord.

OCTOBER 10

I have set before you an open door,
which no one is able to shut.

Revelation 3:8

Saints who remain faithful to the truth of God have an open door before them. My soul, you have resolved to live and die by that which the Lord has revealed in his Word, and therefore before you stands this open door.

I will enter in through the open door of communion with God. Who will prevent me? Jesus has removed my sin and given me his righteousness. Therefore I may freely enter.

Lord, I do so by your grace.

I have also before me an open door into the mysteries of the Word. I may enter into the deep things of God. Election, union to Christ, the second coming—all these are before me, and I may enjoy them. No promise and no doctrine are now locked up so I cannot access them.

An open door of access is before me in private, and an open door of usefulness in public. God will hear me; God will use me. A door is opened for my onward march to the church above, and for my daily fellowship with saints below. Some may try to shut me up or shut me out, but it is all in vain.

Soon I will enter an open door into heaven. The gates of pearl will be my entrance (Rev. 21:21). And then I will go in to my Lord and King and be eternally safe with God.

OCTOBER 11

"I will make them strong in the LORD,
and they shall walk in his name,"
declares the LORD.

Zechariah 10:12

A solace for sick saints. They have grown faint, and they fear that they will never rise from the bed of doubt and fear. But the Great Physician can both remove the disease and take away the weakness which has come of it. He will strengthen the feeble. This he will do in the best possible way, for it will be "in the LORD." Our strength is far better when it is in God rather than in ourselves. In the Lord it causes fellowship; in ourselves it would create pride. In ourselves it would be sadly limited, but in God it knows no bounds.

When strength is given, the believer uses it. He walks up and down in the name of the Lord. What an enjoyment it is to walk around after illness, and what a delight to be strong in the Lord after a season of weakness! The Lord gives his people the freedom to walk up and down, and an inner leisure to use that freedom. He gives us true wealth and spiritual leisure. We are not slaves who know no rest and see no sights. Instead, we are free to travel at our leisure throughout the Immanuel's land.

Come, my heart, do not be sick and sorry any longer. Jesus exhorts you to be strong and walk with God in holy contemplation. Obey his word of love.

OCTOBER 12

And the LORD your God will circumcise your
heart and the heart of your offspring, so that you
will love the LORD your God with all your heart
and with all your soul, that you may live.

Deuteronomy 30:6

Here we read of the true circumcision.

Note *who* it is who circumcises us: "The LORD your God." He alone can deal effectively with our heart, and take away its fleshly ways and pollution. To make us love God with all our heart and soul is a miracle of grace that only the Holy Spirit can work. We must look to the Lord alone for this and never be satisfied with anything short of it.

Note *where* this circumcision takes place. It is not of the flesh, but of the spirit. It is the essential mark of the covenant of grace. Love for God is the sure token of the chosen offspring. By this secret seal the election of grace is certified to the believer. We must ensure we trust in no outward ritual, but are sealed in the heart through the work of the Holy Spirit.

Note the *result* of this circumcision: "That you may live." To be fleshly minded is death. Through the overcoming of the flesh we find life and peace. If our minds are set on the things of the Spirit, we will live (Rom. 8:5–6).

Oh, that the Lord our God may complete his gracious work on our inner natures, that in the fullest and highest sense we may live to the Lord.

If my people who are called by my name humble
themselves, and pray and seek my face and turn
from their wicked ways, then I will hear from heaven
and will forgive their sin and heal their land.

2 Chronicles 7:14

Called by the name of the Lord, we are nevertheless men and women who go astray. What a mercy it is that our God is ready to forgive! Whenever we sin, let us quickly go to the mercy seat of our God, seeking pardon.

We are to humble ourselves. Should we not be humbled by the fact that, after receiving so much love, we still transgress? Oh, Lord, we bow before you in the dust and own our grievous ingratitude. Oh, the shame of sin! Oh, the sevenfold shame of it in people as favored as we have been!

Next, we are to pray for mercy, for cleansing, and for deliverance from the power of sin. Oh, Lord, hear us even now and do not shut out our cry.

In this prayer we are to seek the Lord's face. He has left us because of our faults, and we must ask him to return. Oh, Lord, look on us in your Son Jesus and smile on your servants.

With this must go our own turning from evil. God cannot turn to us unless we turn from sin.

Then comes the triple promise of hearing, pardon, and healing. Our Father, grant us these at once for our Lord Jesus Christ's sake.

OCTOBER 14

Everyone who acknowledges me before men, I also will acknowledge before my Father who is in heaven.

Matthew 10:32

Gracious promise! It is a great joy to me to acknowledge my Lord. Whatever my faults may be, I am not ashamed of Jesus, nor do I fear to declare the doctrines of his cross. Oh, Lord, I have not hidden your righteousness within my heart.

Sweet is the prospect that this text sets before me! Friends forsake and enemies rejoice, but the Lord does not disown his servant. Doubtless my Lord will acknowledge me here and give me new tokens of his favorable regard. But there comes a day when I must stand before the great Father. What bliss to think that Jesus will acknowledge me then! He will say, "This man truly trusted me, and was willing to be accused for my name's sake; and therefore I acknowledge him as mine."

The other day a great man was made a knight, and the queen handed him a jeweled garter. But what of that? It will be an honor beyond all honors for the Lord Jesus to acknowledge us in the presence of the divine Majesty in the heavens. Never let me be ashamed to own my Lord. Never let me indulge a cowardly silence, or allow a fainthearted compromise. Will I blush to acknowledge him who promises to acknowledge me?

OCTOBER 15

As the living Father sent me, and I live because of the Father,
so whoever feeds on me, he also will live because of me.

John 6:57

We live by virtue of our union with the Son of God. As the God-man Mediator, the Lord Jesus lives by the self-existent Father who has sent him, and in the same way we live by the Savior who has given us life. He who is the source of our life also sustains it. Living is sustained by feeding. We must support our spiritual life with spiritual food, and that spiritual food is the Lord Jesus. Our food is not just his life, or death, or offices, or work, or word alone, but Jesus himself—including all these things. On Jesus himself we feed.

This is set before us in the Lord's Supper. But it is actually enjoyed by us whenever we meditate on our Lord. We are nourished as we make him our own by faith, take him into ourselves by love, and assimilate him by the power of the inner life. We know what it is to feed on Jesus, but we cannot speak it or write it. Our wisest course is to practice it, and to do so more and more. We are exhorted to eat abundantly, and it will be to our infinite profit to do so when Jesus is our food and our drink.

Lord, I thank you that this food that is a necessity of my new life is also its greatest delight. So, I do at this time feed on you.

OCTOBER 16

Because I live, you also will live.

John 14:19

Jesus has made the life of believers in him *as certain* as his own. As surely as the Head lives, so the members live as well. If Jesus has not risen from the dead, then we dead are in our sins. But since he has risen, all believers have risen in him. His death has put away our transgressions and broken the chains that held us under the sentence of death. His resurrection proves our justification: we are absolved, and mercy says, "The LORD also has put away your sin; you shall not die" (2 Sam. 12:13).

Jesus has made the life of his people *as eternal* as his own life. How can they die as long as he lives, seeing they are one with him? Because he does not die, and death has no more dominion over him, so they will not return to the graves of their old sins, but will live to the Lord in newness of life. Oh, believer, when, under great temptation, you fear that you will one day fall by the hand of the enemy, let this reassure you. You will never lose your spiritual life, for it "is hidden with Christ in God" (Col. 3:3). You do not doubt the immortality of your Lord; therefore do not think that he will let you die, since you are one with him. The argument for your life is *his life*, and of that you can have no fear. Therefore rest in your living Lord.

OCTOBER 17

He who reveres the commandment will be rewarded.

Proverbs 13:13

Holy awe of God's Word is at a low ebb. People think themselves wiser than the Word of the Lord, and sit in judgment on it. "I did not do so, because of the fear of God" (Neh. 5:15). We accept the inspired Book as infallible, and prove our esteem by our obedience. We have no terror of the Word, but we have a filial awe of it. We are not in fear of its penalties because we have a fear of its commands.

This holy fear of the commandment produces the restfulness of humility, which is far sweeter than the recklessness of pride. It becomes a guide to us in our movements; a drag when we are going downhill, and a stimulus when we are climbing it. Preserved from evil and led into righteousness by our reverence of the command, we gain a quiet conscience, which is a well of wine. We gain a sense of freedom from responsibility, which is as life from the dead. And we gain a confidence of pleasing God, which is heaven below. The ungodly may ridicule our deep reverence for the Word of the Lord; but what of that? The prize of our high calling is a sufficient consolation for us. The rewards of obedience make us scorn the scorning of the scorner.

OCTOBER 18

Those who sow in tears
shall reap with shouts of joy!

Psalm 126:5

Times of weeping are good times to sow. We do not want the ground to be too dry. Seed drenched in the tears of earnest anxiety will come up all the sooner. The salt of prayerful tears will give the good seed a flavor that will preserve it from the maggot. Truth spoken in awe-filled earnestness has a double life about it. Instead of stopping our sowing because we are weeping, let us redouble our efforts because the season is so favorable.

It would not be fitting to sow our heavenly seed while laughing. Deep sorrow and concern for the souls of others are a far more suitable accompaniment of godly teaching than anything like levity. We have heard of men who went to war with a light heart, but they were beaten. And that is how it usually is for those who sow in the same way.

Come, then, my heart, keep on sowing in your weeping. For you have the promise of a joyful harvest. You shall reap. You yourself will see some result from your labor. This will come to you in such a large measure as to give you joy, which a poor, withered, and scanty harvest would not do. When your eyes are blurred by silver tears, think of the golden corn. Bear cheerfully the present toil and disappointment, for the day of harvest will fully reward you.

OCTOBER 19

I will discipline you in just measure.

Jeremiah 30:11

To be left without discipline would be a fatal sign. It would prove that the Lord had said, "[He] is joined to idols; leave him alone" (Hos. 4:17). God grant that this may never be our situation! Uninterrupted prosperity is a thing to cause fear and trembling. Those whom God loves, he reproves and disciplines (Rev. 3:19). But he lets those for whom he has no esteem fatten themselves without fear, like bullocks for the slaughter. It is in love that our heavenly Father chastens his children (Heb. 12:6).

Yet notice that discipline is "in just measure." He gives us love without measure, but chastisement "in measure." Just as under the old law no Israelite could receive more than the "forty lashes less one" (2 Cor. 11:24), which ensured careful counting and limited suffering, so is it with each afflicted member of the household of faith. Every stroke is counted. It is the measure of wisdom, the measure of sympathy, the measure of love by which our discipline is regulated. Far be it from us to rebel against appointments so divine.

Lord, if you stand by to measure the bitter drops into my cup, it is for me cheerfully to take that cup from your hand, and drink according to your directions, saying "Your will be done" (Matt 6:10; 26:42).

OCTOBER 20

He will save his people from their sins.

Matthew 1:21

Lord, save me from my sins. By your name of Jesus I am encouraged to pray like this. Save me from my past sins, that I may not be held captive by the habits of my sins. Save me from the sins of my constitution, that I may not be the slave of my own weaknesses. Save me from the sins which are continually under my eye, that I may not lose my horror of them. Save me from secret sins—sins unnoticed by me because I lack light. Save me from sudden and surprising sins. Let me not be carried off my feet by a rush of temptation. Save me, Lord, from every sin. "Let no iniquity get dominion over me" (Ps. 119:133).

You alone can do this. I cannot snap my own chains or slay my own enemies. You know temptation, for you were tempted. You know sin, for you bore the weight of it. You know how to support me in my hour of conflict. You can save me from sinning, and save me when I have sinned. It is promised in your very name that you will do this. And I pray that you would verify this prophecy to me today. Do not let me give way to temper, or pride, or despondency, or any form of evil. But save me to holiness of life, that your name of Jesus may be glorified in me abundantly.

OCTOBER 21

The least one shall become a clan,
and the smallest one a mighty nation;
I am the LORD;
in its time I will hasten it.

Isaiah 60:22

The Lord's works often begin on a small scale, and they are none the worse for this. Feebleness educates faith, brings God near, and wins glory for his name. Learn to value promises of increase! A mustard seed is the smallest among seeds, and yet it becomes a tree-like plant, with branches which lodge the birds of heaven (Mark 4:30–32). We may begin with one, and it may be "the least one." And yet it will "become a clan." The Lord is great at the multiplication table. How often did he say to his solitary servant, "I will . . . multiply you" (Heb. 6:14)! Trust in the Lord, those who are twos and threes, for he will be among you if you are gathered in his name (Matt. 18:20).

"The smallest one." What can be more despised in the eyes of those who count heads and weigh forces! Yet this is the nucleus of a mighty nation. Only one star shines out at first in the evening, but soon the sky is crowded with countless lights.

Nor should we think the prospect of this increase is remote, for the promise is, "I am the LORD; in its time I will hasten it." There will be no premature haste, like that which we see at meetings where people's emotions are whipped up into an excited frenzy. It will be all in due time. And yet there will be no delay. When the Lord hastens, his speed is glorious.

OCTOBER 22

Now therefore may it please you to bless the house of your
servant, so that it may continue forever before you. For
you, O Lord God, have spoken, and with your blessing
shall the house of your servant be blessed forever.

2 Samuel 7:29

This is a promise pleaded, and so it gives a double instruction to us. Anything which the Lord God has spoken, we should receive as certainly true, and then we should plead it at the throne. Oh, how sweet to quote what our own God has spoken! How precious to be able to turn a promise into a prayer with the word "therefore," as David does in this verse!

We do not pray because we doubt, but because we believe. To pray without believing is not fitting for the Lord's children.

No, Lord, we cannot doubt you. We are persuaded that all your word is a sure foundation for the boldest expectation. We come to you and say, "Do as you have spoken" (2 Sam. 7:25). Bless your servants' house. Heal our sick; save our hesitating ones; restore those who wander; confirm those who live in your fear. Lord, give us food and clothing according to your word. Prosper our undertakings; especially grant success to our endeavors to make known your gospel in our neighborhood. Make our servants your servants, our children your children. Let the blessing flow on to future generations. And as long as any of our descendants remains on earth, may they remain true to you. Oh, Lord God, "let the house of your servant be blessed."

OCTOBER 23

Light is sown for the righteous,
and joy for the upright in heart.

Psalm 97:11

Righteousness is often costly to the person who keeps to it despite the risks. But in the end it will cover its own expenses and return an infinite profit. A holy life is like sowing seed. A lot goes out and apparently gets buried in the soil, never to be gathered up again. We are mistaken when we look for an immediate harvest. But the mistake is very natural, for it seems impossible to bury light. Yet light is "sown," says the text. It lies latent. None can see it. It is sown. We are quite sure that it must one day reveal itself.

We are completely sure that the Lord has planned a harvest for the sowers of light, and they will reap it, each person for themselves. Then their gladness will come. Sheaves of joy for seeds of light. Their heart was upright before the Lord, though people gave them no credit for it, and even censured them. They were righteous, though those about them denounced them as intolerant. They had to wait, as gardeners have to wait for the precious fruits of the earth. But the light was sown for them, and gladness was being prepared on their behalf by the Lord of the harvest.

Courage, brothers and sisters! We need not be in a hurry. Let us possess our souls in patience, for soon our souls will possess light and gladness.

OCTOBER 24

And I will make you to this people
a fortified wall of bronze;
they will fight against you,
but they shall not prevail over you,
for I am with you
to save you and deliver you,
declares the LORD.

Jeremiah 15:20

Stability in the fear and faith of God will make a person like a wall of bronze, which no one can batter down or break. Only the Lord can make such people, but we need them in the church, and in the world, but especially in the pulpit.

This age of shams will fight tooth and nail against uncompromising men of truth. Nothing seems to offend Satan and his people like decisiveness. They attack holy firmness just as the Assyrians besieged fortified cities (2 Kings 18:9–13). The joy is that they cannot overcome those whom God has made strong in his strength. Carried about with every wind of doctrine, others only need to be blown on, and away they go (Eph. 4:14). But those who love the doctrines of grace, because they possess the grace of the doctrines, stand like rocks in the midst of raging seas.

Where does this stability come from? "I am with you . . . declares the LORD." That is the true answer. The Lord will save and deliver faithful souls from all the assaults of the adversary. Hosts are against us, but the Lord of hosts is with us. We dare not budge an inch, for the Lord himself holds us in our place, and there we will dwell forever.

But seek first the kingdom of God and his righteousness,
and all these things will be added to you.

Matthew 6:33

See how the Bible opens: "In the beginning God" (Gen. 1:1). Let your life open in the same way. Seek with your whole soul, first and foremost, the kingdom of God as the place of your citizenship, and his righteousness as the character of your life. As for the rest, it will come from the Lord himself without your being anxious about it. All that is needed for this life and godliness "will be added to you."

What a promise this is! Food, clothing, home, and so forth, God commits to add to you while you seek him. You mind his business, and he will mind yours. If you want wrapping paper and string, you get them thrown in when you buy more important goods. And in the same way, all the earthly things that we need, we will have thrown in with the kingdom. He who is an heir of salvation will not die of starvation. And he who clothes his soul with the righteousness of God cannot be left by the Lord with a naked body. Away with anxious cares. Set all your mind on seeking the Lord. Covetousness is poverty, and anxiety is misery. Trust in God is an estate, and being like God is a heavenly inheritance.

Lord, I seek you; be found by me.

OCTOBER 26

But for the sake of the elect those days will be cut short.

Matthew 24:22

For the sake of his elect the Lord withholds many judgments and shortens others. In great troubles the fire would devour all were it not for the fact that the Lord damps the flame out of regard for his elect. Thus, while he saves his elect for the sake of Jesus, he also preserves the human race for the sake of his chosen.

What an honor is thus put on saints! How diligently they ought to use their influence with their Lord! He will hear their prayers for sinners and bless their efforts for their salvation. He blesses believers that they may be a blessing to those who are in unbelief. Many a sinner lives because of the prayers of a mother, or wife, or daughter for whom the Lord has respect (2 Tim. 1:5).

Have we rightly used this unique power with which the Lord entrusts us? Do we pray for our country, for other lands, and for our age? Do we, in times of war, famine, and disease, stand out as intercessors, pleading that the days may be shortened? Do we lament before God the outbursts of unfaithfulness, error, and promiscuity? Do we urge our Lord Jesus to shorten the reign of sin by hastening his own glorious appearing? Let us get to our knees and never rest until Christ appears.

OCTOBER 27

His servants will worship him.
They will see his face, and his name
will be on their foreheads.

Revelation 22:3–4

Three choice blessings will be ours in the glory land.

"*His servants shall worship him.*" No other lords will oppress us; no other service will distress us. We shall worship and serve Jesus always, perfectly, without weariness, and without error. This is heaven to a saint: in all things to worship the Lord Christ, and to be owned by him as his servant is our soul's highest ambition for eternity.

"*They will see his face.*" This makes the service delightful. Indeed, it is the present reward of service. We shall know our Lord, for we shall see him as he is (1 John 3:2). To see the face of Jesus is the greatest favor that the most faithful servant of the Lord can ask. What more could Moses ask than "Let me see your glory" (Ex. 33:18)?

"*And his name will be on their foreheads.*" They gaze on their Lord until his name is photographed on their brows. They are acknowledged by him, and they acknowledge him. The secret mark of inward grace develops into the public sign of confessed relationship.

Oh, Lord, give us the beginning of these three things here, that we may possess them in their fullness in your own home of bliss!

OCTOBER 28

They shall be forgiven, because it was a mistake.

Numbers 15:25

Because of our ignorance we are not fully aware of our sins of "mistake." Yet we may be sure there are many of them, both of sins of commission and sins of omission. We may be doing, in all sincerity as a service to God, that which he has never commanded and can never accept.

The Lord knows every one of these sins of ignorance. This may well alarm us, since his justice will require the punishment of these trespasses at our hand. But on the other hand, faith spies comfort in the fact that the Lord will wash away stains that are unseen by us. He sees the sin that he may cease to see it by casting it behind his back.

Our great comfort is that Jesus, the true Priest, has made atonement for all the congregation of his children. That atonement secures the pardon of unknown sins. His precious blood cleanses us from all sin. Whether our eyes have seen it and wept over it or not, God has seen it, Christ has atoned for it, the Spirit bears witness to the pardon of it, and so we have a threefold peace.

Oh, my Father, I praise your divine knowledge, which not only perceives my iniquities but provides an atonement that delivers me from their guilt, even before I know that I am guilty.

OCTOBER 29

Thus I will put a division between my people and
your people. Tomorrow this sign shall happen.

Exodus 8:23

Pharaoh has a people, and the Lord has a people. They may dwell together and seem to fare in the same way. But there is a division between them, and the Lord will make it clear. Not forever will one event happen to all in the same way. There will be great difference between the people of the world and the people of the Lord's choice.

This may happen in the time of judgments, when the Lord becomes the sanctuary of his saints. It is very conspicuous in the conversion of believers when their sin is put away, while unbelievers remain under condemnation. From that moment they become a distinct race, come under a new discipline, and enjoy new blessings. Their homes, from then on, are free from the grievous swarms of evils which defile and torment the Egyptians (Exodus 8). They are kept from the pollution of lust, the bite of care, the corruption of falsehood, and the cruel torment of hatred which devour many families.

Rest assured, tested believer, that though you have your troubles, you are saved from swarms of worse ones which infest the homes and hearts of the servants of the world's Prince. The Lord has "put a division." See to it that you keep up that division in spirit, aim, character, and company.

OCTOBER 30

I will sprinkle clean water on you, and you
shall be clean from all your uncleannesses, and
from all your idols I will cleanse you.

Ezekiel 36:25

What an exceeding joy this is! He who has purified us with the blood of Jesus will also cleanse us by the water of the Holy Spirit. God has said it, and so it must be, "You shall be clean."

Lord, we feel and mourn our uncleanness, and it is encouraging to be assured by your own mouth that we shall be clean. Oh, that you would make a speedy work of it!

He will deliver us from our worst sins. The uprisings of unbelief, the deceitful desires that war against the soul, the vile thoughts of pride, and the suggestions of Satan to blaspheme the sacred name—all these will be so purged away that they never return.

He will also cleanse us from all our idols, whether of gold or of clay— our impure loves, and our excessive love of that which in itself is pure. That which we have idolized will either be broken from us, or we from it.

It is God who speaks of what he himself will do. Therefore this word is established and sure. We may boldly look for that which it guarantees to us. Cleansing is a covenant blessing, and the covenant is "ordered in all things and secure" (2 Sam. 23:5).

OCTOBER 31

I shall not die, but I shall live,
and recount the deeds of the LORD.

Psalm 118:17

This is a lovely assurance! It was no doubt based on a promise, inwardly whispered in the psalmist's heart, which he seized on and enjoyed. Is my case like that of David? Am I depressed because the enemy insults me? Are there crowds against me and few on my side? Does unbelief exhort me to lie down and die in despair—a defeated, dishonored man? Have my enemies begun to dig my grave?

What then? Will I give in to the whisper of fear, and give up the battle, and with it give up all hope? Far from it. There is life in me yet: "I shall not die." Vigor will return and remove my weakness: "I shall live." The Lord lives, and I shall live too. My mouth will again be opened: "I shall . . . recount the deeds of the LORD." Yes, and I will speak of the present trouble as another instance of the wonder-working faithfulness and love of the Lord my God. Those who would gladly measure me for my coffin will have to wait a bit longer. For "the LORD has disciplined me severely, but he has not given me over to death" (Ps. 118:18). Glory be to his name forever! I am immortal until my work is done. Until the Lord decides, no burial vault can close over me.

NOVEMBER

NOVEMBER 1

He who calls you is faithful; he will surely do it.

1 Thessalonians 5:24

What will he do? He will sanctify us wholly. See the previous verse. He will carry on the work of purification until we are perfect in every part. He will preserve our "whole spirit and soul and body [to] be kept blameless at the coming of our Lord Jesus Christ" (1 Thess. 5:23). He will not allow us to fall from grace, nor come under the dominion of sin. What great favors these are! Well may we adore the Giver of such unspeakable gifts.

Who will do this? The Lord "who called you out of darkness into his marvelous light" (1 Pet. 2:9), out of death in sin into eternal life in Christ Jesus. Only he can do this; such perfection and preservation can only come from the God of all grace.

Why will he do it? Because he is "faithful"—faithful to his own promise which is committed to saving the believer; faithful to his Son, whose reward it is that his people will be presented to him faultless; faithful to the work which he has started in us by our effectual calling. It is not their own faithfulness, but the Lord's own faithfulness, on which the saints rely.

Come, my soul, here is a grand feast with which to begin a dull month. There may be fogs outside, but there should be sunshine within.

NOVEMBER 2

No good thing does he withhold
from those who walk uprightly.

Psalm 84:11

Many pleasing things the Lord may withhold, but "no good thing." He is the best judge of what is good for us. Some things are certainly good, and these we may have for the asking through Jesus Christ our Lord.

Holiness is a good thing, and this he will work in us freely. Victory over evil tendencies, strong tempers, and evil habits he will gladly grant, and we ought not to remain without it.

Full assurance he will give, and *close communion* with himself, and *access* into all truth, and plenty of *boldness* at the mercy seat. If we do not have these, it is because of a lack of faith to receive, and not from any unwillingness of God to give. "A calm and heavenly frame" (William Cowper), *great patience*, and *fervent love*—all these he will give to holy diligence.

But note well that we must "walk uprightly." There must be no cross purposes and crooked dealings; no hypocrisy nor deceit. If we walk in an unclean way, then God cannot give us favors, for that would be to reward sin. The way of uprightness is the way of heavenly wealth—wealth so large as to include every good thing.

What a promise to plead in prayer! Let us get to our knees.

NOVEMBER 3

For still the vision awaits its appointed time;
it hastens to the end—it will not lie.
If it seems slow, wait for it;
it will surely come; it will not delay.

Habakkuk 2:3

Mercy may seem slow, but it is sure. The Lord in unfailing wisdom has appointed a time for the outpourings of his gracious power, and God's time is the best time. We are in a hurry. The vision of the blessing excites our desire and hastens our longings. But the Lord will keep his appointments. He is never before his time; he is never behind.

God's word is spoken of here as a living thing that will speak and will come. It is never a dead letter, as we are tempted to fear when we have long awaited its fulfillment. The living word is on the way from the living God. And, though it may seem to linger, it is not doing so in reality. God's train is not late. It is only a matter of patience, and we will soon see for ourselves the faithfulness of the Lord. None of his promises will fail; "it will not lie." None of his promises will be lost in silence; "it shall speak" (Hab. 2:3 KJV). What comfort it will speak to the believing ear! No promise of his will need to be renewed like a bill which could not be paid when it fell due—"it will not delay."

Come, my soul, can you not wait for your God? Rest in him and be still in unutterable peacefulness.

NOVEMBER 4

And he said, "Thus says the Lord, 'I will make this
dry streambed full of pools.' For thus says the Lord,
'You shall not see wind or rain, but that streambed
shall be filled with water, so that you shall drink,
you, your livestock, and your animals.'"

2 Kings 3:16–17

Three armies were perishing of thirst, and the Lord intervened. Although
he sent neither cloud nor rain, yet he supplied an abundance of water.
He is not dependent on ordinary methods, but can surprise his people
with novelties of wisdom and power. Thus we are made to see more of
God than ordinary processes could reveal. Although the Lord may not
appear for us in the way we expect, or desire, or suppose, yet he will in
some way or other provide for us. It is a great blessing for our eyes to be
raised above secondary causes, so that we may gaze into the face of the
great First Cause.

Have we grace enough today to make trenches into which the divine
blessing may flow? Sadly, we too often fail to exhibit true and practical
faith. Today let us look out for answers to prayer. Like the child who went
to a meeting to pray for rain and took an umbrella with her, so let us truly
and practically expect the Lord to bless us. Let us make the valley full of
ditches and expect to see them all filled.

NOVEMBER 5

For I will not contend forever,
nor will I always be angry;
for the spirit would grow faint before me,
and the breath of life that I made.

Isaiah 57:16

Our heavenly Father seeks our instruction, not our destruction. He has a kind intention *toward* us when he contends *with* us. He will not always fight against us. We think the Lord's discipline takes a long time, but that is because our patience is short. His compassion endures forever, but not his contending. The night may drag its weary length along, but it must in the end give way to cheerful day. Just as God contends with us only for a limited period, so the wrath that leads to it is only for a small moment. The Lord loves his chosen too much to be always angry with them.

If he were to deal with us always as he does sometimes, then we should faint outright and go down without hope to the gates of death. Courage, dear heart! The Lord will soon end his rebukes. Bear up, for the Lord will bear you up and bear you through. He who made you knows how frail you are and how little you can bear. He will handle tenderly that which he has crafted so delicately. Therefore, do not be afraid because of the painful present, for it hastens to a happy future. He that struck you will heal you (Hos. 6:1). His little wrath will be followed by great mercies.

NOVEMBER 6

Delight yourself in the LORD,
and he will give you the desires of your heart.

Psalm 37:4

Delight in God has a transforming power. It lifts a person above the gross desires of our fallen nature. Delight in the Lord is not only sweet in itself, but it sweetens the whole soul until the longings of the heart become such that the Lord can safely promise to fulfill them. Is that not a grand delight that molds our desires until they are like the desires of God?

Our foolish way is to desire, and then set to work to accomplish what we desire. We do not go to work in God's way, which is to seek him first and then expect all things to be added to us (Luke 12:31). If we let our heart be filled with God until it runs over with delight, then the Lord himself will take care that we will not lack any good thing. Instead of looking around for joys, let us stay at home with God and drink waters out of our own fountain (Jer. 2:13). He can do for us far more than all our friends. It is better to be content with God alone than to go around fretting and pining for the paltry trifles of time and sense. For a while we may have disappointments. But if these bring us nearer to the Lord, they are things to be greatly prized. For in the end, they will secure for us the fulfillment of all our right desires.

NOVEMBER 7

The one who humbles himself will be exalted.

Luke 18:14

It ought not to be difficult for us to humble ourselves, for what have we to be proud of? We ought to take the lowest place without being told to do so. If we are sensible and honest, we will be little in our own eyes. Especially before the Lord in prayer, we will shrink to nothing. There we cannot speak of merit, for we have none. Our one and only appeal must be to mercy: "God, be merciful to me, a sinner!" (Luke 18:13).

Here is a cheering word from the throne. We will be exalted by the Lord if we humble ourselves. For us the way up is downhill. When we are stripped of self, we are clothed with humility, and this is the best garment. The Lord will exalt us in peace and happiness of mind. He will exalt us in knowledge of his Word and fellowship with himself. He will exalt us in the enjoyment of sure pardon and justification. The Lord puts his honors on those who can wear them to the honor of the Giver. He gives usefulness, acceptance, and influence to those who will not be puffed up by them, but will be humbled by a sense of greater responsibility. Neither God nor man will want to lift up a man who lifts up himself. But both God and good men unite to honor modest worth.

Oh, Lord, sink me in self that I may rise in you.

NOVEMBER 8

My grace is sufficient for you, for my
power is made perfect in weakness.

2 Corinthians 12:9

Our weakness should be prized because it makes room for divine strength.
We might never have known the power of grace if we had not felt the
weakness of nature. Blessed be the Lord for the thorn in the flesh and
the messenger of Satan when they drive us to the strength of God (2 Cor.
12:7).

This is a precious word from our Lord's own lips. It has made the
writer laugh for joy. God's grace enough for me! I should think it is. Is not
the sky enough for the bird, and the ocean enough for the fish? The All-
Sufficient is sufficient for my largest need. He who is sufficient for earth
and heaven is certainly able to meet the case of one poor worm like me.

Let us, then, fall back on our God and his grace. If he does not remove our grief, he will enable us to bear it. His strength will be poured
into us until the worm will conquer the mountains; and a nothing will
be victorious over all the high and mighty ones. It is better for us to have
God's strength than our own. For if we were a thousand times as strong
as we are, it would all amount to nothing in the face of the enemy. And
if we could be weaker than we are, which is scarcely possible, we could
nevertheless do all things through Christ.

NOVEMBER 9

And they shall know that I am the LORD their
God with them, and that they, the house of Israel,
are my people, declares the Lord GOD.

Ezekiel 34:30

To be the Lord's own people is a special blessing, but to know that we are such is a comforting blessing. It is one thing to *hope* that God is with us, and another thing to *know* that he is. Faith saves us, but assurance satisfies us. We take God to be our God when we believe in him. But we get the joy of him when we know that he is ours, and that we are his. No believer should be content with hoping and trusting. He should ask the Lord to lead him on to full assurance, so that matters of hope may become matters of certainty.

It is when we enjoy covenant blessings, and see our Lord Jesus has raised up for us "renowned plantations" (Ezek. 34:29), that we come to a clear knowledge of the favor of God toward us. It is not by law but by grace that we learn that we are the Lord's people. Let us always turn our eyes in the direction of free grace. Assurance of faith can never come by the works of the law. Assurance is a gospel virtue and can only reach us in a gospel way. Let us not look within. Let us look to the Lord alone. As we see Jesus, we will see our salvation.

Lord, send us such a flood tide of your love that we will be washed clean from the dirt of doubt and fear.

NOVEMBER 10

He will not let your foot be moved.

Psalm 121:3

If the Lord will not allow it, neither men nor devils can do it. How greatly would they rejoice if they could give us a disgraceful fall, drive us from our position, and bury us out of memory! They could do this to their heart's content were it not for one hindrance, and only one: the Lord will not let it happen. And if *he* "will not let" it, *we* will not suffer it.

The way of life is like traveling among the Alps. Along mountain paths one is constantly in danger of your foot slipping. Where the way is high the head tends to swim, and then the feet soon slide. There are spots that are as smooth as glass, and others that are rough with loose stones. In either of these a fall is hard to avoid. He who is enabled to keep himself upright and to walk without stumbling throughout life has the best of reasons for gratitude. What with pitfalls and snares, weak knees, weary feet, and devious enemies, no child of God would stand fast for an hour were it not for the faithful love that will not let his foot be moved.

Amidst a thousand snares I stand,
upheld and guarded by your hand.
That hand unseen shall hold me still,
and lead me to your holy hill.

Isaac Watts

NOVEMBER 11

For sin will have no dominion over you, since
you are not under law but under grace.

Romans 6:14

Sin will reign if it can. It cannot be satisfied with any place below the throne of the heart. We sometimes fear that it will conquer us, and then we cry to the Lord, "Let no iniquity get dominion over me" (Ps. 119:133). This is his comforting answer: "Sin will have no dominion over you." It may attack you, and even wound you. But it will never establish sovereignty over you.

If we were under the law, our sin would gather strength and hold us under its power. For it is through the punishment of sin that a person comes under the power of sin. As we are under the covenant of grace, we are secured against departing from the living God by the certain declaration of the covenant. Grace is promised to us, by which we are restored from our wanderings, cleansed from our impurities, and set free from the chains of habit.

We might lie down in despair and be content to serve the Egyptians (Ex. 14:12) if we were still like slaves working for eternal life. But since we are the Lord's free people, we take courage to fight against our corruptions and temptations. For we are assured that sin will never bring us under its sway again. God himself "gives us the victory through our Lord Jesus Christ" (1 Cor. 15:57), to whom be glory forever and ever. Amen.

NOVEMBER 12

My people shall be satisfied with my goodness,
declares the LORD.

Jeremiah 31:14

Note the "my" which comes twice: "*My* people shall be satisfied with *my* goodness." The kind of people who are satisfied with God are marked out as God's own. He is pleased with them, for they are pleased with him. They call him their God, and he calls them his people. He is satisfied to take them as his inheritance, and they are satisfied with him as their inheritance. There is a mutual communion of delight between God's Israel and Israel's God.

These people are satisfied. This is a grand thing. Very few of the sons of men are ever satisfied, whatever their circumstances may be. They have swallowed the leech, and it continually cries, "Give! Give!" (see Prov. 30:15 KJV). Only sanctified souls are satisfied souls. God himself must both convert us and content us.

It is no wonder that the Lord's people are satisfied with the goodness of their Lord. Here is goodness without corruption, bounty without restraint, mercy without rebuke, love without change, favor without reserve. If God's goodness does not satisfy us, what will? What! Are we still groaning? Surely there is a wrong desire within us if it is one that God's goodness does not satisfy.

Lord, I am satisfied. Blessed be your name.

NOVEMBER 13

Behold, he who keeps Israel
will neither slumber nor sleep.

Psalm 121:4

The Lord is "the Keeper of Israel." No form of unconsciousness ever steals over him, not deep slumber nor light sleep. He never fails to watch the houses and the hearts of his people. This is a sufficient reason for us to rest in perfect peace. Alexander the Great said that he slept because his friend Parmenio watched. How much more may we sleep because our God is our guard.

"Behold" is set up here to call our attention to the comforting truth. Jacob, when he had a stone for his pillow, fell asleep (Gen. 28:11). But his God was awake and came in a vision to his servant. When we lie defenseless, the Lord himself will cover our head.

The Lord keeps his people as a rich man keeps his treasure, as a captain keeps a city with a garrison, as a sentry keeps watch over his sovereign. No one can harm those who are kept in this way. Let me put my soul into his dear hands. He never forgets us, never ceases actively to care for us, never finds himself unable to preserve us.

Oh, my Lord, keep me, in case I wander and fall and perish. Keep me, that I may keep your commandments. By your unslumbering care prevent my sleeping like the sluggard and perishing like those who sleep the sleep of death.

NOVEMBER 14

If you ask me anything in my name, I will do it.

John 14:14

What a wide promise! Anything! Whether large or small, all my needs are covered by that word "anything." Come, my soul, be free at the mercy seat and hear your Lord saying to you, "Open your mouth wide, and I will fill it" (Ps. 81:10).

What a wise promise! We are always to ask in the name of Jesus. While this encourages *us*, it also honors *him*. This is a constant plea. Occasionally every other basis for our pleas is darkened, especially those we draw from our own relation to God or our experience of his grace. But at such times the name of Jesus is as mighty at the throne as ever, and we may plead it with full assurance.

What an instructive prayer! I may not ask for anything to which I cannot put Christ's hand and seal. I dare not use my Lord's name for a selfish or willful petition. I may only use my Lord's name for prayers that he himself would pray if he were in my situation. It is a high privilege to be authorized to ask in the name of Jesus as if Jesus himself asked. But our love for him will never allow us to put that name where he would not have put it.

Am I asking for that which Jesus approves? Dare I put his seal to my prayer? Then I have that which I seek from the Father.

My God will supply every need of yours according
to his riches in glory in Christ Jesus.

Philippians 4:19

Paul's God is our God and will supply all our needs. Paul felt sure of this
in reference to the Philippians, and we feel sure of it for ourselves. God
will do it, for it is like him: he loves us, he delights to bless us, and it will
glorify him to do so. His compassion, his power, his love, his faithfulness,
all work together to ensure we are not famished.

What a measure the Lord uses: "according to his riches in glory in
Christ Jesus." The riches of his grace are large, but what will we say about
the riches of his glory? And who will come up with an estimate of "his
riches in glory in Christ Jesus"? According to this immeasurable measure
will God fill up the immense abyss of our needs. He makes the Lord Jesus
the receptacle and the channel of his fullness, and then he imparts to us
his wealth of love in its highest form. Hallelujah!

The writer knows what it is to be tested in the work of the Lord.
Faithfulness has been rewarded with anger, and generous givers have
canceled their contributions. But he whom they sought to oppress has not
been one penny the poorer. Instead, he has been richer. For this promise
has been true, "My God will supply every need." God's supplies are surer
than any bank.

NOVEMBER 16

No weapon that is fashioned against you shall succeed,
and you shall refute every tongue that
rises against you in judgment.

Isaiah 54:17

There is great clatter in the forges and blacksmiths of the enemy. They are making weapons with which to strike the saints. They could not even do this much if the Lord of saints did not allow them, for he created the smith who blows the coals in the fire. But see how busily they labor! How many swords and spears they fashion! It matters nothing. For on the blade of every weapon you may read this inscription: *It shall not succeed.*

But now listen to another noise. It is the chatter of tongues. Tongues are more terrible instruments than those that are made with hammers and anvils. The evil which they inflict cuts deeper and spreads wider. What will become of us now? Slander, falsehood, insinuation, ridicule—these are poisoned arrows. How can we meet them? The Lord God promises us that, if we cannot silence them, we will at least escape from being ruined by them. They condemn us for the moment. But we will condemn them in the end, and forever. The mouth of those who speak lies will be stopped, and their falsehoods will be turned to the honor of those good people who suffered by them.

NOVEMBER 17

For the LORD will not forsake his people;
he will not abandon his heritage.

Psalm 94:14

No, and he will not even "forsake" just one of them. Man has his cast-offs, but God has none. For his choice is unchangeable, and his love is everlasting. No one can find a single person whom God has forsaken after having revealed himself to save them.

This grand truth is mentioned in the psalm to comfort the heart of the afflicted. The Lord disciplines his own, but he never forsakes them. The result of the double work of the law and the rod is our instruction. And the fruit of that instruction is a calmness of spirit, a soberness of mind, from which comes rest. The ungodly are left alone until the pit is dug into which they will fall and are taken. But the godly are sent to school to be prepared for their glorious destiny to come. Judgment will return and finish its work on the rebels. But it will equally return to vindicate the sincere and godly. Therefore we may bear the rod of discipline with calm submission. It does not mean anger, but love.

God may chasten and correct,
but he never can neglect;
may in faithfulness reprove,
but he ne'er can cease to love.

Anonymous

NOVEMBER 18

On that day the LORD will protect the inhabitants of
Jerusalem, so that the feeblest among them on that day
shall be like David, and the house of David shall be like
God, like the angel of the LORD, going before them.

Zechariah 12:8

One of the best methods the Lord uses to defend his people is to make
them strong with inner might. People are better than walls, and faith is
stronger than castles.

The Lord can take the feeblest among us and make him like David,
the champion of Israel. Lord, do this with me! Infuse your power into me
and fill me with sacred courage that I may face the giant with sling and
stone, confident in God (1 Samuel 17).

The Lord can make his greatest champions far mightier than they
are. David can be like God, like the angel of the Lord. This would be a
marvelous development, but it is possible, or it would not be spoken of.
Oh, Lord, work in this way with the best of our leaders! Show us what
you are able to do—namely, to raise your faithful servants to a height of
grace and holiness that will be clearly supernatural!

Lord, live in your saints, and they will be like God. Put your power
into them, and they will be like the living creatures who dwell in the presence of the Lord. Fulfill this promise for your entire church in this our
day, for Jesus's sake. Amen.

NOVEMBER 19

From this day on I will bless you.

Haggai 2:19

Future things are hidden from us. Yet here is a mirror in which we may see the years still to come. The Lord says, "From this day on I will bless you."

It is worthwhile noting the day that is referred to in this promise. There had been failures of crops, blighting, and mildew—and all because of the people's sin. Now the Lord saw these disciplined people commencing to obey his word and build his temple. And therefore he says, "Since the day that the foundation of the LORD's temple was laid, consider. . . . From this day on I will bless you" (Hag. 2:18–19). If we have lived in any sin and the Spirit leads us to purge ourselves of it, then we may count on the blessing of the Lord. His smile, his Spirit, his grace, his fuller revelation of his truth, will all prove to be an enlarged blessing for us. We may fall into greater opposition from people because of our faithfulness, but we will rise to closer relations with the Lord our God, and a clearer sight of our acceptance in him.

Lord, I am resolved to be more true to you, and more exact as I follow your doctrine and your commands. And I pray, therefore, by Christ Jesus, to increase the blessing of my daily life from now on and forever.

NOVEMBER 20

For he satisfies the longing soul,
and the hungry soul he fills with good things.

Psalm 107:9

It is good to have longings, and the more intense they are, the better. The Lord will satisfy soul-longings, however great and all-absorbing they may be. Let us greatly long, for God will greatly give. We are never in a right state of mind when we are content with ourselves and are free from longings. Desires for more grace, and groanings that cannot be uttered, are growing pains, and we should wish to feel them more and more.

Blessed Spirit, make us sigh and cry after better things, and for more of the best things!

Hunger is by no means a pleasant sensation. Yet "blessed are those who hunger and thirst for righteousness" (Matt. 5:6). Such persons will not only have their hunger relieved with a little food, but they will be satisfied. They will not be satisfied with any sort of rough food, but their diet will be worthy of their good Lord. For they will be filled with goodness by the Lord himself.

Come, let us not worry because we long and hunger. But let us hear the voice of the psalmist as he also longs and hungers to see God magnified. "Let them thank the Lord for his steadfast love, for his wondrous works to the children of man!" (Ps. 107:8, 31).

NOVEMBER 21

Turn to me and be saved,
all the ends of the earth!
For I am God, and there is no other.

Isaiah 45:22

This is a promise of promises. It lies at the foundation of our spiritual life. Salvation comes through turning to look to him who is "a righteous God and a Savior" (Isa. 45:21). How simple is the direction! "Turn to me." How reasonable is the requirement! Surely the creature should turn toward the Creator. We have looked elsewhere long enough. It is time to look alone to him who invites our expectation and promises to give us his salvation.

Only a look! Will we not turn to look at once? We are to bring nothing in ourselves, but to look outward and upward to our Lord on his throne, to where he has gone up from the cross. A look requires no preparation, no vigorous effort. It needs neither wit nor wisdom, wealth nor strength. All that we need is in the Lord our God. If we turn to him for everything, that everything will be ours, and we will be saved.

Come, far-off ones, look to him! All the ends of the earth, turn your eyes this way! Men from the furthest regions of the world may see the sun and enjoy his light. In the same way, you who lie in death's borders at the very gates of hell may by a look receive the light of God, the life of heaven. You may receive the salvation of the Lord Jesus Christ, who is God, and therefore able to save.

NOVEMBER 22

In those days and in that time, declares the LORD,
iniquity shall be sought in Israel, and there shall be
none, and sin in Judah, and none shall be found, for
I will pardon those whom I leave as a remnant.

Jeremiah 50:20

A glorious word indeed! What a perfect pardon is promised here to the sinful nations of Israel and Judah! Sin is to be so removed that it cannot be found; so blotted out that there will be none left. Glory be to the God of pardons!

Satan seeks out sins with which to accuse us. Our enemies seek them that they may add them to our account. And our own conscience seeks them with a morbid eagerness. But when the Lord applies the precious blood of Jesus, we fear no form of search. For "there shall be none" and "none shall be found." The Lord has caused the sins of his people to cease to be. He has finished the transgression and put an end to sin (Dan. 9:24). The sacrifice of Jesus has "cast all our sins into the depths of the sea" (Mic. 7:19). This makes us dance for joy.

The reason for the obliteration of sin lies in the fact that the Lord himself pardons his chosen ones. His word of grace is not only royal but divine. He speaks absolution, and we are absolved. He applies the atonement, and from that moment his people are beyond all fear of condemnation. Blessed be the name of the sin-annihilating God!

NOVEMBER 23

The LORD your God will clear away these
nations before you little by little.

Deuteronomy 7:22

We are not to expect to win victories for the Lord Jesus with a single blow. Evil principles and practices die hard. In some places it takes years of labor to drive out even one of the many vices which defile the inhabitants. We must carry on the war with all our might, even when favored with little obvious success.

Our business in this world is to conquer it for Jesus. We are not to make compromises but to exterminate evils. We are not to seek popularity but to wage unceasing war against iniquity. Infidelity, heresy, drunkenness, impurity, oppression, worldliness, error—all these we are to "clear away."

Only the Lord our God can accomplish this. He works through his faithful servants. And—blessed be his name—he promises that he will work in this way. "The LORD your God will clear away these nations before you." He will do this by degrees, that we may learn perseverance, may increase in faith, may earnestly watch, and may avoid fleshly security. Let us thank God for a little success and pray for more. Let us never put away the sword until the whole land is won for Jesus.

Courage, my heart! Go on little by little, for many "littles" will make a great whole.

NOVEMBER 24

He will not always chide,
nor will he keep his anger forever.
Psalm 103:9

He will sometimes chide, or he would not be a wise Father to such poor wayward children as we are. His discipline is very painful to those who are true, because they feel how sadly they deserve it, and how wrong it is on their part to grieve him. We know what this chiding means, and we bow before the Lord, mourning that we should cause him to be angry with us.

But what a comfort we find in these lines! "Not always" will he chide. If we repent and turn to him with hearts broken *for* sin and broken *from* sin, he will smile on us at once. He takes no pleasure in turning a frowning face toward those whom he loves with all his heart. It is his joy that our joy should be full.

Come, let us seek his face. There is no reason for despair, nor even for despondency. Let us love a chiding God, and before long we will sing: "Your anger turned away, that you might comfort me" (Isa. 12:1). Go away, dark misgivings, the ravens of the soul! Come in, humble hopes and grateful memories, the doves of the heart! He who pardoned us long ago as a judge will again forgive us as a father. And we will rejoice in his sweet, unchanging love.

Who are you, O great mountain? Before Zerubbabel
you shall become a plain. And he shall bring forward
the top stone amid shouts of "Grace, grace to it!"

Zechariah 4:7

At this hour a mountain of difficulty, distress, or necessity may be in our way. Natural reason sees no path over it, or through it, or round it. Let faith come in, and immediately the mountain disappears and becomes a plain. But faith must first hear the word of the Lord: "Not by might, nor by power, but by my Spirit, says the LORD of hosts" (Zech. 4:6). This grand truth is a prime necessity for meeting the insurmountable trials of life.

I see that I can do nothing, and that all reliance on man is meaningless. "Not by might." I see that no visible means can be relied on, but the power is in the invisible Spirit. God alone must work, and men and means must be reckoned as nothing. If the Almighty God takes up the concerns of his people, then great mountains are nothing. He can remove worlds as children throw balls about, or kick them with their foot. This power he can lend to me. If the Lord tells me to move an Alpine peak, I can do it through his name. It may be a great mountain, but even before my feebleness it will become a plain; for the Lord has said it. What can I be afraid of with God on my side?

NOVEMBER 26

Your sorrow will turn into joy.

John 16:20

Their particular sorrow was the death and absence of their Lord. And it was turned into joy when he rose from the dead and showed himself to them. All the sorrows of saints will be transformed in this way—even the worst of them that look as if they must remain fountains of bitterness forever.

Then the more sorrow the more joy. If we have loads of sorrow, then the Lord's power will turn them into tons of joy. The more bitter the trouble, then the sweeter the pleasure. The swinging of the pendulum far to the left will cause it to go all the more to the right. The memory of the grief will heighten the flavor of the delight. We will set the one in contrast with the other, and the brilliance of the diamond will be seen more clearly because of the black foil behind it.

Come, my heart, cheer up! In a little while I will be as glad as I am now gloomy. Jesus tells me that by a heavenly alchemy my sorrow will be turned to joy. I do not see how this will be, but I believe it, and I begin to sing in anticipation. This depression of spirit is not for long. I will soon be up among the happy ones who praise the Lord day and night. And there I will sing of the mercy which delivered me out of great afflictions.

And he said, "My presence will go with
you, and I will give you rest."

Exodus 33:14

Precious promise! Lord, enable me to make it all my own.

We must go at certain times from our home, for here on earth "we have no lasting city" (Heb. 13:14). It often happens that when we feel most at home in a place, we are suddenly called away from it. Here is the antidote for this sorrow. The Lord himself will keep us company. His presence, which includes his favor, his fellowship, his care, and his power, will always be with us in every one of our journeys. This means far more than it says, for in fact it means all things. If God is present with us, then we possess heaven and earth.

Go with me, Lord, and then command me where you will!

But we hope to find a place of rest. The text promises it. We are to have a rest that is God's own giving, making, and preserving. His presence will cause us to rest even when we are on the march, yes, even in the midst of battle. *Rest*—what rich blessing it is! Can it ever be enjoyed by mortal beings? Yes, there is the promise, and by faith we plead it. Rest comes from the Comforter, from the Prince of Peace, and from the glorious Father who rested on the seventh day from all his works. To be with God is to rest in the most emphatic sense.

NOVEMBER 28

The LORD will command the blessing on you in
your barns and in all that you undertake.

Deuteronomy 28:8

If we obey the Lord our God, then he will bless that which he gives us.
Riches are no curse when blessed by the Lord. When men have more
than they require for their immediate needs, and begin to lay up stores in
barns, the dry rot of covetousness or the blight of hard-heartedness tends
to follow the accumulation. But with God's blessing it is not so. Prudence
arranges the saving, generosity directs the spending, gratitude maintains
consecration, and praise sweetens enjoyment. It is a great mercy to have
God's blessing in one's iron safe and in one's bank account.

What a favor is given to us by the last clause! "The LORD will command the blessing . . . in all that you undertake." We would not undertake anything on which we dare not ask God's blessing; neither would
we go about it without prayer and faith. But what a privilege to be able
to look for the Lord's help in every enterprise! Some talk of a lucky
man—the blessing of the Lord is better than luck. The support of great
people is nothing compared to the favor of God. Self-reliance is all very
well, but the Lord's blessing is infinitely more than all the fruit of talent,
genius, or tact.

NOVEMBER 29

Whoever believes will not be in haste.

Isaiah 28:16

They will make haste to keep the Lord's commandments. But they will not make haste in any impatient or improper sense.

They will not be in a hurry to run away, for they will not be overcome with the fear which causes panic. When others are flying here and there as if their wits had failed them, believers will be quiet, calm, and deliberate. And so they will be able to act wisely in the hour of testing.

They will not be in a hurry with their expectations, craving their good things at once and on the spot. Instead they will wait for God's time. Some are in a desperate hurry to have the bird in the hand; for they regard the Lord's promise as a bird in the bush, that is, not likely to be theirs. Believers know how to wait.

They will not be in a hurry to plunge into wrong or questionable actions. Unbelief must be doing something, and thus its works are its own undoing. But faith makes no more haste than good speed. And so it is not forced to go back sorrowfully along the way that it followed carelessly.

What about me? Am I believing, and am I therefore keeping to the believer's pace, which is walking with God? Be at peace, fluttering spirit! Oh, rest in the Lord, and wait patiently for him! Heart, see that you do this at once!

NOVEMBER 30

It is the LORD who goes before you. He will
be with you; he will not leave you or forsake
you. Do not fear or be dismayed.

Deuteronomy 31:8

In the presence of a great work or a great warfare, here is a text which should help us to buckle on our harness. If the Lord himself goes before us, it must be safe to follow. Who can obstruct our progress if the Lord himself is in the lead? Come, fellow soldiers, let us make a prompt advance! Why do we hesitate to press on toward victory?

Nor is the Lord only ahead of us; he is also with us. Above, beneath, around, within is the omnipotent, omnipresent One. In all time, even on to eternity, he will be with us just as he has been. How this should nerve our arm! Press forward at it boldly, soldiers of the cross, for the Lord of hosts is with us!

Being before us and with us, he will never withdraw his help. He cannot fail in himself, and he will not fail toward us. He will continue to help us according to our need, right to the end. As he cannot fail us, so he will not forsake us. He will always be both able and willing to grant us strength and help until our fighting days are over.

Let us not fear nor be dismayed. For the Lord of hosts will go down to the battle with us. He will bear the brunt of the fight and give us the victory.

DECEMBER

DECEMBER 1

Whoever walks in integrity walks securely.

Proverbs 10:9

His walk may be slow, but it is sure. He that hurries to be rich will not be innocent nor sure. But steady perseverance in integrity, even if it does not bring riches, will certainly bring peace. In doing that which is just and right, we are like one walking on a rock, for we have confidence that every step we take is on solid and safe ground. On the other hand, the highest success through questionable transactions must always be hollow and treacherous. The man who has gained it must always be afraid that a day of reckoning will come, and then his gains will condemn him.

Let us stick to truth and righteousness. By God's grace let us imitate our Lord and Master, in whose mouth no deceit was ever found (1 Pet. 2:22). Let us not be afraid of being poor, nor of being treated with contempt. Never, on any account whatever, let us do that which our conscience cannot justify. If we lose inward peace, we lose more than money can buy. If we keep in the Lord's own way, and never sin against our conscience, our way is sure against all comers. Who can harm us if we are followers of that which is good? We may be thought fools by fools if we are firm in our integrity, but in the place where judgment is infallible, we will be approved.

DECEMBER 2

I have set the LORD always before me;
because he is at my right hand, I shall not be shaken.

Psalm 16:8

This is the way to live. With God always before us, we will have the noblest companionship, the holiest example, the sweetest consolation, and the mightiest influence. This must be a resolute act of the mind: "I have set." It must be maintained as a set and settled thing. Always to have an eye to the Lord's eye, and an ear for the Lord's voice—this is the right state for the godly person. His God is near him, filling the horizon of his vision, leading the way of his life, and furnishing the theme of his meditation. What vanities we should avoid, what sins we should overcome, what virtues we should exhibit, what joys we should experience if we did indeed set the Lord always before us! Why not?

This is the way to be safe. When the Lord is always in our minds, we come to feel safe and certain because he is so near. He is at our right hand to guide and aid us. And so we are not shaken by fear, nor force, nor fraud, nor fickleness. When God stands at a person's right hand, that person is sure to stand. Come on, then, opponents of the truth! Rush against me like a furious tempest if you want. God upholds me. God remains with me. "Whom shall I fear?" (Ps. 27:1).

DECEMBER 3

I will make with them a covenant of peace and banish
wild beasts from the land, so that they may dwell
securely in the wilderness and sleep in the woods.

Ezekiel 34:25

It is the height of grace that the Lord should be in covenant with human-ity—feeble, sinful, and dying creatures. Yet the Lord has solemnly entered into a faithful contract with us, and from that covenant he will never turn aside. Because of this covenant we are safe. Just as lions and wolves are driven away by shepherds, so will all noxious influences be chased away. The Lord will give us rest from disturbers and destroyers. The wild, evil beasts will be banished from the land.

Oh, Lord, make good your promise even now!

The Lord's people are to enjoy security in places of greatest exposure: wildernesses and woods are to be like pastures and folds to the flock of Christ. If the Lord does not change the place for the better, he will make us the better in the place. The wilderness is not a place to dwell in, but the Lord can make it so. In the woods one feels bound to watch rather than to sleep. Yet the Lord gives his beloved sleep even there. Nothing outside or within should cause any fear to the child of God. By faith the wilderness can become the suburbs of heaven, and the woods the hallway of glory.

DECEMBER 4

He will cover you with his pinions,
and under his wings you will find refuge;
his faithfulness is a shield and buckler.

Psalm 91:4

A gracious simile indeed! Just as a hen protects her brood and allows them to nestle under her wings, so the Lord will defend his people and let them hide away in him. Have we not seen the little chicks peeping out from under the mother's feathers? Have we not heard their little cries of contented joy? In this way let us shelter ourselves in our God and feel overflowing peace in knowing that he is guarding us.

While the Lord covers us, we trust. It would be strange if we did not. How can we distrust when the Lord himself becomes house and home, refuge and rest to us?

This done, we go out to war in his name and enjoy the same guardian care. We need a shield and buckler, and when we implicitly trust God, even as the chick trusts the hen, we find his truth arming us from head to foot. The Lord cannot lie; he must be faithful to his people; his promise must stand. This sure truth is all the shield we need. Behind it we defy the flaming darts of the enemy (Eph. 6:16).

Come, my soul, hide under those great wings; lose yourself among those soft feathers! How happy you are!

DECEMBER 5

He will dwell on the heights;
his place of defense will be the fortresses of rocks;
his bread will be given him; his water will be sure.

Isaiah 33:16

The person to whom God has given grace to live a blameless life dwells in perfect security.

He dwells on the heights above the world, out of gunshot of the enemy and near to heaven. He has high aims and motives, and he finds high comforts and company. He rejoices in the mountains of eternal love, where he is at home.

He is defended by fortresses of stupendous rock. The firmest things in the universe are the promises and purposes of the unchanging God. And these are the safeguard of the obedient believer.

He is provided for by this great promise: "His bread will be given him." As the enemy cannot climb the fort, nor break down the defenses, so the fortress cannot be captured by siege and famine. The Lord, who rained manna in the wilderness (Exodus 16), will keep his people with good stores even when they are surrounded by those who would starve them.

But what if water should fail? That cannot be: "His water will be sure." There is a never-failing well within the impregnable fortress. The Lord sees that nothing is lacking. No one can touch the citizen of the true Zion. However fierce the enemy, the Lord will preserve his chosen.

DECEMBER 6

When you pass through the waters, I will be with you;
and through the rivers, they shall not overwhelm you;
when you walk through fire you shall not be burned,
and the flame shall not consume you.

Isaiah 43:2

There is no bridge. We must go through the waters and feel the rush of the rivers. The presence of God in the flood is better than a ferryboat. We must be tried, but we will be triumphant. For the Lord himself, who is mightier than many waters, will be with us. Even though it sometimes feels as if God is absent, the Lord will surely be with us in difficulties and dangers. The sorrows of life may rise to extraordinary heights, but the Lord is equal to every occasion.

The enemies of God can put in our way dangers of their own making, namely, persecutions and cruel mocking. These are like a burning, fiery furnace. What then? We will walk through the fires. Because God is with us, we will not be burned. Indeed, not even the smell of fire will remain upon us (Dan. 3:27).

Oh, the wonderful security of the heaven-born and heaven-bound pilgrim! Floods cannot drown him, nor fires burn him.

Your presence, oh, Lord, is the protection of your saints from the varied dangers of the road. Look on me; in faith I commit myself to you, and my spirit enters into rest.

DECEMBER 7

May the LORD give strength to his people!
May the LORD bless his people with peace!

Psalm 29:11

David had just heard the voice of the Lord in a thunderstorm and had seen his power in the hurricane whose path he had described (Ps. 29:3–9). Now in the cool calm after the storm, that overwhelming power by which heaven and earth are shaken is promised to be the strength of the chosen. He who sends the thunderbolt winging with unerring accuracy will give to his redeemed the wings of eagles. He who shakes the earth with his voice will terrify the enemies of his saints and give his children peace. Why are we weak when we have divine strength to flee to? Why are we troubled when the Lord's own peace is ours? Jesus, the mighty God, is our strength. Let us put him on and go out to our service. Jesus, our blessed Lord, is also our peace. Let us rest in him today, and end our fears. What a blessing to have him for our strength and peace both now and forever!

The same God who rides on the storm in days of tempest will also rule the hurricane of our troubles and, before long, send us days of peace. We will have strength for storms, and songs for fair weather. Let us begin to sing at once to God, our strength and our peace. Away, dark thoughts! Up, faith and hope!

DECEMBER 8

If anyone serves me, he must follow me; and
where I am, there will my servant be also. If
anyone serves me, the Father will honor him.

John 12:26

The highest service is imitation. If I would be Christ's servant, I must be his follower. To do as Jesus did is the surest way to bring honor to his name. Let me keep this in mind every day.

If I imitate Jesus, I will have his company. If I am like him, then I will be with him. In due course he will take me up to live with him above, if I have tried to follow him here below in the meantime. After his suffering, our Lord came to his throne. In the same way, after we have suffered a while with him here below, we also will arrive in glory. The pattern of our Lord's life will be the pattern of ours. If we are with him in his humiliation, then we will be with him in his glory. Come, my soul, pluck up courage and put down your feet in the blood-soaked footprints that your Lord has left you.

Do not let me fail to notice that the Father will honor those who follow his Son. If he sees me true to Jesus, then he will put marks of favor and honor on me for his Son's sake. No honor can be like this. Princes and emperors bestow the mere shadows of honor; the substance of glory comes from the Father. Therefore, my soul, cling you to your Lord Jesus more closely than ever.

DECEMBER 9

And Jesus said to him, "'If you can'! All things
are possible for one who believes."

Mark 9:23

Our unbelief is the greatest obstacle in our way. In fact, there is no other real difficulty for our spiritual progress and prosperity. The Lord can do everything. But when he makes a rule that, according to our faith so will it be to us, then our unbelief ties the hands of his omnipotence.

Yes, the allies of evil will be scattered if we can only believe. The truth which the world so despises will nevertheless lift its head if we can only have confidence in the God of truth. We can bear a whole load of trouble and pass uninjured through the waves of distress if we first prepare for action by buckling on the belt of peace with the hands of trust.

What! Can we not believe? Is everything possible except believing in God? Yet he is always true. Why do we not believe him? He is always faithful to his word. Why can we not trust him? When we are in a right state of heart, faith involves no effort. It is then as natural for us to rely on God as for a child to trust its father.

The worst of it is that we can believe God about everything except the present pressing trouble. This is folly. Come, my soul, shake off such sinfulness, and trust your God with the load, the labor, the longing of this moment. This done, all is done.

DECEMBER 10

But if you carefully obey his voice and do all that
I say, then I will be an enemy to your enemies
and an adversary to your adversaries.

Exodus 23:22

The Lord Christ in the midst of his people is to be acknowledged and obeyed. He is the vice-regent of God, and speaks in the Father's name. It is for us implicitly and immediately to do as he commands. We will lose the promise if we disregard the command.

How large the blessing promised to full obedience! The Lord enters into an alliance with his people, offensive and defensive. He will bless those who bless us, and curse those who curse us. God will go heart and soul with his people, and enter in deepest sympathy into their position. What a protection this gives us! We need not concern ourselves about our adversaries when we are assured that they have become the adversaries of God. If the Lord has taken up our quarrel, then we may leave the enemy in his hands.

So far as our own interest is concerned, we have no enemies. But for the cause of truth and righteousness we take up arms and enter into conflict. In this sacred war we are allied with the eternal God. And, if we carefully obey the law of our Lord Jesus, he is committed to extend all his power on our behalf. Therefore we fear no man.

DECEMBER 11

Trust in the LORD, and do good;
dwell in the land and befriend faithfulness.

Psalm 37:3

"Trust" and "do" are words that go well together, in the order that the Holy Spirit has placed them. We should have faith, and that faith should work. Trust in God leads us on to holy doing. We trust God for good, and then we do good. We do not sit still because we trust. Instead, we rouse ourselves, and expect the Lord to work through us and by us. It is not ours to worry and do evil, but to trust and do good. We neither trust without doing, nor do without trusting.

Enemies would root us out if they could. But by trusting and doing, we dwell in the land. We will not go into Egypt, but we will remain in Immanuel's land—the providence of God, the Canaan of covenant love. We are not so easy to get rid of as the Lord's enemies suppose. They cannot thrust us out, nor stamp us out. Where God has given us a name and a place, there we remain.

But what about the supply of our needs? The Lord will surely provide for those who dwell within his care. Their role is to trust and to do; the Lord's role is to do according to their trust. If not fed by ravens, or fed by an Obadiah, or fed by a widow, even so they shall be fed somehow (1 Kings 17:6, 15–16; 18:4). Away, oh, fears!

DECEMBER 12

In quietness and in trust shall be your strength.

Isaiah 30:15

It is always a weakness to be fretting and worrying, questioning and mistrusting. What can we do if we wear ourselves down to skin and bone? Can we gain anything by fearing and fuming? Do we not make ourselves unfit for action and unhinge our minds for wise decision making? We are sinking by our struggles when we might float by faith.

Oh, for grace to be quiet! Why run from house to house to repeat the weary story that makes our hearts more and more sick every time we tell it? Why stay at home to cry out in agony because of wretched, foreboding thoughts that may never be fulfilled? It would be good to have a quiet tongue, but it would be far better to have a quiet heart. Oh, to be still and know that the Lord is God (Ps. 46:10)!

Oh, for grace to trust in God! The Holy One of Israel must defend and deliver his own people. He cannot run back from his solemn declarations. We can be sure that his every word will stand, though the mountains should depart (Isa. 54:10). He deserves to be confided in. And if we display trust and therefore quietness, we will be as happy as the spirits before the throne.

Come, my soul, return to your rest, and lean your head on the breast of the Lord Jesus.

DECEMBER 13

At evening time there shall be light.

Zechariah 14:7

It is a surprise that it should be so. For at evening time all things threaten to make it dark. Yet God has a tendency to work in a way that is far above our fears and beyond our hopes. As a result, we are greatly amazed and are led to praise his sovereign grace. No, what happens to us will not be what our hearts were predicting: the dark will not deepen into midnight, but it will suddenly brighten into day. Never let us despair. In the worst times let us trust in the Lord who "turns deep darkness into the morning" (Amos 5:8). It is when the task of making bricks gets harder that Moses appears (Exodus 5), and it is when troubles abound that the end is nearest.

This promise should assist our patience. The light may not fully come until our hopes are almost gone as a result of waiting all day to no purpose. To the wicked, the sun goes down while it is still day. To the righteous, the sun rises when it is almost night. May we not with patience wait for that heavenly light, which may be long in coming, but is sure to prove well worth waiting for?

Come, my soul, take up your song and sing to him who will bless you in life and in death, in a manner surpassing anything that nature at its best has ever seen.

DECEMBER 14

And he who was seated on the throne said,
"Behold, I am making all things new."

Revelation 21:5

Glory be to his name! All things need making new, for they are sadly battered and worn by sin. It is time that the old clothing was rolled up and laid aside, and that creation put on her Sunday suit. But no one else can make all things new except the Lord who first made them. For it needs as much power to make out of evil as to make out of nothing. Our Lord Jesus has undertaken the task, and he is fully competent to complete it. He has already started his labor, and for centuries he has persevered in making new the hearts of people and the order of society. Eventually he will make new the whole constitution of human government, and human nature will be changed by his grace. There will come a day when the body will be made new and raised like his glorious body.

What a joy to belong to a kingdom in which everything is being made new by the power of its King! We are not dying out; we are speeding on toward a more glorious life. Despite the opposition of the powers of evil, our glorious Lord Jesus is accomplishing his purpose. He is making us, and all things about us, "*new.*" He is making us as full of beauty as when they first came from the hand of the Lord.

DECEMBER 15

And they shall beat their swords into plowshares,
and their spears into pruning hooks;
nation shall not lift up sword against nation,
neither shall they learn war anymore.

Isaiah 2:4

Oh, that these happy times would come! At present the nations are heavily armed and are inventing more and more terrible weapons. It is as if the chief end of man is the destruction of thousands of his fellow human beings. Yet one day peace will prevail. Indeed, it will so prevail that the tools of destruction shall be beaten into other shapes and used for better purposes.

How will this come about? By trade? By civilization? By arbitration? We do not believe it. Past experience prevents us trusting in such feeble means. Peace will be established only by the reign of the Prince of Peace. He must teach people by his Spirit, renew their hearts by his grace, and reign over them by his supreme power. Only then will they cease to wound and kill. Man is a monster once his blood is up, and only the Lord Jesus can turn this lion into a lamb. By changing our hearts, our bloodthirsty passions are removed.

Let every reader of this book of promises offer a special prayer today to the Lord and Giver of peace. Pray that he would soon put an end to war and establish harmony over the whole world.

DECEMBER 16

You shall drive out the Canaanites, though they have
chariots of iron, and though they are strong.

Joshua 17:18

To be assured of victory is a great encouragement to be courageous. For
then a person goes out to war with confidence and ventures where otherwise they would have been afraid to go. Our warfare is with the evil
within us and around us. And we ought to be persuaded that we can get
the victory, and that we will do so in the name of the Lord Jesus. We are
not riding for a fall, but to win; and win we will. The grace of God in
its omnipotence is sent out to overthrow evil in every form—hence the
certainty of triumph.

Some of our sins are like chariots of iron in our constitution, our former habits, our associations, and our occupations. Nevertheless we must
overcome them. They are very strong, and compared to them we are very
weak. Yet in the name of God we must master them, and we will. If one
sin has control over us, we are not the Lord's free men. A man who is held
by only one chain is still a captive. There is no going to heaven with one
sin ruling within us, for of the saints it is said, "Sin will have no dominion
over you" (Rom. 6:14). Up, then, and slay every Canaanite, and break to
pieces every chariot of iron! The Lord of hosts is with us, and who will
resist his sin-destroying power?

DECEMBER 17

So we will always be with the Lord.

1 Thessalonians 4:17

While we are here the Lord is with us, and when we are called away we are with him. There is no dividing the saint from his Savior. They are one, and they must always be one. Jesus cannot be without his own people, for he would be a Head without a body. Whether caught up into the air, or resting in paradise, or journeying here, we are with Jesus. And who will separate us from him?

What a joy this is! Our supreme honor, rest, comfort, and delight is to be with the Lord. We cannot conceive of anything that can surpass or even equal this divine company. By holy fellowship we must be with him in his humiliation, rejection, and travail, and then we will be with him in his glory. Before long we will be with him in his rest and in his royalty, in his expectation and in his manifestation. We will fare as he fares, and triumph as he triumphs.

Oh, my Lord, if I am to be with you forever, I have an incomparable destiny. I will not envy an archangel. To be forever with the Lord is my idea of heaven at its best. Not the harps of gold, nor the unfading crowns, nor the unclouded light is glory to me. My glory is Jesus, Jesus himself, and myself forever with him in nearest and dearest fellowship.

DECEMBER 18

Like birds hovering, so the LORD of hosts
will protect Jerusalem.

Isaiah 31:5

With a hurrying wing the mother bird rushes to protect her young. She wastes no time on the way when coming to supply them with food or guard them from danger. In the same way, the Lord will come to the defense of his chosen as if on eagle's wings. Indeed, he will ride on the wings of the wind (Ps. 18:10; 104:3).

With outstretched wings the mother covers her little ones in the nest. She hides them away by interposing her own body. The hen gives her own warmth to her chicks and makes her wings a house in which they dwell at home. In the same way, the Lord himself becomes the protection of his elect. He himself is their refuge, their home, their all.

Like birds flying and birds *covering* (for the word "hovering" means both), so the Lord will be to us. And this he will be repeatedly and successfully. We will be defended and preserved from all evil. The Lord who likens himself to birds will not be like them in their feebleness, for he is "the LORD of hosts." Let this be our comfort, that almighty love will be swift to help and sure to cover. The wings of God are more quick and more tender than the wing of a bird. We will put our trust under its shadow from now on and forever.

DECEMBER 19

He keeps all his bones;
not one of them is broken.

Psalm 34:20

In context, this promise refers to the much-afflicted righteous man: "Many are the afflictions of the righteous, but the LORD delivers him out of them all" (Ps. 34:19). He may suffer skin wounds and flesh wounds, but no great harm will be done: "Not one of [his bones] is broken."

This is a great comfort to a tested child of God, and comfort that I dare accept. For up to this hour I have suffered no real damage from my many afflictions. I have neither lost faith, nor hope, nor love. Instead of losing these bones of character, they have gained in strength and energy. I have more knowledge, more experience, more patience, more stability than I had before my trials came. Not even my joy has been destroyed. I have had many bruises through sickness, bereavement, depression, slander, and opposition. But the bruises have healed, and there has been no compound fracture of a bone, not even a simple one. The reason is not difficult to find. If we trust in the Lord, he keeps all our bones; and if he keeps them, we may be sure that not one of them is broken.

Come, my heart, do not sorrow. You are smarting, but there are no bones broken. Endure hardness, and defy fear.

DECEMBER 20

I, I am he who comforts you;
who are you that you are afraid of man who dies,
of the son of man who is made like grass,
and have forgotten the LORD, your Maker,
who stretched out the heavens
and laid the foundations of the earth,
and you fear continually all the day
because of the wrath of the oppressor,
when he sets himself to destroy?
And where is the wrath of the oppressor?

Isaiah 51:12–13

Let the text itself be the portion for today. There is no need to enlarge on it. Those who are trembling read it, believe it, feed on it, and plead it before the Lord. He whom you fear is only a human being after all. Meanwhile, he who promises to comfort you is God, your Maker, the Creator of heaven and earth. Infinite comfort more than covers a very limited danger.

"Where is the wrath of the oppressor?" It is in the Lord's hand. It is only the fury of a dying creature—fury that will end as soon as the breath is gone from the nostril. Why, then, should we stand in awe of one who is as frail as ourselves? Let us not dishonor our God by making a god of puny man. We can make an idol of a man by regarding him with excessive fear as well as by giving him inordinate love. Let us treat men as men, and God as God. Then we will go calmly on in the path of duty, fearing the Lord and fearing nobody else.

DECEMBER 21

He will again have compassion on us;
he will tread our iniquities underfoot.
You will cast all our sins
into the depths of the sea.

Micah 7:19

God never turns from his love, but he soon turns from his wrath. His love to his chosen is according to his nature; his anger is only according to his office. He loves because he is love; he frowns because it is necessary for our good. He will come back to the place in which his heart rests, namely, his love to his own. And then he will take pity on our grief and bring it to an end.

What a choice promise is this: "He will tread our iniquities underfoot"! He will conquer them. They try to enslave us, but the Lord will give us victory over them by his own right hand. Like the Canaanites, they will be beaten, brought under control, and ultimately slain.

As for the guilt of our sins, how gloriously is that removed! "All our sins"—yes, the whole lot of them; "you will cast"—only an almighty arm could perform such a wonder; "into the depths of the sea"—where Pharaoh and his chariots went down (Ex. 14:27–28). Our sins will not be hurled into the shallows from which they might be washed up by the tide, but into the "depths." They are all gone. They sank to the bottom like a stone. Hallelujah! Hallelujah!

DECEMBER 22

God is our refuge and strength,
a very present help in trouble.

Psalm 46:1

A help that is not present when we need it is of small value. The anchor that is left at home is of no use to the seaman in the storm. The money that he used to have is of no worth to the debtor when a court order is made against him. Very few earthly helps could be called "very present." They are usually far away when we seek them, far away when we need them, and farther still when once they have been used. But as for the Lord our God, he is present when we seek him, present when we need him, and present when we have already enjoyed his aid.

He is more than "present," he is "*very* present." More present than the nearest friend can be, for he is in us in our trouble; more present than we are to ourselves, for sometimes we lack presence of mind. He is always present, effectively present, sympathetically present, altogether present. He is present now if this is a gloomy period. Let us rest ourselves on him. He is our refuge; let us hide in him. He is our strength; let us arm ourselves with him. He is our help; let us lean on him. He is our very present help; let us rest in him now. We need not have a moment's care or an instant's fear. "The LORD of hosts is with us; the God of Jacob is our fortress" (Ps. 46:7).

DECEMBER 23

And of Joseph he said,
"Blessed by the LORD be his land,
with the choicest gifts of heaven above,
and of the deep that crouches beneath."

Deuteronomy 33:13

We may be rich in the kind of things that Joseph received, and we may have them in a higher sense. Oh, for "the choicest gifts of heaven above"! Power with God and the manifestation of power from God are most precious. We would enjoy the peace of God, the joy of the Lord, the glory of our God. We prize the blessing of the three divine Persons in love, grace, and fellowship beyond the finest gold. The things of earth are as nothing compared with the things of heaven.

"The choicest gifts of heaven above" includes "the dew" (Deut. 33:31 KJV). How precious is this! How we pray and praise when we have the dew! What refreshing, what growth, what fragrance, what life there is in us when the dew is about! Above all things else, as plants planted by the Lord's own right hand, we need the dew of his Holy Spirit.

"The deep that crouches beneath." Surely this refers to that unseen, underground ocean that supplies all the fresh springs that make the earth glad. Oh, to tap into the eternal fountains! This is an unspeakable blessing. Let no believer rest until they possess it. The all-sufficiency of the Lord is ours forever. Let us resort to it now.

DECEMBER 24

Your enemies shall come fawning to you,
and you shall tread upon their backs.

Deuteronomy 33:29

That archenemy, the devil, is a liar from the beginning. But he is so very plausible that, like our mother Eve, we all too easily believe him. Yet in the end, we will prove him a liar, gain victory over him, and so tread him down beneath our feet.

Satan says that we will fall from grace, dishonor our profession, and perish along with apostates. But, trusting in the Lord Jesus, we will remain on track and prove that Jesus loses none whom his Father gave him (John 6:39). Satan tells us that our bread will fail, and we will starve with our children. Yet the Feeder of the ravens has not forgotten us yet, and he will never do so (Luke 12:24). He will prepare us a table in the presence of our enemies (Ps. 23:5).

Satan whispers that the Lord will not deliver us out of the testing that is looming in the distance. He threatens that the last straw will break the camel's back. What a liar he is! For the Lord will never leave us, nor forsake us (Heb. 13:5). "Let him deliver him now!" cries our false foe (Matt. 27:43). But the Lord will silence him by coming to our rescue.

Satan takes great delight in telling us that death will prove too much for us.

"What will you do in the thicket of the Jordan?" (Jer. 12:5). But there also he will prove to be a liar. For we will pass through death singing psalms of glory.

DECEMBER 25

This Jesus, who was taken up from you into heaven, will come in the same way as you saw him go into heaven.

Acts 1:11

Many are celebrating our Lord's first coming today. Let us turn our thoughts to the promise of his second coming. This is as sure as the first advent and derives a great deal of its certainty from it. He who came as a lowly man to serve will certainly come to receive the reward of his service. He who came to suffer will not be slow in coming to reign.

This is our glorious hope, for we will share his joy. Today our glory is hidden and we are humiliated, just as he was when here below. But when he comes, it will be our manifestation, just as it will be his revelation (Col. 3:4). Dead saints will live at his appearing. The slandered and despised "will shine like the sun in the kingdom of their Father" (Matt. 13:43). Then the saints will appear as kings and priests, and the days of their mourning will be ended (Isa. 60:20). The long rest and inconceivable splendor of Christ's coming reign will be an abundant reward for the ages of witnessing and warring.

Oh, that the Lord would come! He is coming! He is on the road and traveling quickly. The sound of his approach should be music to our hearts! Ring out, bells of hope!

DECEMBER 26

Peter answered him, "Though they all fall away
because of you, I will never fall away."

Matthew 26:33

"Why?" someone cries, *"This is not a promise from God!"* Just so. But it was a promise of a man, and therefore it came to nothing. Peter thought he was saying what he should certainly carry out. But a promise that has no better foundation than human resolve will fall to the ground. No sooner did temptations come than Peter denied his Master and used oaths to confirm his denial (Matt. 26:69–75).

What is man's word? An earthen pot broken with a blow. What is your own resolve? A blossom which with God's care may bear fruit, but that left to itself will fall to the ground with the first wind that moves the branches.

On human words hang only what they will bear.

On your own resolve do not depend at all.

On the promise of your God hang time and eternity, this world and the next, your all and the all of all your beloved ones.

This volume is a checkbook for believers, and this page is meant as a warning concerning which bank they draw from and whose signature they accept. Rely on Jesus without limit. Do not trust yourself nor anyone born of woman beyond appropriate limits. But trust only and wholly in the Lord.

DECEMBER 27

"For the mountains may depart
and the hills be removed,
but my steadfast love shall not depart from you,
and my covenant of peace shall not be removed,"
says the LORD, who has compassion on you.

Isaiah 54:10

One of the most delightful qualities of divine love is its abiding character. The pillars of the earth may be moved out of their places, but the kindness and the covenant of our merciful Lord never leaves his people. How happy my soul feels with a firm belief in this inspired declaration! The year is almost over, and the years of my life are growing few. But time does not change my Lord. New lamps are taking the place of the old. Perpetual change affects all things, but our Lord is the same. Force overturns the hills, but no conceivable power can affect the eternal God. Nothing in the past, the present, or the future can cause the Lord to be unkind to me.

My soul, rest in *the eternal kindness* of the Lord, who treats you as a close relative. Remember also *the everlasting covenant*. God always has it in mind—see that you remember it as well. In Christ Jesus the glorious God has pledged himself to you to be your God and to hold you as one of his people. Kindness and covenant—dwell on these words as sure and lasting things that eternity itself will not take from you.

DECEMBER 28

He has said, "I will never leave you nor forsake you."

Hebrews 13:5

Several times in the Scriptures the Lord has said this. He has often repeated it to make our assurance doubly sure. Let us never harbor any doubt about it. In itself the promise is especially emphatic. In the Greek it has five negatives, each one definitely shutting out the possibility of the Lord's ever leaving one of his people so that we might justly feel forsaken by God. This priceless scripture does not promise us exemption from trouble, but it does secure us against desertion. We may be called to travel strange ways, but we will always have our Lord's company, assistance, and provision. We need not covet money, for we will always have our God. God is better than gold, and his favor is better than fortune.

Surely we ought to be content with such things as we have, for he who has God has more than everything else in the world. What can we have beyond the Infinite? What more can we desire than almighty Goodness?

Come, my heart. If God says he will never leave you, nor forsake you, then be much in prayer for grace that you may never leave your Lord, nor even for a moment forsake his ways.

DECEMBER 29

Even to your old age I am he,
and to gray hairs I will carry you.
I have made, and I will bear;
I will carry and will save.

Isaiah 46:4

The year is very old, and here is a promise for our aged friends; indeed for all of us since age creeps over everyone. If we live long enough, we will all have gray hairs. Therefore we may as well enjoy this promise with the foresight of faith.

When we grow old, our God will still be the "I AM," remaining forever the same. Gray hairs tell of our decay, but he does not decay. When we cannot carry a burden, and can hardly carry ourselves, the Lord will carry us. Just as in our younger days he carried us like lambs in his breast, so will he carry us in our years of infirmity.

He made us, and he will care for us. When we become a burden to our friends, and a burden to ourselves, the Lord will not shake us off. Instead, he will take us up and carry and deliver us more fully than ever. In many cases the Lord gives his servants a long and calm evening. They worked hard all day and wore themselves out in their Master's service, and so he said to them, "Now rest in anticipation of that eternal Sabbath that I have prepared for you." Let us not dread old age. Let us grow old graciously, since the Lord himself is with us in the fullness of grace.

DECEMBER 30

Having loved his own who were in the
world, he loved them to the end.

John 13:1

This fact is essentially a promise. For what our Lord was, he is, and what he was to those with whom he lived on earth, he will be to all his beloved so long as the moon remains.

"*Having loved.*" Here was the wonder! That he should ever have loved these men at all is the marvel. What was there in his poor disciples that he should love them? What is there in me?

But once he has begun to love, it is his nature to continue to do so. Love made the saints "*his own*"—what a choice title! He purchased them with blood, and they became his treasure. Being his own, he will not lose them. Being his beloved, he will not cease to love them. My soul, he will not cease to love you!

The text is good as it stands: "*to the end.*" Even at this, his death, the ruling passion of love for his own reigned in his heart. It means also "to the uttermost." He could not love them more: he gave himself for them. Some read it "to perfection." Truly he lavished on them a perfect love in which there was no flaw nor failure, no folly, no unfaithfulness, and no reserve.

Such is the love of Jesus to each one of his people. Let us sing to our Well-Beloved a song.

DECEMBER 31

You guide me with your counsel,
and afterward you will receive me to glory.

Psalm 73:24

From day to day and from year to year my faith believes in the wisdom and love of God, and I know that I will not believe in vain. No good word of his has ever failed (Josh. 21:45), and I am sure that none will ever "fall to the ground" (1 Sam. 3:19).

I put myself into his hands for guidance. I do not know the way I should choose; the Lord will choose my inheritance for me. I need counsel and advice, for my duties are convoluted and my condition is complex. I seek the Lord, as the high priest of old looked to his Urim and Thummim (Ex. 28:30). I seek the counsel of the infallible God in preference to my own judgment or the advice of friends. Glorious Lord, you will guide me!

Soon the end will come. A few more years and I must depart this world to the Father. My Lord will be near my bed. He will meet me at heaven's gate. He will welcome me to the land of glory. I will not be a stranger in heaven. My own God and Father will receive me to endless bliss.

Glory be to him who will guide me here on earth and receive me into his presence when the time comes. Amen.

INDEX OF BIBLE PROMISES

Index of Bible Promises